Campaigning in America

CAMPAIGNING IN AMERICA

A HISTORY OF ELECTION PRACTICES

Robert J. Dinkin

Contributions in American History, Number 135

GREENWOOD PRESS
New York • Westport, Connecticut • London

Library of Congress Cataloging-in-Publication Data

Dinkin, Robert J.
    Campaigning in America.

    (Contributions in American history,
  ISSN 0084–9219 ; no. 135)
    Bibliography: p.
    Includes index.
    1. Electioneering—United States—History.
  I. Title II. Series.
  JK1971.D56 1989   324.7′0973   88–29627
  ISBN 0–313–26167–9 (lib. bdg. : alk. paper)

British Library Cataloguing in Publication Data is available.

Copyright © 1989 by Robert J. Dinkin

Library of Congress Catalog Card Number: 88–29627
ISBN: 0–313–26167–9
ISSN: 0084–9219

First published in 1989

Greenwood Press, Inc.
88 Post Road West, Westport, Connecticut 06881

Printed in the United States of America

The paper used in this book complies with the
Permanent Paper Standard issued by the National
Information Standards Organization (Z39.48–1984).

10 9 8 7 6 5 4 3 2 1

Contents

Acknowledgments

In completing this study, I have been aided by many people. Ronald P. Formisano of Clark University, Jean H. Baker of Goucher College, and Michael E. McGerr of the Massachusetts Institute of Technology each read chapters in their field of expertise and made many useful recommendations. My colleagues at Fresno State Don Broyles, Lyman Heine, and David Jones also read and criticized parts of the manuscript. Peter Klassen, dean of the School of Social Sciences, and John Kendall, chairman of the History Department, as well as former chairman Stephen Benko, have long been supportive of my work. History Department secretaries Diane Rivera-Pasillas and Penny Yagura helped with several phases of manuscript preparation. Joan C. Palestine typed the first draft of most of the chapters. My son Sam Dinkin transferred the material to the word processor and my daughter Leslie Dinkin spent several weeks entering the numerous additions and corrections. I would also like to acknowledge the efforts of the staff at Greenwood Press, expecially my copyeditor Todd Adkins, who saved me from many errors and improved the overall quality of the work. Finally, I would like to thank my wife Roxane Head, who was very helpful during the revising stage and has also succeeded in revising my life.

Introduction

For more than two hundred years political campaigning has held a special fascination for the American public. As early as the 1750s one of George Washington's correspondents observed that at election time, "the flame of burgessing seemed to enter every heart."[1] Three-quarters of a century later the remarks of an English visitor were even more pronounced: "the spirit of electioneering . . . seems to enter as an essential ingredient into the composition of everything."[2] Numerous similar statements can be found in subsequent periods as well. Yet despite its pervasive quality vote-seeking never has enjoyed wide esteem nor have most participants in the process truly relished going out on the hustings. Indeed, except in those cases where a candidate forced the public to confront a necessary or otherwise ignored issue, the campaign rarely has been a politician's finest hour. (Sometimes it has been the worst.) Perhaps this is one of the reasons why no one ever has written a history of American electioneering, at least from the standpoint of the practices used. There have, of course, been studies of battles for the presidency and works on the tactics employed in individual contests. There also have been analyses of separate aspects—for instance, campaign finance—and of the major developments in particular eras. But no full-scale treatment of campaign activities over the entire span of American history has been produced. This book seeks to correct that omission by surveying the changing nature of vote-getting from its rather simple forms in colonial times to the highly complex methods of today.

The book is divided chronologically into seven chapters, the early ones coinciding with traditional political watersheds, especially the rise and fall of party systems, the later ones corresponding more to new directions in campaigning. Although it is difficult to create exact boundaries or cut-off points, the delineations I have chosen mark as near as possible the moments of distinct changes in electioneering styles. The five chapters that contain the more recent epochs are separated into two parts. The first and most essential part discusses the general attributes of campaigning in the period, the second focuses on each of the presidential elections in these years. The presidential elections are presented in order to furnish continuity and to demonstrate more clearly how techniques evolved from one contest to the next. This format also allows certain notable occurrences—William Jennings Bryan's long speaking tour and William McKinley's "front-porch" gatherings in 1896—to be seen in the context of the particular race and not just as isolated events. While each chapter deals with both continuity and change, the emphasis is mainly on the latter so as to avoid repetition.

This book makes no attempt to be exhaustive or definitive and at times only gives limited attention to state and local activities. Nor is there much analysis of the symbolic elements of campaigning. Murray Edelman in *The Symbolic Uses of Politics* previously has shown how elections reinforce democracy by giving people "a chance to express discontents and enthusiasms, to enjoy a sense of involvement."[3] Other writers have noted how campaigns provide for a mutual exchange of ideas and help keep the electorate informed. Louis W. Koenig has explored the manner in which campaigns foster a social and political consensus that influences public policy. Dan Nimmo has looked at elections as ritual drama and tells how myths and traditions have been created from it. In a related essay Bruce E. Gronbeck has demonstrated the way in which campaigning "ultimately legitimates itself as much as it does instrumental output."[4] These and other works attest to the fact that this subject already has been well covered.

Besides downplaying the symbolic aspects of campaigning, the present work does not say much about the critical events and issues of each era, nor does it delve deeply into the structure of political parties at different points in time. Nevertheless, it is impossible to discuss the history of election campaigns without devoting at least some attention to parties and issues and the way candidates framed their public positions. Naturally a certain amount of emphasis is given to the methods of party organization and the operation of state and national committees. But little space is allotted to the behind-the-scenes political maneuvering or to the struggles for the party nomination at national conventions because they do not involve direct appeals to the electorate. The bulk of the volume concerns the techniques involved in the actual search for votes. Most of the examples are taken from presidential elections, for it was usually in these large and prolonged quests that most breakthroughs in campaigning first took place.

In surveying the past two-and-a-half centuries, one finds a good deal of change in the manner in which candidates have attempted to gain votes. In the beginning office seekers made few personal appearances for it was not usually considered proper to ask for support. Eventually this attitude was altered as elections became more competitive and the people themselves wanted to judge the candidates before casting their ballots. Political parties on the local, state, and national levels would for a long time play an expanding role in the process. Campaigns would grow even more elaborate and costly as the public increasingly was bombarded with messages and materials. By the mid–nineteenth century the so-called "army style" with its heavy use of hoopla became the norm. Later on came the "merchandising style" and its application of modern advertising techniques. New technology, especially in the twentieth century, also would affect the way votes were sought after. Yet the changes in electioneering generally have occurred in a gradual fashion without abrupt departures. Old ways often would be employed along with the new until the former were shown to be completely obsolete.

Whether campaign tactics have become nastier and messages more distorted in recent times is not easy to judge. Surely some of the name-calling and unsavory schemes unleashed in the nineteenth century are hard to top. In his book on new forms of electioneering, Richard Armstrong argues that it would be most unlikely for contemporary candidates and their managers to create "a blatantly false and misleading image" like William Henry Harrison's "Log-Cabin and Hard Cider" campaign of 1840. Nor, he says, would it be possible today as it was in the past for a person to get away with falsely accusing an opponent of having fathered an illegitimate child or having been a pimp. Yet he himself notes the case of Democratic Congressman George E. Brown, Jr., of California, who in the early 1980s was hit with direct-mail attacks that improperly claimed he had "refused to vote against the mailing of pornography to children . . . voted to allow scientific experiments on live fetuses . . . and advocated a national program to fund sterilization."[5] Perhaps it would be safe to say that campaigning in America always has been subject to falsehood and distortion.

What effect campaigning has had on the outcomes of elections is difficult to ascertain. We have no way of measuring a campaign's effectiveness, and some have viewed its influence as minimal. When asked about the impact of the Republican effort on behalf of Richard Nixon in 1972, Jeb Magruder, one of the key figures in the operation (who later was indicted in the Watergate scandal), asserted that it would not have made a difference of more than "2, 4 or 5 percent." A generation earlier the highly respected political scientists Charles E. Merriam and Harold F. Gosnell claimed that superior vote-getting techniques may have been significant in local races, but in presidential contests, "where the floodgates of national publicity are focused on both major candidates, it may be that the direction of the tide of public opinion is more important than the skill of propagandists."[6] Recent studies indicate that in national competitions roughly two-thirds of the electorate already has made its decision by the time of the party conventions. Yet while campaigning may change few minds, it does have the function of reinforcing a person's preferences. Moreover, even if it can be argued that the methods of electioneering have had little to do with the voting results, they can tell us much about our culture and how people have behaved in the political sphere over the course of time.

Campaigning in America

1

The Colonial and Revolutionary Periods

1607–1789

Electioneering techniques developed slowly in early America. No political parties existed, and in some colonies elections were irregularly held. Only property owners, a group consisting of anywhere from half to four-fifths of all adult white males, were allowed to vote; indentured servants, women, blacks, and numerous religious dissenters were ineligible. Interest in politics naturally was low in an age when survival was the main concern in life. Given the limited forms of communication, the majority of people had little knowledge of political events anyway. Even among the politically aware, few saw much reason to take part in the electoral process because most major offices were appointive. In almost every colony the governor and members of the upper house of the legislature received their appointment from the British Crown or from a proprietor. Administrative and judicial posts also were not subject to public choice. Rhode Island and Connecticut were unique in having popularly elected governments throughout the colonial period. Elsewhere, only the lower house of the legislature and certain local offices continued to be elective.[1]

In the seventeenth century actual encounters for elective office were extremely rare. Elections for the Virginia House of Burgesses—the first legislature in America, established in 1619—commonly went uncontested. Bacon's Rebellion, a popular uprising in colonial Virginia in 1676, caused some turnover of representatives but involved no open appeal for votes. New York, colonized by the Dutch in the 1620s, had no elected assembly until it came under British rule in the mid–1660s. Only at the end of the century did any competition develop at the polls. Massachusetts, Rhode Island, and Connecticut, founded in the 1630s, occasionally had competitive races, but these left little evidence of open electioneering. Other colonies, such as the

Carolinas and Pennsylvania, were not settled until the last third of the century and experienced almost no contention at the ballot box for many years.

By the middle of the eighteenth century, however, elections in several colonies became more competitive. The homogeneity and close-knit leadership that characterized some of the early New England settlements had begun to break down. Here and elsewhere many challenges were raised against traditional authority. New York and Pennsylvania contained a mixture of ethnic and religious groups—English (Anglican, Presbyterian, and Quaker), Dutch, German, French, and Scottish—and grew into hotbeds of factionalism. Even in less-divided Virginia and Maryland, clashing interests frequently caused heated rivalries. Moreover, increasing numbers of individuals now had the affluence and leisure time that allowed them to participate in politics. Rising young men often coveted a seat in the legislature to enhance their position. All these factors led to a considerable upsurge in vote-getting activity.

The reasons for contested elections varied. In some instances competition stemmed from divisions over local problems—perhaps involving differences over land allocations, the apportionment of taxes, or religious regulations. In others colonywide matters dominated, for example, whether to print paper money to reduce economic strain or build forts to defend against Indian attacks. Sometimes legislators who disliked the governor's policies would form a "country party" and oppose the election of the chief executive's supporters, known as the "court party." In about as many cases, however, neither local nor provincial issues were of much consequence, so outcomes mainly hinged upon each candidate's rank and personal qualities. As Lucille Griffith has written about contests in mid-eighteenth-century Virginia: "It seems not to have been so much a question of *what* as *who*."[2] Robert Munford's play *The Candidates* (1770) clearly illustrates this theme, for when the lead character, Worthy, at first declines to stand for reelection with his colleague, Wou'dbe, a number of questionable figures enter the race. Among them we find Sir John Toddy, "an honest blockhead" with little ability except in consuming liquor, and Smallhopes and Strutabout, two fellows of doubtful virtue. Eventually, Worthy reconsiders, joins the fray, and easily defeats the undesirables.

To be sure, elections in many places (most notably in the Carolinas and Georgia) continued to be uncontested. Even in increasingly competitive districts further north, a well-to-do planter or merchant could secure a legislative seat without openly appealing for votes. In colonial times the common person's deference toward members of the elite was particularly strong. This was reinforced by the system of voice voting that existed in many colonies, in which the candidate was present at the polls on election day. Moreover, custom dictated that a provincial office seeker remain above the conflict and not actively solicit support. As William Livingston of New York warned in an essay published in the *Independent Reflector* (1753): "To ask a man for his vote is a confession in the candidate that he is suspicious of his own merit. 'Tis a proof of his apprehensions that the sense of the public is against him."[3] In spite of the strictures against open campaigning, more and more persons wishing to be elected felt the need to forego their passive stance.

The main method of campaigning during the colonial period was canvassing and handshaking. Probably more so than today, people felt it important to be personally acquainted with the men for whom they voted. Having less populous election districts gave representation a greater personal meaning. Thus persons running for office sought to meet members of the electorate individually—at church, at taverns, at court, or at a militia training. Candidates in urban areas often went from door to door or buttonholed voters in the street on the way to the polls. The closer the contest, the more active someone would have to be. In 1752 William Parsons of Northampton County, Pennsylvania, noted that his opponent for an assembly seat, James Burnside, was "going from place to place, beating his breast," in order to become chosen.[4]

In addition to making a canvass, one of the most accepted forms of campaigning in those days was treating the electorate to food and drink. Contemporaries often referred to this practice as "swilling the planters with bumbo."[5] In the southern and middle colonies, especially Virginia, Maryland, and New York, it was customary for the candidates to provide refreshments for the voters before or after the balloting. George Washington was not unusual in spending thirty-nine pounds on "treats" for his first assembly election in 1758. This included payment for 160 gallons of various beverages, an average of a quart-and-a-half per voter.[6] If a candidate ignored the custom of treating, he often found himself in great difficulty. In 1777, James Madison, believing "the corrupting influence of spiritous liquors, and other treats," to be "inconsistent with the purity of moral and republican principles," tried to introduce a "more chaste mode of conducting elections in Virginia." He found, however, that "the old habits were too deeply rooted to be suddenly reformed," and was defeated by an opponent who continued to use "all the means of influence familiar to the people."[7]

In the northern colonies, the press, particularly newspapers, had some significance as an electioneering aid. Candidates used newspapers in two ways—by inserting short announcements of their intent to seek a particular office and by contributing anonymous essays on important issues.[8] Partly because of the strict libel laws of the time, writers of such essays usually refrained from personal attacks and simply called for the election of new legislators. As one opponent of the Quaker faction wrote in the *Pennsylvania Gazette* in 1737: "I am of Opinion that the Majority of the Members of the last Assembly, are entirely unworthy of your Notice in the next Election. And I believe when you have read their Minutes, and considered their Behavior as I have done, you will be of the same Sentiment."[9] Besides newspapers, a variety of pamphlets and broadsides made their appearance in urban elections. Hundreds of copies of these materials were handed out before a contest in such towns as Boston, New York, and Philadelphia.

Despite the rise of active campaigning, elections in colonial America tended to be conducted on a more modest scale than those in later times. The period given to soliciting votes was usually quite brief. Rarely did it extend beyond a week, and sometimes it lasted no longer than the morning of election day itself. The large majority of campaigns remained local in nature, with candidates relying on their own resources and the support of a few trusted friends. Even in colonies where highly partisan activity occurred during the legislative sessions, members from each constituency normally managed their own reelection bids without seeking outside help.

There were times when campaigning went much further. In New York, Pennsylvania, and Maryland, for example, in periods of extreme conflict between "court" and "country" factions, partisans engaged in rather elaborate electioneering schemes. Political leaders such as James DeLancey of New York, William Allen of Pennsylvania, and Stephen Bordley of Maryland attempted to organize campaign operations on a broad basis, sometimes covering the entire colony. These three men would send emissaries to different counties to meet with local officials and help supervise the vote-getting process. As part of their strategy, they arranged the tickets well in advance of the balloting, inserted material in the press, provided money to get out the vote, and sent letters to friends and relatives requesting their assistance. If the scope of their activities did not equal that of later party managers, certain aspects of their approach surely pointed in a modern direction.[10]

Perhaps the colony that engaged in the most widespread campaigning of all was Rhode Island, where family and sectional rivalry kept elections competitive for many years. During the Ward–Hopkins controversy (1755–70), which set the Providence-based faction headed by Stephen Hopkins against that led by Samuel Ward of Newport, the two sides made an immense effort to achieve victory in the annual gubernatorial race. No area of the colony was ignored, no expense was ever denied. Despite the fact that the Ward faction captured the governorship just three times in the fifteen-year period, the balloting always was very close and its leaders maintained their optimism. "We could undoubtedly obtain the Election this Year," Samuel Ward told one of his backers in 1764, "if our Friends in the Country will but exert themselves. They may depend upon all proper Support and Assistance."[11] In these hard-fought contests, even bribery was acceptable. Voters were paid either with food and drink or directly in currency. As one contemporary wrote: "Generally he that distributes the most cash, and gives the best entertainments . . . is the man who obtains a majority of votes, which fixes him in the [governor's] chair . . . for that year."[12]

Competitive elections and extensive campaigning fell off in Rhode Island and most other colonies in the 1770s. As Americans unified in opposition to British encroachment, it reduced the amount of rivalry at the polls. Only in deeply divided Pennsylvania and Delaware did serious struggles still occur up until 1776. When war broke out, factional differences were put into the background in most of the new states. As the fighting expanded, wartime dislocation and the presence of the British army often prevented any meaningful voting. Once peace was established early in the 1780s and new state governments were put into full operation, the number of contests picked up considerably. By 1785, Archibald Stuart of Virginia told Thomas Jefferson that "Competition for seats in the house run higher than ever they Did under the Old government."[13] Over the next few years, partisan activity before election day would be stimulated even further.

One reason for greater electoral competition in the postwar period was the growing politicization of common people. Those who had passively accepted rule by the rich and wellborn in the past were no longer willing to do so. Direct participation in protests against the British and in the war itself had made average citizens aware of political issues and conscious of their rights. Many, having rejected aristocratic British rule, became wary of rule by this country's upper class. They began to act and speak out publicly on crucial matters. "Every drabbling dishclout politician, however various their opinions, have all some kind of observation to make upon the time," insisted one contemporary.[14] When election day neared, "the curiosity and interest of the inhabitants were aroused," remarked another.[15] Nevertheless, the world was not turned completely upside down. One astute foreign visitor, Count Francesco Dal Verme of Milan, after watching the assembly contest in Philadelphia in 1783, noted that despite a wider range of participants, "the rich," here as elsewhere, were "more influential than others."[16] On the whole, however, men of affluence did not dominate elections to the extent they did before independence.

An equally important reason for the upswing in competition was the heavy increase in factionalism. In many states postwar problems led to the rise of factions that were more organized, stable, and far-reaching than before. Traditional historians normally have referred to the competing sides as Conservatives and Radicals, but as Jackson T. Main has pointed out, they might more accurately be called Cosmopolitans and Localists. The first group comprised chiefly business and professional men plus some large landholders who had similar economic interests. Many were well educated and had a broad or "continental" outlook. They also wished to perpetuate elite rule. Their Localist adversaries usually were small farmers who did not produce goods for distant markets. They lived mostly in the interior—in isolated rural areas far from trading and cultural centers. Unlike the Cosmopolitans, the less-educated, less-worldly Localists frequently displayed a narrow and provincial outlook.[17]

Concerning political attitudes, the Cosmopolitans favored a stronger central government that would promote economic growth. They disapproved of the Articles of Confederation, which had created a weak national government without power to tax or regulate commerce. The Cosmopolitans more willingly accepted taxation and government spending but wanted a hard and stable currency. They also showed greater sympathy for former Tories and criticized confiscation of their property. In general, they feared the democratic tendencies emerging in the new nation. The Localists, on the other hand, wanted no change in the form of government, preferring the decentralized system under the articles. They opposed any new spending and taxation and disliked any leniency toward the Tories. While neither group had the permanence and clear identity of later parties, both operated in much the same fashion as subsequent party organizations. The two sides, Main asserts, normally voted along strict partisan lines in the legislature and soon began contending with each other at the ballot box.[18]

Due to the growth of sharp political divisions, elections gradually became more issue-oriented than in colonial times. As noted above, earlier clashes at the polls had often been more a question of who rather than what. Issues generally had been local, temporary, and not overly consequential. Now they were becoming more national, ongoing, and extremely significant. Those issues pertaining to such postwar problems as paper currency, treatment of Loyalists, western lands, and prewar British debts created widespread public concern and deeply affected the outcome of numerous state races. "Paper money or not seems to agitate the generality of the counties," reported Edmund Randolph shortly before the Virginia election of 1787.[19] Similar words frequently were echoed elsewhere. Of course, issues and factional conflicts did not lie at the basis of all elections. In many places, personality clashes and local matters continued to be the chief sources of competition, but an overall change was clearly noticeable.

Campaigns tended to be longer than those in the provincial period. While some races still lasted only a few days or a week, others proceeded for an entire month or longer. "Columbia County is five Weeks gone with Electioneering sickness," exclaimed Killian Van Rensselaer amid the New York gubernatorial contest in 1789.[20] Elections in the cities of the faction-ridden Middle Atlantic states often involved the most vigorous activity. Describing what went on in New York City in the late 1780s, Samuel Blachley Webb declared: " 'Tis all confusion—parties for different sides appear publicly and sometimes blows ensue."[21] Partisans often distributed handbills in the streets and placed notices in taverns and on the fronts of buildings. In Philadelphia, the "City of Brotherly Love," persons went "from house to house, ransacking every story from cellar to garret, begging, preying and insisting on votes— and extorting promises of them." On election day itself, individuals were known to stop people on the way to the polls, "forcing tickets into their hands."[22] Even small southern communities had their share of contests. Having entered the legislative race in Edenton, North Carolina, in 1785, Doctor Hugh Williamson, later a delegate to the Constitutional Convention, told a friend: "Electioneering was carry'd on with great Zeal.... A couple of Gentlemen," he said, had "canvassed all the Town over" for his opponents, spreading many "falsehoods."[23]

While most campaigns were still local in nature, some states engulfed in factional disputes, such as Pennsylvania, planned strategy on a broader basis. County leaders corresponded with the top figures in Philadelphia and some-times dispatched emissaries to different locales to promote the ticket. This was also true at times in New York and New England, where the governor was popularly chosen. Although gubernatorial candidates in this area did not openly seek votes, they did send agents to visit various parts of the state to drum up support. The lawyer William Plumer, after canvassing much of the interior of New Hampshire for former General John Sullivan in the winter of 1787, reported back: "In a late tour through a very considerable number of towns in the Connecticut River, I was pleased to find, notwith-standing the many little and infamous tricks practised by the agents and tools of *certain Characters*, that very many of the people, and many of the most respectable, were zealous advocates of your reelection."[24]

Electioneering may have reached statewide proportions in some instances, but it usually did not go beyond that realm. The only interstate activity of any kind occurred in the selection of delegates to the various constitutional ratifying conventions in 1787–88. Indeed, the battle over ratification of the federal Constitution represented a major advance in the electioneering pro-cess. More concerted activity took place at that time than in any previous instance. Although there was no national organization directing these efforts, party strategists on both sides sent messengers carrying campaign literature from one state to another, especially into New York, Virginia, and New Hampshire, three states slow to ratify. The Antifederalist Committee in New York City, headed by John Lamb, also wrote letters containing strategic proposals to the Constitution's opponents in many areas—even as far away as South Carolina. Furthermore, New York and Philadelphia newspapers carried essays on several aspects of the constitutional question that guided editorialists all along the seaboard.[25]

Besides expansion of geographic bounds, other new vote-getting tactics were introduced. Public speeches, previously used to stir up Americans against British rule, were now used to stir up voters for and against the new federal document. Before choosing delegates to the state ratifying convention in New York both Federalists and Antifederalists in the spring of 1788 spoke at county meetings in search of support. A few months earlier in Baltimore, Samuel Chase, running for a seat in the legislature, addressed a "numerous and respectable body of citizens" at the courthouse on the shortcomings of the Constitution. Then, when seeking election to the Maryland ratifying convention from Anne Arundel County, Chase talked before sizable crowds in Annapolis and Elkridge, again taking a strong Antifederalist stand. This new method must have been effective, for it was soon reported in the press that "Anne Arundel county, though naturally Federal, . . . elected four Antifederalists, owing to the popular electioneering talents of Mr. Chase."[26]

In addition to prepared speeches, this era witnessed the first formal campaign debates between candidates. While vying for a spot in the Massachusetts ratifying convention in late 1787, Theodore Sedgwick of Stockbridge publicly discussed the contents of the new federal Constitution with his Antifederalist opponent John Bacon. According to Sedgwick, Bacon eventually became convinced by his arguments and wound up supporting the new document, although Bacon vehemently denied it.[27] Clearly the most celebrated series of preelection exchanges featured James Madison and James Monroe in Culpeper County, Virginia, during the first congressional contest in the winter of 1789. After Madison's initial appearance in the area, Monroe followed suit in order to "erase any false impressions." Subsequently, the two men agreed to appear together to comment on the Constitution and other matters. For two weeks they traveled about the county presenting their contrary political views to the populace. Madison later described one encounter, which had been held before a gathering of German farmers whose votes were believed to be crucial. The meeting took place on a cold evening at a small Lutheran church. "Service was performed," he said, "and then they had music with two fiddles. . . . When it was over we addressed these people and kept them standing in the snow listening to the discussion of constitutional subjects. They stood it out very patiently—seemed to consider it a sort of fight of which they were required to be spectators. I then had to ride in the night twelve miles to quarters; and got my nose frostbitten, of which I bear the scar now."[28]

Along with the introduction of new forms of vote getting came the enhancement of popular older forms, particularly that of treating the electors to food and drink. While the custom already had shifted from being an impartial distribution of rewards to a means of securing votes, it now moved much further in that direction. In many places the candidates provided even more in the way of refreshment than their colonial forebears. Rum punch, wine, and beer were served in ever-larger quantities, together with all sorts of other fare. On election day in Washington County, Maryland, in January 1789, the local Federalists prepared a lavish feast near the courthouse. "An ox roasted whole, hoof and horn, was divided into morsels, and every one would taste a bit," declared an onlooker. The people, he added, "were so happy to get a piece of Federal Ox as ever superstitious Christians or Anti-Christians were to get relics from Jerusalem."[29]

Easily the most significant development in electioneering during this era was the expanded use of the press. In the few weeks before an election, the public prints often carried numerous essays related to the contest; some also offered lists of candidates for the people to consider. By 1789 about ninety separate newspapers were in circulation—almost twice the number in 1775—

many of them triweeklies and dailies. Newspapers now operated not only in large cities but also in smaller urban centers like Worcester, Massachusetts, Poughkeepsie, New York, and Carlisle, Pennsylvania. Several southern towns such as Fredericksburg, Petersburg, and Winchester, Virginia, and New Bern, North Carolina, had begun publishing newspapers on a regular basis as well.[30]

Besides enlarging their preelection coverage, newspapers of this period started printing much more frankly partisan material. Many contributors began taking sides, no longer simply calling for the election of "good men." Increasingly, they extolled the alleged virtues of one candidate and brutally attacked the supposed shortcomings of his opponent, finding it most advantageous to emphasize the latter. Even in New England, where personal assaults had long been considered improper, malicious statements about those running for office became widespread. Some newspapers eventually went beyond carrying a few partisan items and started to reflect a distinct political point of view. By the late 1780s a numbers of major sheets, such as the *Independent Gazetteer* in Philadelphia and the *Massachusetts Centinel* in Boston, were firmly in either the Antifederalist or Federalist camp. Although not official party organs, they served much the same purpose. Thus even before the emergence of a party system in the 1790s, a politically active and partisan press was developing.[31]

The increasingly vigorous campaigns of the Confederation era brought forth many critical comments. While most were from disgruntled partisans, some reflected an honest belief that free and open elections, and by implication the American system of government, stood in imminent danger of destruction. Although such statements had appeared once in a while during the colonial period, they became more frequent and angry in tone a decade after independence. A Philadelphian in 1786 asked, "Through what mud and dirt will not the tools and runners of party wade, and what horrid meanness will they not stoop to answer and serve the vile purposes of party and faction?"[32] A New Hampshirite condemned those "who wish to bribe our votes by emissaries, handshakes, and holiday sociabilities, and those who address us with the more silent, but not less sophistical artifice of newspaper panegyric."[33]

Regardless of the criticism, it is evident that electioneering during the revolutionary period had proceeded in a modern direction. While the quest for votes occasionally had been strenuous in the years before 1776 and would become much more so after 1790, the intervening era provided an important bridge. Candidates went to greater lengths to get elected and adopted new methods to garner votes. Of course, George Washington was designated the first president in 1788–89 without having made any effort on his own behalf; his name and stature carried him to a unanimous victory. Otherwise, the gentlemanly approach, whereby the office sought the man, was definitely on the wane.

2

The Early National Period

1790–1820

Having expanded during the revolutionary era, electioneering accelerated even further in the early national period. The gradual formation of the first regular political parties—the Federalists and the Republicans—stimulated greater competition for office and resulted in a major rise in campaigning over the next quarter century. Many of the methods and practices used in earlier times were enhanced considerably because of the emerging party struggle. Instead of local groups working individually to get out the vote, statewide organizations began setting up machinery for that purpose. More interstate operations were initiated, as prominent politicians sometimes traveled outside their section to make arrangements. Of course, some statewide and even interstate activity had occurred before this juncture, most notably in the process of ratifying the federal Constitution. As David Hackett Fischer has noted, however, "there is a point at which a difference in degree becomes a difference in kind."[1] And the new parties of the Federalist–Jeffersonian years soon reached that stage.

The new federal experiment in government did not begin with organized parties. Indeed, most of America's founders saw political parties as factious and divisive, the bane of republican government. Nevertheless, when in the early 1790s Alexander Hamilton, the secretary of the treasury under President Washington, introduced his controversial finance program—to fund the debt, place an excise tax on whiskey, and establish the Bank of the United States—it led to growing partisanship in Congress and in the public at large. Thomas Jefferson, the secretary of state, and James Madison, a key figure in the House of Representatives, both believed that these and other steps rapidly were bringing into being an all-powerful central government and destroying the balance of forces that the Constitution had envisioned. They also thought that the administration's actions clearly favored the small urban commercial class at the expense of the majority of the people, particularly in the South and West, who were involved in agriculture. As a counter-measure Jefferson helped set up a partisan newspaper, the *National Gazette*, edited by Philip Freneau, which severely criticized the new federal policies. Shortly thereafter, Jefferson and Madison began to correspond with and then meet political leaders from various states, seeking to build a formal opposition group. When this happened, Hamilton felt the need to organize administration supporters to oppose the "vigorous and general effort" made by "factious men" to promote for office "persons unfriendly to the measures, if not the constitution, of the National Government."[2] Soon the two sides—the Jeffersonian Republicans and the Hamiltonian Federalists—were battling one another at the polls.

To be sure, many elections in the early 1790s remained uncontested or centered on personal rather than party matters. Only a few states such as New York, Pennsylvania, Maryland, and Delaware witnessed well-coordinated campaigns from the onset of the party conflict. In much of the South and New England, it took considerable time for formally organized groups to develop. Those who voted in a partisan manner in Congress frequently ran as independents back home. In addition, most candidates continued to rely on their own resources and those of friends to get elected. When James Madison stood for reelection to the House in 1790, he simply wrote to a few of the leading gentlemen in his district and asked that they back his cause. As he was too busy to return to Virginia to attend the proceedings on election day, he told his father to have someone present at the county seat in his place.[3]

Even where no party contests took place, most candidates had to make a greater effort to get elected than before. Throughout the upper South extensive canvassing came to be an almost essential part of the process. While celebrated figures such as Madison could stay on the sidelines without jeopardizing their position, the majority of office seekers could not afford to remain idle. They had to devote a number of days and sometimes weeks to getting acquainted with the electors. During a two-month campaign in the late 1790s, Henry (Light-Horse Harry) Lee of Virginia said he had spent "no more than five or six nights under his own roof."[4] By 1806 a Kentuckian would claim (though perhaps with a bit of exaggeration) that to obtain a congressional seat a man "must for at least a year before the election totally neglect his private affairs" and perpetually "take the rounds, through the district with the velocity of a race rider."[5]

THE OLD AND THE NEW

As candidates stopped at places on their itinerary, some fell into the habit of delivering public speeches. Although preelection speechmaking had been practiced on occasion in the late 1780s, it grew into a widespread phenomenon in the 1790s, especially in the upper South. In quite a few Maryland counties, "stump speaking" or "haranguing the voters" became the high point of the contest. According to one observer such oratory primarily took place "where there is known to be a great concourse of people—at a horse race—a cock-fight—or a Methodist quarterly meeting. Here, the candidates for political honors or preferment, assemble with their partisans—they mount the Ros-trum, made out of an empty barrel or hogshead, Harangue the Sovereign people—praise and recommend themselves at the expence of their adversary's character and pretensions."[6]

Still more common than speechmaking at this time was the practice of treating. Many states now had laws against the offering of "Victuals, Drink or other Consideration" before an election, but such statutes seldom were enforced.[7] Particularly in the South, providing voters with food and drink proved to be as popular as ever. Ferdinand Bayard, a Frenchman traveling through Virginia in 1791, observed that "the candidates offer drunkenness openly to anyone who is willing to give them his vote."[8] One North Carolinian who desired a seat in the legislature was said to have driven to the courthouse in an old-fashioned one-horse sulky, "with a couple of tin cups, and a ten-gallon keg between his legs."[9] Elaborate barbecues became the fashion in this region, and an expenditure of several hundred dollars to cover the costs was not unknown. The type of fare served at these events varied. In the state of Delaware in 1795, one office seeker had "roasted a steer and half a dozen sheep . . . as a kind of snack for his friends." Another gave a "fish feast" and also a "turtle feast."[10] Amid these goings-on, the candidate would greet prospective voters.

Some representatives, however, refused to engage in open campaigning of this kind. For example, Congressman John Page of Virginia, a member of an old and respectable family, found it demeaning and improper. As he wrote to his constituents in 1794:

Courting popularity as it is called, and attempting to gain the affections or *votes* of the people, is so nearly connected with an officious attention to them, and an un-wearied effort to gratify their curiosity or their wishes, that any one of the citizens of these United States who is acquainted with the history of mankind and the frailty of human nature, will agree with me, that the more attention I pay my business in Congress, and the less to my constituents, the greater must be my respect for them, their dignity and permanent interests. For such a man must know, that courting popularity has oftener produced tyrants, or demagogues, and revolutions attended with confusion and slaughter, than patriots and good government.[11]

The number of Virginians engaged in politics who still held such views is difficult to estimate. In any case, most of them realized that refusing to campaign could possibly lead to defeat.

In parts of New England in the 1790s, open solicitation of votes was still frowned upon. When an occasional vote-getting foray occurred it met with a good deal of public derision. As a Connecticut congressman insisted: "Should any person have the effrontery or folly to make such an attempt, he may be assured of meeting with the general contempt and indignation of the people, and of throwing an insuperable bar in the way of obtaining the object of his pursuit."[12] Even in the Middle Atlantic states electioneering "out of doors" was not yet fully respectable. One New Jersey critic declared that a candidate is a "detestable and dangerous wretch when his popularity has been 'sought after' by *day light* and by *candle light*."[13] Many men who went about looking for votes had to disguise their campaigning activities. Some claimed that their traveling was connected with business purposes. Others maintained that they were simply visiting friends.

In spite of the negative attitude exhibited by traditionalists, vote seeking met with less disapproval as time went on. By the turn of the century it had become an accepted fact of political life in most locales. Although some persons still privately expressed their misgivings about what transpired, few public pronouncements appeared, at least outside of Connecticut. Of course, extensive campaigning continued to be more acceptable in the South and the Middle Atlantic states than in conservative New England. Nevertheless, as Noble Cunningham has pointed out: "Everywhere the growth of parties brought both necessity and respectability to electioneering. Whether a candidate issued an address to the voters over his own name or left this to be done by a committee, whether a candidate himself campaigned or relied on an election committee, the voters were increasingly solicited for their suffrages."[14]

The mounting party rivalry also tended to break down the traditional notion that men should be elected to office on the basis of their community standing or former service. Where one stood on current issues came to hold greater importance. The impact was not uniform, but even in states slow to organize politically the change became evident. As historian J. R. Pole has written about Virginia at this time: "Although a two-party system hardly took root the party contest helped to splinter the fences of the old regime. It encroached on the personal character of the relationship between representative and electors by introducing considerations of general and impersonal policy. . . . Electors began to meet to inform their representatives of their opinions of their performances; and, an equally unusual departure, representatives began to report the proceedings of the [legislative or congressional] session to their constituents."[15]

PRINTED MATTER

Congressmen kept their constituents abreast of events by mailing various documents from the capital. Most useful in this regard was the circular letter. Since they could not reach everyone in their district either in person or by separate notices, many incumbent legislators sent general printed letters to the people back home. Such works usually ran two to four pages in length, though sometimes longer, and were aimed particularly at knowledgeable persons who had previously expressed concern with state and national affairs. Some letters primarily contained factual accounts of the proceedings of Congress, others included the personal views of the author on government policies. The phenomenon of circular letters had its greatest utility in the South and West, less densely settled regions without many sources of news and lacking in formal party machinery. Although not distributed solely in election years, these letters and related materials became obvious campaign devices.[16]

Circular letters may have been helpful but for most locales in the new republic newspapers constituted the chief electioneering tool. The number of papers being published climbed from 91 (70 weeklies, 10 semiweeklies, 3 triweeklies, 8 dailies) in 1790 to 234 (178 weeklies, 29 semiweeklies, 3 triweeklies, 24 dailies) in 1800.[17] More important than rising numbers was the high degree of partisanship exhibited. Some newspapers had begun to take sides in the struggle over the Constitution. But this generally did not represent a permanent commitment, and most sheets subsequently returned to an independent stance. By the late 1790s, however, a large percentage of them had come to display firm partisan leanings. Statements on issues and candidates increasingly reflected only one point of view. In fact, after a while many publications were founded expressly for political purposes. Although they often printed a few pages of business news like their predecessors, the basic purpose of these journals lay in promoting a particular party and position. By 1810 at least half the newspapers in the country were political rather than commercial in orientation.[18]

Distributing newspapers was often the only way the party could reach the prospective voter. With over ninety percent of the population living in rural areas, the gazettes, as they frequently were called, became indispensable. Some partisan papers deliberately were sold below cost because of the political influence they could exert. Indeed, a certain quantity might be given away to the public without any charge. The Republican committee in Norfolk County, Massachusetts, for example, resolved "That the Printer of the SALEM REGISTER be requested to print an extra number of papers from this time to the time of the election, to be distributed GRATIS among the people by the committees of the various towns, and that these committees be EARNESTLY REQUESTED to send by all opportunities to Salem for the same, in as great a number as they can use adventageously, and that the same be delivered to said committees FREE OF EXPENCE."[19]

As newspapers turned into partisan organs the person in charge, formally known as the printer, began to act more like a modern editor—not simply taking items from other journals but actually writing lead essays or editorials. By 1796 Noah Webster, a Federalist, who had set up the *American Minerva* in New York City, regularly included editorials under the masthead, and his counterparts at other publications soon followed suit. Several men in this era, in fact, would gain notoriety for their scurrilous attacks upon state and national leaders. Benjamin Franklin Bache, grandson of Benjamin Franklin and founder of the *Aurora* (Philadelphia), served as the chief Republican hatchetman, denouncing John Adams as a monarchist and assailing even George Washington as a "debaucher of his country." Prominent on the Federalist side stood William Cobbett, an English émigré who became a master of invective as the publisher of *Porcupine's Gazette* (Philadelphia). On one occasion Cobbett condemned Pennsylvania gubernatorial candidate Thomas McKean as a "secret Catholic," a "coward," and a "turncoat."[20]

ELECTION OF 1792

In the early 1790s the heaviest amount of all forms of electioneering took place in the states of New York and Pennsylvania, where factional division was strongest. The race for the New York governorship in 1792 between George Clinton and John Jay was typical of the battles being waged. (Although contemporaries referred to the rivalry as one between Clintonians and Jayites, it essentially represented a Republican–Federalist encounter, as each group had national connections.) Key figures on both sides created committees of correspondence to promote their respective interest. Governor Clinton started sending "expresses"—fast riders carrying direct dispatches— to all corners of the state urging a full mobilization of forces. Jay's backers, seeing their opponents using "every exertion to influence the public mind in favor of their candidate," felt it necessary to act in a like fashion. They told county leaders to do everything possible "to bring forward the electors, and to see that the election is held, and the returns made in strict conformity to the law."[21] Nevertheless, the Jay-Federalist campaigners could not match the Clinton-Republican network, and Clinton won the election.

An equally large effort was made by competing forces during the 1792 congressional contest in Pennsylvania, though here too the Republicans went to greater lengths. Operations began with a small group of party officers in Philadelphia, headed by Dr. James Hutchinson and Alexander Dallas, who formed a statewide ticket. Then letters were sent to their associates in various locales around the state asking that a thorough canvass be made. Hutchinson told Albert Gallatin, future secretary of the treasury, who was then in charge of Republican affairs in Luzerne County: "we rely on you for making the ticket universally known among our friends to the West of the Alleghenny." He carefully instructed Gallatin about the need for a heavy turnout on election day. "I hope all your influential characters will be active," he wrote. "No exertion will be wanting here."[22]

On the presidential level, as had happened in the first federal election, no contest ever developed. Partisans in both camps wanted George Washington to continue to occupy the chief executive's office. (Washington was perhaps the only president who did not in some way angle for the exalted post he held.) Some Republican leaders, however, seemed dissatisfied with the idea of John Adams remaining in the vice presidency and sought his removal. Adams had irritated many people with his writings on government, which included positive words about the British monarchy. In a few states Republicans gave their support to George Clinton of New York. Yet most of the campaigning against Adams went on behind the scenes, and it soon became apparent tht he would be reelected by a substantial margin.[23]

The party struggle broadened over the next few years, especially as it became caught up with problems in foreign affairs. The French Revolution took an extremely violent turn, and in 1793 a troubled France went to war against England. This placed immense pressure on the United States, which during its war for independence had signed a treaty of alliance with France. President Washington believed he was following the right course by keeping the country neutral amid these tumultuous developments. But many Republicans were disappointed that the United States had failed to come to the aid of the beleaguered French, who had sent an emissary (Citizen Genêt) to solicit American support. They were further angered when the president's special envoy, Chief Justice John Jay, concluded a treaty with England in 1794 that brought the United States only insignificant commercial concessions and left several key questions unresolved. Jay's Treaty and other matters relating to foreign policy would be major issues in the congressional and state contests in 1794–95.[24]

Among the new forces on the election scene in several states were popular associations known as Democratic or Republican societies. These groups had been formed in defense of republicanism and in opposition to the Federalist agenda, particularly in regard to foreign relations and the use of government troops to put down the so-called Whiskey Rebellion in Pennsylvania. Members of such organizations actively supported Republican state and congressional candidates, playing a large role in many contests. Although they passed resolutions, drew up addresses, circulated broadsides, and paraded in the streets to promote their cause, there is no evidence that they ever managed campaigns or functioned as official agencies of the Republican party. They acted more like interest or pressure groups and never gained full respectability. The original societies died out within a few years, but they served as a model for local political clubs founded later on in the next century.[25]

The Federalists, while faced with heavier competition, continued to dominate the national government, much to the dismay of the Republican leaders. Thomas Jefferson resigned his post as secretary of state in 1793, finding himself at odds more than ever with the Washington–Hamilton administration. From his home in Virginia he led the opposition against the central government's increasingly pro-Federalist policies. Jefferson did not at first express any desire to seek the presidency when Washington chose to step down in 1796, but it was clear that he would accept a call from fellow

Republicans to stand for that office if they requested his services. And within a short time they did.[26]

ELECTION OF 1796

Distinguished by competing individuals as much as by competing issues, the election of 1796 marked the first real battle for the presidency in American history. The publication of Washington's farewell address late that summer provided "a signal, like dropping a hat, for the party racers to start," wrote Fisher Ames of Massachusetts.[27] Actually, Republican leaders had begun making preparations some months before, nominating by consensus (without a formal caucus) Thomas Jefferson as the party's standard-bearer. Little attention was paid to naming a running mate, although Senator Aaron Burr in New York had acquired the backing of key men in several states. The Federalists, in a similarly informal manner, designated John Adams of Massachusetts, the incumbent vice president, and Thomas Pinckney of South Carolina, negotiator of the recent treaty with Spain, for the top two spots on their side.[28]

The Adams–Jefferson contest in 1796 did a great deal to stimulate the growth of campaign machinery. Competing party tickets listing the names of presidential electors were created for the first time in a number of states— New York, Pennsylvania, Delaware, and Massachusetts. In almost all cases, the tickets were framed at party meetings with many members of the party faithful in attendance. In Delaware, for instance, "deputies from the several hundreds" in Kent County met at Dover "for the purpose of preparing a ticket, to be recommended to the Republican Citizens . . . at the ensuing general election."[29] To be sure, formal organization of the party did not proceed as far elsewhere; no other competing statewide tickets seem to have been put forth. The Federalists lacked party apparatus in most of the South, and the Republicans faced the same problem in the North. Moreover, only half of the sixteen states permitted the popular choice of presidential electors, limiting the possibilities for greater activity to some degree.

Much of the presidential struggle was carried out in the press. Federalist journals attacked the Republicans as supporters of French radicalism, Citizen Genêt, the Whiskey Rebellion, and antifederalism. Republican papers responded by condemning the Federalists for their pro-British sympathies and principally for their defense of the Jay Treaty. Both sides, however, devoted the most space to the candidates' characters. Indeed, the background and personal traits of the two major contenders became the main issue in the race. Editorialists described their favorite as a glorious patriot while portraying the opponent as a virtual traitor. At the hands of Republican writers, Adams was seen as a friend of monarchy and aristocracy; Jefferson, according to the Federalists, represented Jacobinism and revolution. The candidates themselves remained publicly silent throughout the war of words, setting a precedent that would be largely observed for many years.[30]

The state that experienced the greatest amount of electioneering in 1796 was large and populous Pennsylvania. The two sides stood about evenly matched, and both realized that tremendous exertions would be necessary to achieve victory. The Republican campaign became noteworthy for producing the first full-fledged party manager in American politics, John Beckley. Beckley, a Virginia-bred Republican who held the position of clerk in the House of Representatives, took charge of every detail in the multidistrict vote-getting operation. No previous effort could compare with Beckley's. From his post in Philadelphia, he wrote letters to local leaders urging their cooperation. Because the Federalists controlled the urban areas, Beckley had his followers concentrate on rural voters. He also showed his ingenuity by creating an attractive ticket—one that included the well-known Thomas McKean and Peter Muhlenberg—and then sent out an enormous quantity of hand-written ballots to help familiarize the inhabitants with the names of the Republican electors. At one point he informed Madison that "30,000 tickets are gone thro' the State by express into every county." Later on he shipped over a thousand copies of an important pamphlet, circulating it first in the western region so as to prevent any effective Federalist rebuttal in the east. Beckley's maneuvers surely helped make it possible for Jefferson to win fourteen of Pennsylvania's fifteen electoral votes. While his direct influence on contemporaries is hard to measure, Beckley continued to play a major role as organizer and propagandist.[31]

One unusual aspect of the race, at least from a modern perspective, was the brazen attempt by France to influence the result through its minister, Pierre Adet. As one historian has written: "Never before or since has a foreign power acted so openly in an American election."[32] During the summer, Adet made a trip to New England to promote Jefferson's candidacy and also sent agents to tour the western states for the same purpose. Later on he wrote a number of newspaper articles blaming the Federalists for the decline in Franco-American relations and threatening the possibility of naval action against U.S. shipping. Then, in November, just at the moment the presidential electors were to cast their ballots, Adet announced that he had been recalled because the French Directory felt the government had become unmistakably pro-British. Adet believed that France's sympathizers in this country would react to these moves by doing whatever was necessary to have Jefferson chosen president. But, if anything, his scheme had a negative effect, for many Americans disliked, and would always staunchly oppose, foreign interference in the nation's electoral process.[33]

Whether Adet's activities had any impact upon the outcome, the Federalists won. Even with the loss in Pennsylvania, the administration party acquired enough electoral votes to come out on top. It swept every state in the Northeast and picked up scattered support in the upper South, where voting had proceeded on a district basis. Jefferson took most of the southern votes as well as those in the new states of Kentucky and Tennessee, but he completely failed in New York, New Jersey, and New England. Adams gained the presidency notwithstanding an attempt by Alexander Hamilton to make vice presidential designee Pinckney the chief executive by having Adams's name left off the ballot in a few southern states. In fact, Hamilton's strategy backfired, for some northern Federalists got wind of his scheme and deliberately left off Pinckney's name so that Jefferson wound up with the second highest total in the electoral college and became vice president.[34]

Although Adams defeated Jefferson in the presidential balloting in 1796, party strife did not come to an end. In fact, it soon accelerated to an even higher level. This was plainly apparent in the congressional elections of 1798–99, which took place at a time of growing U.S. conflict with France and division at home over passage of the Alien and Sedition Acts. Fierce struggles at the ballot box sprang up in several states.[35] One in Virginia, which had national consequences, pitted future chief justice John Marshall against a feisty Republican incumbent John Clopton. In the press Clopton and others sharply censured Marshall for hiding his Federalist views and for his allegedly extravagant campaigning style. They reported that he had danced around bonfires at a public gathering and had spent the unheard-of sum of five thousand dollars on barbecues. One editorialist ridiculed Marshall as "the pay-master of strong liquors, the barbecue representative of Richmond." Yet despite the charges, the better-known Marshall prevailed at the polls by the slim margin of 108 votes.[36]

Many other eminent Federalists around the country also obtained narrow victories, capitalizing on the heightened anti-French sentiment and Adams's sincere quest for peace. There were now 63 Federalists and 43 Republicans in Congress, but it nevertheless proved difficult for the Federalists to maintain their position because of popular resentment toward the Alien and Sedition Acts and other administration policies that threatened personal liberty. Internal tensions remained high during the next year-and-a-half as dramatic court cases and legislative measures highlighted partisan differences. The continuing discord helped set the stage for the powerful party clash in the year 1800.

ELECTION OF 1800

The presidential election of 1800, with Jefferson again challenging Adams, easily ranks as the largest and most heated encounter in the early years of the republic. The magnitude of electioneering would not be surpassed for almost a quarter of a century. Without question, more people were involved, more literature was distributed, more canvassing went on, and more interstate coordination took place than in any presidential race before the Jacksonian era. Prominent figures corresponded constantly, and a few like Aaron Burr and Alexander Hamilton traveled to several states trying to influence the outcome. Yet for all the activity this was by no means a national campaign. No national organizations existed on either side and no overall direction was attempted. State groups may have received some party literature and advice from national leaders, but each one acted more or less independently. Moreover, the election system still lacked uniformity. Voting in the sixteen states occurred at different times under different laws, and in some cases the electoral results hinged upon local legislative contests. Only five states permitted the designation of presidential electors by direct popular choice. In certain others, the majority party, fearing the worst, tried to limit the popular will. The Republican-dominated legislature in Virginia, for example, switched from election by districts to a general ticket, which prevented their opponents from acquiring any electoral votes. In similarly partisan fashion Federalist forces in New Hampshire and Massachusetts transferred the responsibility for naming electors to the legislature. Such legal maneuvers reduced campaigning in these states, but elsewhere it flourished far beyond the level of 1796.[37]

The Republicans showed themselves to be much better organized in 1800 than in the previous national election. At least forty-three senators and representatives met in a formal caucus and nominated Thomas Jefferson and Aaron Burr as the official party candidates. For the first time several state committees inaugurated a wide range of vote-getting activities. New Jersey Republicans, who heretofore had been rather inactive, established various local and county groups in addition to the main state committee to promote the candidates. County committees usually ran all aspects of the operation in their area; they published addresses, circulated handbills, arranged party meetings, and sent delegates to statewide gatherings. In Virginia, a legislative caucus put together a complete slate of electors and formed a Republican General Committee to manage the campaign. The party ticket was distributed throughout the Old Dominion, and the General Committee's official statement endorsing Jefferson was reprinted regularly in the leading Republican newspapers.[38]

The Federalists, though somewhat divided and slow to react, also held a congressional nominating caucus, where they once more agreed to support John Adams, along with General Charles Cotesworth Pinckney of South Carolina. (In a situation similar to the one in 1796, Hamilton and some of his friends hoped that Pinckney could obtain a higher proportion of the electoral votes.) The Federalists then set up coordinating committees and county organizations in key states, but the scope of their effort did not match that of the Republicans. Groups remained small and often had to depend on a few elite figures in each locale. In charge of the Federalist vote-getting machinery were a number of office holders—customs collectors, internal revenue clerks, postmasters, judges, and so on—who owed their livelihood to the incumbent administration. For example, Lucius Stockton, a federal attorney in New Jersey, spent almost a month traveling on horseback speaking out in favor of Adams and against Jefferson.[39]

Neither party created formal platforms in the modern sense, but Jefferson previously had set forth a list of principles that would be repeated by Republicans over the course of the campaign. Besides vowing to uphold the Constitution and oppose monarchy, Jefferson called for "a government rigorously frugal and simple," "the discharge of the national debt," plus limitations on military spending and on the size of the federal bureaucracy. He also supported "free commerce with all nations, political connections with none." This program was printed by the *Aurora* (Philadelphia) in a modified form, which provided a statement of Republican aims in one column that was contrasted with the Federalist record of high taxes, standing armies, and violations of civil liberties in an adjoining column.[40]

In their pronouncements the Federalists ignored the charges made by the Jeffersonians and instead emphasized peace and prosperity. The creation of the federal government plus the leadership shown by Washington and Adams, they said, had provided the country with a successful start. As the Federalist Committee of Virginia declared: "To the adoption of our constitution, to the sage maxims of administration established by the immortal WASHINGTON, and steadily pursued by his virtuous successor, may be fairly ascribed our present prosperous situation."[41] The men in power had fostered economic recovery, prevented involvement in two wars, and fully maintained our national honor. Now the proposed election of a Republican president threatened to ruin it all. One Federalist newspaper in New York put it quite bluntly: "The question to be settled is, whether we shall retain that Constitution, under whose influence we have all flourished . . . or whether we shall be plunged into scenes of horror and misery, similar to those experienced in France."[42]

While official party literature usually refrained from personal diatribe, many unofficial writings did not, and the campaign often deteriorated into a series of attacks upon individual character. Federalists blasted Jefferson for his religious convictions or, to be more precise, his alleged lack thereof. Reverend William Linn of New York, in an essay entitled "Serious Considerations on the Election of a President," argued that the designation "of any man avowing the principles of Mr. Jefferson would . . . destroy religion, introduce immorality, and loosen all the bonds of society."[43] On the front page of the highly partisan *Gazette of the United States*, published in Philadelphia, voters were asked the question: "shall I continue in allegiance to

GOD—AND A RELIGIOUS PRESIDENT
 Or impiously declare for
JEFFERSON—AND NO GOD!!!"[44]

John Adams too faced a mountain of slanderous abuse. He provided an easy target for Republican penmen, as historian John C. Miller has pointed out: "Having written a book and spoken his mind freely on all occasions, he had in effect delivered himself into the hands of his enemies. From his own words, sometimes garbled and quoted out of context, he was convicted of being an advocate of monarchy, life tenure for senators, an alliance with Great Britain, and a fighting Navy." One of Adams's biggest critics was none other than high Federalist Alexander Hamilton, who wrote a scathing pamphlet claiming that the president's conduct and character made him unfit to be retained in office. Although this work originally had been intended for private consideration among Federalist leaders, its eventual public circulation caused immense division within the party at a critical stage of the contest.[45]

Neither Adams nor Jefferson said or wrote anything for public consumption, but both candidates did play a more active role in 1800 than in 1796. Jefferson carried on correspondence with Republican officials in several states and distributed numerous pamphlets to them. Whereas he himself did not write letters to the press, he often urged his friends to do so. Adams also consulted with his supporters around the country, and while he never made a direct appeal for votes, he did take a roundabout route when he journeyed to the new federal capital that year. He briefly stopped at Lancaster, Pennsylvania, greeting onlookers, then traveled to Frederickstown, Maryland, doing more of the same. Next, he shifted directions and visited Annapolis and Baltimore. "Why," if not to campaign, inquired a Jeffersonian editor, "must the President go fifty miles out of his way to make a trip to Washington?"[46]

The final result in 1800 largely was determined at a very early stage in the voting—by the outcome of the legislative contest in New York in May. New York possessed twelve crucial electoral votes that were to be designated by its newly chosen house and senate. Because the overconfident Federalists refused to adopt the district system, it became winner take all. Aaron Burr, in charge of the state's Republican campaign, thus set out to achieve a total victory for his side. New York City held the key, and to entice straddlers Burr put together an attractive ticket, persuading such notables as ex-governor George Clinton, General Horatio Gates, and Brockholst Livingston to be on the slate. He also built an innovative local machine to capture the vote—creating a finance committee, setting up ward and precinct meetings, compiling a card index of past voter preferences, and stationing men at the polls to guard against fraud. While the balloting went on, Burr was indefatigable, appearing at several voting places to harangue the people as they came to make their choices. Alexander Hamilton, supervising the Federalist forces, tried to exert a similar influence by parading on horseback and addressing the freemen before they voted. But the Federalist ticket proved less appealing (ironically, the party of "aristocracy" had named several artisans and shopkeepers), and the organizational structure did not measure up to their opponents. This put New York in the Republican column.[47]

Even with the loss of New York, the Federalists still had a chance to win.

They controlled most of New England, and if they could have mustered enough support from the South, their party might have been victorious. In many southern states the campaign generated great excitement. This was particularly true in politically divided North Carolina. By August a Raleigh newspaper declared that the election had crowded out every other topic of conversation. Leaders of both parties distributed huge quantities of literature over a wide area hoping to influence as many voters as possible. In Maryland, where interest rose even higher, stump speakers proved extremely active. As one bystander observed: "The candidates, on both sides, are now traveling through their districts, soliciting the favor of individuals, with whom they associate on no other occasion, and men of the first consideration condescend to collect the dissolute and ignorant mobs of hundreds of individuals, to whom they make long speeches in the open air."[48]

The Federalists ran fairly well in North Carolina and Maryland, taking roughly half the electoral vote in each. But in South Carolina they suffered a critical defeat. At first it seemed as if the Federalists might win, for the tally in the city of Charleston stood heavily in their favor. Notwithstanding greater Republican successes in the outlying areas, the outcome remained in doubt when the presidential electors gathered at the capital. There, Charles Pinckney, cousin of the Federalist candidate but strongly inclined to the Jeffersonian side, managed to convince several uncommitted electors to vote a straight Republican ticket, giving the party a clear majority. (During the negotiations Charles Cotesworth Pinckney might have been able to gain enough support for the presidency or vice presidency, but he refused to accept any votes separate from Adams.)[49] The victory in South Carolina, after a sweep of Pennsylvania, Virginia, Kentucky, and Tennessee, put Jefferson and his running mate Aaron Burr over the top with 73 electoral votes to Adams's 65 and Pinckney's 64.

This seemed to conclude the election, but then a major complication arose. The federal Constitution recognized no distinction between presidential and vice presidential candidates, and Burr had accumulated the same number of electoral votes as Jefferson. It was assumed that Burr immediately would step aside. When the wily New Yorker chose not to, there ensued many weeks of behind-the-scenes intrigue as the election was thrown into the House of Representatives. Some Federalist congressmen saw an opportunity to thwart their Republican enemies by designating Burr for the chief executive's spot. Eventually, however, after thirty-five indecisive ballots, they withdraw their backing. Influenced to some degree by Alexander Hamilton, they came to believe that Jefferson would be less likely than Burr to change previous policies or ruin the country. Thus "the sage of Monticello," the acknowledged leader of the Republicans, finally became the third president.[50]

FEDERALIST RESURGENCE

With Jefferson in the White House and an overwhelming Republican majority in Congress, the Federalists now appeared doomed as a major party.

Besides having a narrow appeal, they had not been as politically active as their opponents at election time. All through the previous decade the party had not been deeply involved in organized electioneering. To be sure, they had set up newspapers and in some states like New York had established formal machinery. But widespread partisan activity through corresponding committees, broad-based canvassing, and treating had been more characteristic of the other side. Many of the older, traditional Federalists had, in fact, always detested open campaigning. One contemporary noted that gentlemen of the old school "did not mingle with the mass," for this would have been "too degrading for them." Indeed, the Federalists during the 1790s mainly had relied on their control of the apparatus of government for continued success. They depended on the prestige of the presidency to awe the public and the Alien and Sedition Acts to coerce their enemies.[51]

After the party's crushing defeat in 1800, some Federalist leaders, particularly of the younger generation, saw the need for change. If they ever hoped to retain federal power or prevent further deterioration at the state level, it was imperative for them to give up their relatively passive stance and begin courting popular favor. These men, of course, did not wish to become democrats, but they realized the importance of adopting some democratic techniques. "In order to preserve the commonwealth," said Harrison Gray Otis of Massachusetts, one of the new guard, "our organization must be more complete and systematic. It must extend through every county and town, and an ample fund must be provided for the distribution of political truth."[52] Soon the Federalists began developing a more sophisticated campaign apparatus than they had ever thought possible. In nearly all the states from New Hampshire to Maryland, Federalists set up formal statewide committees and eventually created an elaborate structure of county and local committees that arranged nominations and supervised campaigns.[53]

Expanding on the techniques employed by their adversaries, Federalists in Connecticut, Massachusetts, and New Hampshire made a vigorous attempt to recruit new voters to their cause. Using more or less the same sophisticated approach in each state, party leaders requested that town committees divide their towns into districts and "procure a list of all voters in the town unquestionably Federal." After identifying loyal members, they needed to "procure a list of all doubtful characters." The object of the first list was "that the Federalists may be known and brought to town meeting." The object of the second was "that the men may be known, who may be influenced by correct information to vote on the federal side." Subcommittees in each district comprising "active, prudent, popular federalists" were supposed to inspect the situation to make certain that the plans were being carried out. Such efforts, the leaders hoped, would bring their side "an encrease of many thousands of votes."[54]

In a major switch from past policy, the Federalists, who had earlier appealed primarily to the "respectable citizens," now sought to attract the working-class vote. Urban committees hosted get-togethers for various groups of artisans. The writer Washington Irving, promoting the Federalist cause in New York City, spent a number of evenings drinking beer, shaking hands, and talking with the multitude. At the same time, newspaper editors prepared essays aimed at winning over specific groups such as cartmen and shoemakers. On one occasion a Federalist writer asserted that shoemakers had been "grossly deceived" by Republicans in the legislature. In general, he warned that Republicans were hypocrites who would expound "on every corner" that "all men are created equal" yet, when meeting a man who differed from them, would attempt to "knock out his eye for a damned rascal." Looking for any new source of support, the Federalists even courted free blacks with promises of local offices and "enormous supplies of home crackers and cheese."[55]

Although in the 1790s the Federalists had scorned the so-called Republican Societies fostered by their opponents, they now decided to establish a variation of their own. Founders of these groups generally called them Washington Benevolent Societies, associating themselves with the name and deeds of their renowned and recently departed leader. While only a few such societies sprang up immediately, by the year 1808 they were operating widely from Maryland northward. Besides promoting Federalist principles, members often contributed money to campaigns or helped out at election time by distributing literature and preparing handwritten tickets. Sometimes they held public exercises on the Fourth of July, on Washington's birthday (February 22), or on April 30, the anniversary of the president's first inaugural, which in certain states coincided with election day.[56]

An important part of the Federalist electioneering surge involved making sure that most of their adherents voted. In both inland towns and coastal cities, the party took great pains to encourage and convey voters to the polling place. As the partisan Newburyport, Massachusetts, newspaper announced just before the balloting in 1804: "Let every Federalist on [election] day quit his shop, his farm, his office, or his counting house, and make everything subservient to the great duty he owes his country.[57] In Boston, according to Samuel Eliot Morison, "vigilant ward committees made life miserable for the stay-at-homes," harassing them in several ways. Ticket distributors were employed in each of the twelve wards and "bully boys" were stationed at the polls. Federalists in other cities hired conveyances to ensure a heavy turnout. Coachmen in New York City went through the streets offering rides. In Delaware partisans rented three ships to transport voters from Wilmington to Dover.[58]

All in all, the Federalists were fairly successful in expanding their vote-getting operations during the first decade of the new century. They formed numerous committees and initiated a variety of measures to increase popular support. Yet as David Hackett Fischer has pointed out: "Try as they might, the young Federalists were probably never able to equal in volume the electioneering of their opponents." On the same day that the party arranged a barbecue in Anne Arundel County, Maryland, in 1809, Fischer notes, the "Jeffersonians sponsored no fewer than nine barbecues in the same county."[59] Just as the Federalists celebrated Washington's birthday and inauguration day, so the Republicans developed festivities commemorating what they considered big occasions and often in a more elaborate fashion. Easily the most notable event on their calendar was that honoring Jefferson's inauguration on March 4. "The 4th of March forms an epoch in the political history of the United States, which ought to awaken the purest sensations of the American Patriot," announced a Virginia Republican.[60]

Some of the biggest and bitterest campaigns of those years occurred in the governorship races in Massachusetts and New York, where support for the two parties was evenly divided. Although speechmaking and treating rarely went on in the Bay State, plenty of partisan literature was passed around. As Nathaniel Ames recorded in his diary in March 1808, "Electioneering opened. Pamphlets flying like wild geese in a storm.[61] Two years earlier Republican candidate James Sullivan exclaimed: "The arts, frauds, bribes and calumnies used by the federalists this year were never equalled but in one instance. Bribery is boasted of without a blush, and the most attrocious slanders smoothed over with an apology that they were only for an electioneering purpose."[62] In the heated New York contest of 1804, when the Federalists aligned themselves with the slippery Aaron Burr, many charges of corruption sailed back and forth. References also appeared regarding Burr's alleged *amours*. It was claimed that he had developed a liaison with the young daughter of a Washington tradesman, whom he secretly had lured to New York City. One handbill even mentioned specific houses of ill repute that he was supposed to frequent.[63]

Even though the war for independence had ended more than two decades earlier, Republicans campaigning in these states and elsewhere still sought to equate Federalists with Tories. New Yorkers favoring Burr's candidacy in 1804 found themselves condemned as "sons of sworn king's men." Broadsides three years later linked "Tory-Federalists" with many atrocities of the Revolution. One sheet published in Massachusetts in 1808 even declared them responsible for the Boston Massacre. In 1810 the *New York Journal* habitually referred to the "Federalist Tories" as men who had gained their wealth while true Whigs were sacrificing everything for the Patriot cause. In about every election prior to the War of 1812, "Anglo Federalists" faced accusations of sympathizing with British impressment of seamen and other misdeeds perpetrated upon Americans. Federalist writers, for their part, harped on past Republican sympathy for the French Revolution and "Jacobinism."[64]

Both sides used various deceptive means to influence election outcomes. These included the distribution of misleading handbills and the dispatching of illegal voters. One technique increasingly employed was the gerrymander, that is, the manipulation of districts in such a way as to give one party a greater majority than their voting strength deserved. Although engaged in by Patrick Henry and a few others before 1790, the practice became particularly common in the period from 1798 to 1812. There were, in fact, more than a dozen incidents in this fourteen-year span—five in New York alone between 1802 and 1809. The actual term gerrymander originated in Massachusetts in 1812. A group of Federalists noted the fact that the outer portion of Essex County had been made into a monster-shaped election district. When artist Elkanah Tisdale drew a sketch of it looking like a salamander, someone spoke up and called it a gerrymander after Republican governor Elbridge Gerry, who had allowed the bill to become law.[65]

ELECTIONS OF 1804–20

While statewide contests through 1816 often involved considerable electioneering, national campaigns for the presidency tended to be rather limited in scope. The election of 1804, with Thomas Jefferson certain to be chosen a second time, led to little activity beyond some newspaper editorials praising or criticizing his administration. The Republican press proudly pointed to the reduced taxes and national debt, the elimination of the Alien and Sedition Acts, and, of course, the recently completed Louisiana Purchase (1803), which had doubled the size of the nation. The Federalists again condemned Jefferson's character, referring to him as an infidel and an atheist. They also tried to show that his policies had weakened the country and brought on the threat of war. Even the acquisition of Louisiana was looked on by them as a mistake. But the vast majority of people, including many onetime northern Federalists, rejected these views and supported the Virginia Republican. Jefferson took more than ninety percent of the electoral vote, scoring an easy victory over the Federalist candidate Charles C. Pinckney (162 to 14).[66]

The competition in 1808 grew somewhat more intense, as the country had become enmeshed in the protracted military conflict between England and France. Besides being the victim of naval assaults by both belligerents, the nation suffered from the effects of the administration's Embargo Act, which especially damaged New England shipping. In these circumstances the Federalist party began to revive on the national level, helped along by a sizable division among Republicans regarding the choice of Jefferson's successor. The majority in the congressional caucus supported Secretary of State James Madison, but a significant minority favored James Monroe, and did not enthusiastically endorse Madison after he was nominated. Federalist leaders from eight states held a secret meeting in New York and considered naming George Clinton, the Republican vice president, as their party's standard-bearer before finally settling upon Charles C. Pinckney again. There was little personal campaigning on behalf of the candidates, but many charges and countercharges appeared in the press. The Federalists focused on the issue of the embargo and the terrible hardship it had caused. They also claimed that Madison was subservient to Napoleon and unfairly hostile toward England. Yet the Republicans successfully defended their record, and Madison emerged victorious by a margin of 122 to 47 in the final electoral tally.[67]

The next presidential election, coinciding with the preliminary phases of the War of 1812, wound up being a much closer contest. Many Americans, particularly those living along the northeastern coast, were unhappy about the war and its early mismanagement. They wanted James Madison ousted. The Federalists, as part of their effort to capitalize on these circumstances and return to power, held a secret gathering that had many of the characteristics of a nominating convention. Seventy delegates representing all sections of the country were present at this meeting. While not everybody there accepted the outcome, De Witt Clinton of New York (a Republican and nephew of the former governor and vice president) became the party's standard-bearer against the incumbent Madison. Shortly before, Madison had been unanimously renominated by the Republican congressional caucus (80 to 0).

The coalition of Clintonians and Federalists in 1812 pushed much harder than those who were involved in the two preceding anti-Republican efforts. They fiercely attacked Madison's foreign-policy blunders, charging the president with incompetency and calling him an agent of France. "Madison and War! or Clinton and Peace," they shouted over and over in the northern states. Madison supporters tried to defend his policies and his conduct of the war, claiming it was wrong "to impute to Mr. Madison the failure of every military expedition." They also warned that the election of Clinton would mean a restoration of unpopular Federalist programs. These latter arguments helped Madison retain his hold on traditionally Republican areas below the Mason-Dixon line, but in the more divided North, Clinton took almost the entire electoral vote. Indeed, had he won in Pennsylvania, he would have gone to the White House. But Madison prevailed in the Keystone State, where there was considerable prowar sentiment, and in virtually the entire South and West, gaining a total of 128 votes to 89 for his opponent.[68]

The Madison–Clinton encounter in 1812 turned out to be the last national battle seriously waged by the Federalists. The party would soon be totally disgraced as a result of obstructionist tactics exhibited during the war, culminating in the Hartford Convention, where some members even talked of secession. In 1816 the leadership went through the motions of putting up a presidential candidate, but they did not really contest the election in an active manner. Few articles appeared in the press. Certain states such as Rhode Island did not even put forth a Federalist slate of electors. Rufus King of New York, who allowed his name to be entered as the party designee, managed just 34 electoral votes, compared to 183 for the Republicans' James Monroe, longtime diplomat and former secretary of state, who now succeeded

Madison. Like his predecessors, Monroe did not openly campaign—of course, he had no need to. Four years later, in 1820, Monroe faced no opposition of any kind in his reelection bid and acquired every electoral vote but one.[69]

On the state level as well, contests after 1815 diminished in number and intensity, with competition in some places becoming almost nonexistent. The elaborate vote-getting machinery of a few years earlier, including the corresponding committees, soon slipped into inactivity. By 1817 the Republicans had come to dominate every state government with the exception of Delaware and Massachusetts. Only a handful of New England and Middle Atlantic states still possessed any active Federalist opposition. In certain states like Pennsylvania and New Hampshire, the chief encounters involved rival factions of the Republican party. Indeed, probably the most vigorous electioneering of the time occurred here. Throughout the South and West, where parties were less organized to begin with, Republican candidates for Congress and other offices generally ran unopposed. As the country entered the 1820s, the first party system, which had once seen a number of hard-fought election campaigns, came to an end.[70]

In the Federalist–Jeffersonian era of 1790 to 1820, election campaigning, while it fell off in the last stages, advanced considerably beyond what had developed before the federal government was created. The competing parties came up with many innovations to attract voters to the polls, some of which have been wrongly credited to subsequent periods. There were, however, no truly national campaigns, and the amount of preelection activity remained somewhat limited in certain sections like New England. But even in the more competitive areas, the vote-getting methods of the Federalists and Republicans, compared to the later Whigs and Democrats, "remained half-developed and not explicitly institutionalized." Growth was uneven and depended upon immediate political circumstances. At crucial moments the parties worked hard to create organizations and get out the vote, but when major issues receded from view competition and heavy campaigning diminished. In some states high offices went uncontested for years. As Ronald Formisano has pointed out, a strong correlation existed between organizational efforts and the appearance of big events and issues. Later on, as parties became fully developed, the presence or absence of issues did not have too much effect on the amount of preelection activity. In the heyday of the second party system, fierce contests occurred regardless of the temper of the times.[71]

3

The Jacksonian Period

1824–52

With the old party conflict gone and only a few states still engaging in competitive politics, electioneering in the early 1820s started out in a rather subdued fashion. But over the following two-and-a-half decades, known as the Jacksonian era, the magnitude and style of political campaigning would change dramatically. On every level more innovation occurred in this period than at any time until the next century. The resurgence of political parties in the latter half of the 1820s brought about the first extensively coordinated nationwide campaigns. In conjunction with this movement came the rise of institutions that have remained as basic parts of the electoral system: nominating conventions, party platforms, central committees, complex candidate organizations, massive demonstrations, and other elaborate vote-getting techniques.

NEW PARTIES, NEW CONCEPTS

The new pattern of electioneering did not take hold everywhere at once. In quite a few locales, during the formative stages, the quest for votes did not proceed any faster than before. Certain states, especially in the South and West, were slow to adopt an effective two-party system, so that competition remained limited and men often ran unopposed. Even where politics was more advanced, some office seekers continued to act in the same manner as their predecessors, sending out a few letters, and perhaps making a modest canvass. However, the new campaigning style gradually laid down its roots. By the mid–1830s many congressional and state races became highly competitive and frequently were tied to the struggles of the ascending national parties. Getting elected thus required effort and organization on a far bigger scale. Money had to be raised and newspapers put into operation. For all offices below the presidency, personal appearances and speechmaking now seemed a necessity. Legislative aspirants in Alabama soon were "riding ten or twelve miles in the hot sun and speaking every day" for a whole month. When James K. Polk sought the governorship of Tennessee in 1843, he logged 2,300 miles over a four-month period and sometimes spoke for as long as five to six hours a day.[1]

The upsurge in campaigning resulted not only from the rise in competition but from societal and structural changes that brought a greater proportion of the populace into the political sphere. Deference clearly was on the wane in this new democratic age. The average American had grown more politically aware, as improvements in transportation and communication reduced isolation and made news of major events widely available. In these years, also, the nation's voting population rapidly expanded. Added to the Union were several new states whose laws contained fewer franchise restrictions than in the past. At the same time, nearly all the older states had removed property and other traditional requirements so that by 1825, outside of Virginia, Louisiana, and Rhode Island, suffrage had been extended to virtually all white men. Then, too, numerous political offices that previously had been appointive were now elective. Governors and other state officials increasingly became subject to popular choice. Presidential electors, formerly designated by the legislatures, began to be chosen directly by the people on general tickets. This last-mentioned modification gave a broader dimension to the presidential contest, which heretofore had been outside the purview of many voters.

With the suffrage extended and many positions to fill, it became imperative for those in charge to mobilize voters on a regular, statewide basis. There soon emerged a new kind of leader who proved adept at this task, a job not very pleasing to the old gentleman planter or merchant. The latter remained involved in political life either as candidates for office or in an advisory capacity. The key role of partisan organizer, however, was taken over by a new breed of professional politicians. These men, such as Martin Van Buren and Thurlow Weed of New York and Amos Kendall of Kentucky, typically came from humbler backgrounds and enjoyed the give-and-take of politics, hoping to make it a full-time career. They had worked their way up from the local and state levels to the national level, making important contacts as they moved along. Although not without vision, they usually were more interested in power and place than in any set of high principles. Of course, a few party managers in the past had possessed similar outlooks—for example, John Beckley. But they had been an exception and did not operate at a time when one could exert influence on such an extensive basis.[2]

To achieve their goals the new political architects sought to build more disciplined parties than the earlier ones, organizations that could maintain widespread public support. By and large these men had formed a positive attitude toward political parties, in contrast to the founders' generation, which had considered them a lamentable evil. During the 1820s and 1830s the modern view of parties as necessary democratic devices for shaping and presenting options for popular choice slowly gained acceptance. Most Jacksonian politicians even tolerated the existence of opposition parties. As Van Buren pointed out in 1827: "In a Government like ours founded upon freedom in thought and action, imposing no unnecessary restraints, and calling into action the highest energies of the mind, occasional differences are not only to be expected, but to be desired."[3] Parties, as one historian has written, gave concrete expression to these differences, channeling potentially violent conflict into regularly held electoral contests between competing political groups.

The newly formed parties initially developed in the Middle Atlantic and southern border states, then in New England and the Deep South, and last of all in the West. This second party system not only spread further geographically but became more deeply embedded in society than the first. The two parties created various institutions for mobilizing mass opinion as well as the apparatus for getting out the vote. In addition, their remarkable ability to provide patronage for their followers helped solidify their existence and assured them of continuing support. By midcentury, it is estimated that 50,000 appointments were available in the federal bureaucracy, and many thousands more in state and municipal governments. As party organizations grew and an increasing proportion of the electorate internalized party norms, writes Paul Kleppner, turnout surged upward and then stabilized at a high level. In contrast to the 27 percent recorded in the preparty election of 1824, approximately eighty percent of the eligible voters cast ballots in the 1840 presidential race, and nearly as many participated in subsequent national contests. Voting in state elections did not lag too far behind. Sixty to seventy percent turnouts in congressional and gubernatorial races were not uncommon.[4]

One outgrowth of the new system was the emergence of conventions as the chief method of selecting candidates. Most designations formerly had been made by secret legislative caucuses or mixed caucuses (consisting of elected legislators and other key party members). However, by 1824 such bodies had come to be seen as undemocratic and unrepresentative. Over the next several years nominating conventions started to appear on the state level, and in the early 1830s on the national level. Conventions helped promote unity behind a single candidate and allowed the people to have a greater role in the election process. To be sure, conventions were not necessarily run by the rank and file. In many cases a small clique took over and manipulated the proceedings for its own narrow purposes. But the convention concept must be judged as more democratic than the legislative or mixed caucus. In addition, it encouraged compromise among varying interests, gave official sanction to the party ticket, and served as an important vehicle for launching a campaign.[5]

Some persons naturally remained opposed to the new formations and repeatedly cited the dangers associated with competitive politics. As one New York congressman insisted: "Faction is at war with the vital principle of freedom. It destroys independence of sentiment, and the freedom of election; it subjects the understanding of the People to the influence of their passions."[6] In fact, this age of rising democracy and partisanship fostered a win-at-all-cost attitude that soon reduced the standards of campaigning to an all-time low. Demagoguery, particularly in presidential elections, became widespread, as every candidate was subjected to the most vicious forms of character assassination. To be sure, Thomas Jefferson had been vilified as a radical and John Adams condemned as a monarchist in 1800, but abuse now went beyond all previous bounds. Not all elections, of course, were heavily tainted. But the higher the stakes and the closer the contest, the greater the likelihood that personal assaults would occur.

A few campaigners still capitalized upon their position as gentlemen in their quest for votes, but the majority adapted their approach to fit the new democratic age. This was best accomplished by identifying oneself with the "common man" and claiming to be a "candidate of the people." Some rich men even wore old homespun clothes when out canvassing among prospective voters. "I have always accomodated [sic] my habits and Dress when electioneering," confessed well-to-do North Carolinian James Graham.[7] It became fashionable to talk about one's early hardships, avoiding any mention of current affluence and status. Daniel Webster, who had risen to prominence as a corporate lawyer, usually ignored this fact while on the stump, portraying himself instead as a man of the soil. On a western tour in the 1830s, Webster informed his listeners: "What I am my fellow countrymen you all know; I am a plain man. I never set up for anything: whatever else you may accuse me of, it can never be said that I have set myself up for anything. I am a farmer and on the yellow sands of the east, many a time I have tilled my father's field and followed my father's plough."[8]

While stressing his own common-man status, an office seeker was apt to describe his adversary as an aristocrat. It became standard procedure to attack a rival's wealth and extravagant life–style. This soon extended beyond individuals to entire groups. According to one contemporary, a defeated party had only to brand the opposition as aristocratic in order to regain office. Jacksonian Democrats, in fact, liked to refer to the other side as Federalists.[9] Even more common was the effort to denigrate an opponent's character and accuse him of being unprincipled and corrupt. Some candidates attempted to link their adversary to a political scandal, perhaps an incident of thievery or fraud. When this could not readily be done, it usually was easy to denounce a rival for acting in a duplicitous or underhanded manner. Martin Van Buren, according to the outspoken frontiersman and Whig politician Davy Crockett, "had always two ways to do a thing." As a young child, he could laugh on one side of his face while crying on the other, and by the age of twelve had accomplished the art of reading a book upside-down "to acquire a shifting *nack* for business, and a ready turn for doing things more ways than one."[10]

Besides damning their opponent in one way or another, party leaders on the national level worked to associate their own candidate with notable figures from the past. Displays on behalf of Andrew Jackson often included a portrait of George Washington next to his. In campaign statements supporters depicted "Old Hickory" as a second Washington, the embodiment of true patriotism. "Under Washington our independence was achieved; under Jackson our independence has been preserved," read one handbill in 1824.[11] Jackson also was linked to Jefferson and his "republican" principles, as were other Democratic leaders of the time. Even Whigs such as William Henry Harrison claimed ties with Jefferson. Jefferson had, of course, challenged the Hamiltonian idea of an all-powerful executive branch and stood against all forms of corruption. Harrison would tell a large audience in Ohio in 1840 that "if the Augean stable is to be cleaned, it will be necessary to go back to the principles of Jefferson."[12]

If Jacksonian politicians often emphasized individual character, issues were not neglected. Indeed they became critical factors in most campaigns, particularly on the state level. To be sure, questions involving broad-based reform—abolition of slavery, protection of the Indians, rights of workers— generally were avoided or dealt with only indirectly by the major parties. Each side nevertheless took firm stands on such economic issues as government-financed internal improvements, a protective tariff for industry, and rechartering the Bank of the United States. The Bank ultimately became the biggest issue of Jackson's presidency; regardless of its effectiveness in stabilizing the financial system, it stood to many as a symbol of aristocracy and monopolistic control. Whether or not to retain the institution seemed so momentous a matter by the mid–1830s that Senator Thomas Hart Benton of Missouri predicted that "Every election State or Federal, now and for years to come, will be contested on the question of *Bank or no Bank*.[13] Also of great concern during the Jackson–Van Buren years, at least to the opposition party, was governmental corruption. Charges of flagrant abuse by Jacksonian spoilsmen were heard over and over in every campaign.

Of course, what people viewed as most significant often varied from one state to another. In Pennsylvania, the tariff continued to be the all-important question for many years; in Rhode Island, the extension of the franchise remained crucial; in Missouri, nothing surpassed federal policy toward public land. In the upper Midwest, which was first settled by New Englanders and then inhabited by non-English immigrants, cultural issues sometimes predominated. The evangelical Yankees saw the mass of recent arrivals, especially Catholic Irish and Germans, as threatening the established Anglo-Protestant culture, and sought to prevent the newcomers from acquiring political power. Alien suffrage became a key issue dividing the parties in states like Michigan, Wisconsin, Iowa, and Illinois in the 1840s. In these places as well as in certain northeastern states, the subjects of temperance, Sabbath observance, and Bible reading in the schools also stirred voter interest. Regardless of the issues raised, it is clear that their discussion constituted a basic part of election-time rhetoric.[14]

Perhaps equally as vital as current issues in campaign pronouncements was reiteration of the fundamental principles on which each party stood. The Democrats, claiming that their political creed sprang from the popular will, repeatedly stated their belief in a federal government of limited power, derived solely from the Constitution, which did not interfere in the domestic institutions of the several states. Holding this view, Jackson and his successors always stressed rigid economy and spoke out against heavy federal spending. The National Republicans and later Whigs, on the other hand, argued that the government should play a more positive role in finance and otherwise. "Government," exclaimed a Whig spokesman, "need not and should not be an institution of purely negative, repressive usefulness and value, but . . . should exert a beneficient, paternal, fostering influence upon the Industry and Prosperity of the People. . . . It may promote the welfare and happiness of the People by every means legitimately within its power."[15]

SPEECHMAKING AND HOOPLA

Whatever their view or affiliation, candidates used a variety of methods to get their message across to the public, building on existing practices but carrying them much further. Stump speaking, employed in a few areas during the Federalist–Jefferson era, became extremely widespread in the Jackson period. Aspirants for most state and national offices could not hope to succeed without spending several weeks on the stump. Platform styles differed: some individuals spoke extemporaneously, others delivered prepared speeches or engaged their opponent in open debate. Sometimes rival office seekers wishing to reduce expenses would travel together on a tour of the district. During their days on the hustings they would arrive at a particular town late in the morning, share the podium for the afternoon—each man speaking for a couple of hours—then, following dinner and separate meetings with local officials, the two might occupy the same hotel room, before leaving at dawn for the next stop on the itinerary. Amid national campaigns, major figures would be brought in to speak at huge party gatherings and keep an audience spellbound long into the night. "One of the most remarkable peculiarities of the present time," declared John Quincy Adams in 1840 "is that the principal leaders are traveling about . . . holding forth, like Methodist preachers, hour after hour, to assembled multitudes under the canopy of heaven."[16]

Stump speaking would be supplemented in many instances by a kind of slick showmanship that enhanced the excitement of the new politics. Feeling the need to create high-level enthusiasm for their party ticket, Jacksonian politicians organized huge parades, rallies, barbecues, and tree plantings. They also prepared an abundance of songs and slogans for the campaigners to chant. A few of these phenomena had been introduced previously, but not on anything near the scale applied in this period. While a discussion of the issues and candidates remained basic, hoopla and display proved more effective in whipping up interest among the voters. Thus most crucial elections "would contain a large dose of ballyhoo to amuse and delight an otherwise 'lethargic' public."[17] The volume reached such a point that in 1844 the *Baltimore Sun* would report: "Even those who closely confine their attention to their business cannot remain in ignorance unless they bandage their eyes so that they may not . . . see the poles, flags, and banners or stop up their ears and thus shut out the music accompanying the numerous processions."[18]

Naturally, not all elections caused so much uproar. Moreover, electioneering styles continued to differ from section to section as they had in the past. Contests in New England still were less lively than those in other regions, particularly before 1840. Little ostensible canvassing seems to have been undertaken. While some preelection rallies, picnics, and clambakes took place, the pursuit of votes rarely reached high levels of intensity. It was hard to break with a tradition that frowned on anyone openly seeking support. However, there is evidence of at least a few men spending time on the stump. One was John Clifford, a New Bedford, Massachusetts, judge and fervent Whig. Clifford said that in 1839, "*Every night* save Sundays, I [spoke] literally for three weeks previous to the election." Then he claimed that in 1840 he had been "driving about from Dan to Beersheba 'sleeping in unaccustomed beds' and making speeches of unreasonable length" in the weeks prior to the balloting.[19]

In southern border states such as Maryland and Tennessee, campaigners engaged in far greater activity. Organized speaking tours were common here, and the candidate's friends frequently arranged big gatherings for him along the route. During James Polk's first gubernatorial campaign in Tennessee in 1838, one of his supporters wrote him that the people of Overton "are resolved to give you a dinner. I am going to Winchester tomorrow to consult . . . upon the propriety of getting up two Democratic festivals in the Mountain District." Polk's appearance in Murfreesboro that year was attended by close to 2,000 persons. Following several hours of speechmaking, members of the crowd shared in a spread that consisted of "forty fat sheep, forty fine shoats, six beeves, three hundred pounds of fine ham, and bread and vegetables without limit." Then they washed it down with "the generous juice of the grape, whiskey, and old cogniac [sic]."[20]

There were fewer mass gatherings in the newly settled areas of the South and West but there was more individual contact between candidate and voter. As someone aboard a Mississippi riverboat told Alexis de Tocqueville in 1831: "out here a candidate must go and harangue his partisans in the public places, and drink with them in the taverns."[21] W. R. W. Cobb, known as the "most successful vote-puller" in mid-nineteenth-century Alabama, resorted to all sorts of tricks to catch the elector's eye, including the "rattling of tinware and crockery." He also "delighted in the singing of homely songs composed for stump purposes." Office seekers in certain rural areas seemed willing to go to any length to acquire a vote. In the backwoods near Natchez, Mississippi, where two aspirants for Congress stopped at a farmhouse overnight, both did a number of family chores. One man even helped with the milking, "holding the calf by its tail," after having removed "red bugs" from the body of the farmer's baby son.[22]

The Middle Atlantic states perhaps went furthest in inaugurating spectacular statewide campaigns. In practically every town numerous partisan demonstrations were scheduled before election day. The first major event would often be a pole raising, a ceremony with roots in the revolutionary period. Seen as a symbol of liberty, a pole, usually twenty to one hundred feet high and adorned with party emblems, was erected in a central location as a cheering crowd looked on. Party organizers subsequently staged enthusiastic rallies featuring famous speakers from both inside and outside the district. At the climax of the campaign came the grand parade, in which hundreds and perhaps thousands of the party faithful marched through the streets at night "to the glare of torches." Alongside the participants would be elaborate floats carrying colorful banners, transparencies, and portraits of the chief candidates.[23]

The following account of a pro-Jackson parade in New York City in 1832, provided by foreign observer Michel Chevalier, gives a vivid description of what transpired on such occasions. "The procession was nearly a mile long; the Democrats marched in good order," he said. On some of the banners "were inscribed the names of the Democratic societies or sections; *Democratic young men of the ninth or eleventh ward*; others bore imprecations against the Bank of the United States," one containing the prayer "Deliver us from evil." "Then came the portraits of General Jackson afoot and on horseback; there was one in the uniform of a general and another in the person of a Tennessee farmer with the famous hickory cane in his hand." In addition to the many inanimate objects exhibited, Jackson's partisans brought along a live eagle— "tied by the legs, surrounded by a wreath on leaves and hoisted upon a pole, after the manner of the Roman standards."

In evaluating what he had observed, Chevalier noticed a strong similarity between the Jacksonian preelection parade and solemn religious processions he had encountered in Mexico. "The American standard-bearers," he pointed out, "were as grave as the Mexican Indians who bore the sacred candles. The Democratic procession, like the Catholic procession, had its halting places; it stopped before the houses of Jackson men to fill the air with cheers and halted at the doors of the leaders of the Opposition to give three, six, or nine groans."[24] One might say that the Americans, who had few official ceremonies, were inventing political rituals that corresponded to the religious rituals in other lands. Although certain rituals eventually were eliminated, new ones would be added, such as the practice of party members serenading candidates outside their home or hotel-room window as a demonstration of loyalty.

PRINTED MATTER

As did stump speaking and ritualistic events, newspapers played a more important role than in former epochs by not only promoting the immediate ticket but instilling party values over the long run. Editors, themselves key party servants, would be rewarded with patronage and printing contracts for aiding the party cause. Some like Horace Greeley of the *New York Tribune* had influence far beyond their immediate locale.[25] The number of papers almost tripled in these years, and most of them could be characterized as partisan sheets. As newspapers normally lacked independent financial backing, neutrality became almost impossible. Probably less than five percent of the American press in 1850 remained unaligned. The major parties established dozens of new journals before each national election. On the state and county levels, almost every candidate for major office set up one or more papers to promote his own cause. Failure to do so meant almost certain defeat. As Martin Van Buren said about his chief organ in upstate New York, *The Argus:* "Without a paper [soundly and discreetly] edited in Albany, we may hang our harps on the willows. With it, a party can survive a thousand convulsions."[26]

A new creative mode that ought to be mentioned in connection with journalism was the political cartoon. As commercial lithography developed in this era, many cartoons depicting the candidates and issues began to appear. Like other forms of journalism at the time, cartoons or caricatures were highly partisan, with Jackson often portrayed by opponents as a monarch—"King Andrew"—and Van Buren as a sly fox. One of the most devastating showed the Whig candidate in 1848, General Zachary Taylor, holding a bloody sword while sitting on a mound of Mexican War victims' skulls. The quality of the artwork in these lithographs did not equal that found in later ones; the pictures were often cluttered with many individuals and statements, making it difficult to determine their meaning. Also, the settings were usually quite conventional—a presidential contest shown as a horserace, a boxing match, or a card game. Nevertheless, some of these drawings did provide rather powerful images for the voter to consider as election day neared.[27]

Candidates and party officials prepared considerable quantities of other printed material to get their views across. As in the past, broadsides, pamphlets, and circular letters comprised the most common forms. One major addition, which would become a recurring feature of presidential races, was the campaign biography. Generally written with the cooperation of the nominee, it furnished the largest source of information about him in a single package. As William Burlie Brown, who has investigated this subject, points out, such works "are neither scholarly productions nor pure fabrications. They are what an advertising-conscious civilization calls 'promotional literature,' designed to 'sell the customer,' a presidential candidate."[28] Some of them were compiled by campaign managers, some by journalists, some by famous authors—Nathaniel Hawthorne wrote the biography of Franklin Pierce in 1852. Regardless of authorship, almost every book in this genre sought to create a symbol—a symbol based on many ideals and images that the public admired. During the Jacksonian period biographers stressed images closely associated with the early republic. The archetypal candidate was depicted as being "self-reliant and self-made, a transcendant patriot, a staunch nationalist, a champion of human liberty."[29]

CAMPAIGN FINANCE

Due to the immense growth of electioneering in these years, fund-raising became a key factor for the first time. Considerable sums were now needed, especially to publish the many kinds of reading matter. According to one estimate, it took approximately $3,000 to finance a congressional campaign in a midwestern state and perhaps $4,000 in a Middle Atlantic state. (Vote-getting operations in the Deep South and New England continued to be somewhat less costly.) Gubernatorial races, covering larger areas, required much heavier financing than those for Congress. One such contest in Kentucky around 1830 was said to have involved $10,000 to $15,000. Of course, national campaigns proved infinitely more expensive because they encompassed a far broader range of activities. No exact figures are available for these years, but it probably took close to $50,000 to elect a president by midcentury (even more if the money spent by the state parties for the whole ticket is included). Thus only a wealthy person or one who could find wealthy backers was able to seek high office in this new era of democratic politics.[30]

Campaign funds were accumulated in a number of ways. Local organizations at times solicited contributions among their membership. Delegates to county conventions often had to be taxed a small amount to pay for publications. Many groups sponsored public dinners or banquets, charging five dollars a plate. At party meetings, the rank and file sometimes paid admission or the well-to-do were called upon to contribute a particular sum to help underwrite expenses. For instance, New Yorker Philip Hone recorded in his diary that at a Whig gathering in the fall of 1838, some sixty to eighty prominent men jointly subscribed several thousand dollars for the upcoming gubernatorial contest. From 1840 onward, some state officials began making assessments on the salaries of political appointees. Not infrequently, party leaders attempted to shift a part of campaign expenses to the U.S. government through the franking privilege. It is estimated that at least $40,000 a year in federal funds went for the distribution of franked newspapers in this era. A few individual members of the House of Representatives spent over one hundred dollars each—not a small sum at that time—to mail reelection material to their constituents.[31]

ELECTION OF 1824

Although many factors helped bring on the new style of campaigning, perhaps the most important one was the presidential election of 1824. Because there existed neither a unified national party nor an indisputable successor to the retiring James Monroe, several aspirants actively competed for the highest office in the land. In fact, the jockeying and maneuvering started more than two years before the balloting. In 1822 the journalist Hezekiah Niles wrote on the great "buz" in Washington about "who should succeed Mr. Monroe."[32] The leading contenders included three members of the president's cabinet: Secretary of the Treasury William H. Crawford, Secretary of State John Quincy Adams, and Secretary of War John C. Calhoun. (The latter would ultimately withdraw and seek the vice presidency.) Also among the favorites in the race were influential Kentucky congressman Henry Clay and General Andrew Jackson, who had gained fame at the Battle of New Orleans.

Each of these men nominally was a Republican, though Adams and Clay both favored a more vigorous use of the federal government than either Crawford or Jackson. Nevertheless, it is not clear whether this represented a crucial distinction; support for each man depended to a greater degree upon political and sectional considerations. At first, Crawford seemed to hold the advantage, having won the backing of powerful figures in New York and Virginia. Even though he suffered a stroke and remained in questionable condition for some time, he still was nominated to succeed Monroe by a majority of the congressional caucus in early 1824. Friends of the other candidates, however, refused to accept the caucus decision and undertook efforts to discredit it. They attacked the caucus as undemocratic and, because less than a third of Congress attended, the tool of faction. Indeed, the congressional caucus as well as Crawford's candidacy appeared doomed after this. (Crawford eventually recovered but finished well behind the top two in both the popular and electoral votes.)[33]

In lieu of caucus approval the other contestants began to vie for broad public support. While the overall amount of electioneering was small compared to later contests, the groundwork for larger operations was established. The first national campaign managers appeared in the person of Josiah S. Johnston for Henry Clay and John H. Eaton for Andrew Jackson. (Adams took no part in any organizational efforts, but several friends acted on his behalf.) Associates of each contender set up newspapers and distributed literature. Each side also sought the endorsement of as many state and county caucuses and conventions as they could acquire. Through all these endeavors both Adams and

Clay maintained a customary silence, but Jackson took the unprecedented step of issuing public statements on various policy questions. In another departure Jackson's strategists attempted to create a truly heroic image for their candidate. John Eaton's *Wyoming Letters* and later his *Life of Jackson*—the first formal campaign biography—glorified Old Hickory not only for his military prowess but as a defender of republican virtues.[34]

Another innovation in this campaign was the public opinion poll. During the spring and summer of 1824, the *Star* in Raleigh, North Carolina, the *American Watchman* in Wilmington, Delaware, and the *Harrisburg Pennsylvanian*, all pro-Jackson newspapers, began to publish tallies of voter preferences recorded at a number of popular gatherings. The *Star* reported that at militia trainings around the state the count was heavily in favor of Jackson, and the *Pennsylvanian* announced that Jackson received more Fourth of July toasts at public meetings than any other candidate. The *American Watchman* of July 24 printed the results of a poll, allegedly taken "without discrimination of parties," in the towns of Wilmington and Newark. It showed Jackson with a total of 335 supporters, Adams with 169, Clay with 19, and 9 for Crawford. Although one can question the procedure used—the figures may even have been invented—such polls would become a normal part of nineteenth-century elections. Through them partisans hoped to create a groundswell of public support for their favorite candidate.[35]

The campaign of 1824 in several ways foreshadowed the more famous one of 1828. There was little debate about current issues but much regarding the purported virtues and shortcomings of the candidates. Each camp supplied favored journalists with ammunition to use against its rivals. Such material not only brought each man's accomplishments into question but also his personal character. Adams was criticized as being aristrocratic, Crawford as corrupt, Clay as immoral, and Jackson as uncouth and tyrannical. Jackson, in particular, was judged unfit for the presidency because of his limited education and political experience. Also, his being a military man supposedly made him a threat to the republic. Yet amid all the charges and countercharges, it soon became apparent that Jackson—a westerner and war hero, the nominee least connected with Washington politics—had captured the public fancy.[36]

In the popular vote Jackson easily outdrew his nearest rival Adams, acquiring 43 percent of the total compared to Adams's 31 percent. But in the electoral college the Tennessean did not obtain the needed majority—the count showed Jackson having 99, Adams 84, Crawford 41, and Clay 37—which meant that the final decision would be made in the House of Representatives. During the House proceedings Clay and his backers, disliking Jackson, eventually threw their support to the New Englander Adams, making him the sixth president. However, when Adams later appointed Clay as secretary of state, Jackson became irate, screaming loudly that a "corrupt bargain" had been secretly contracted between the two men. Old Hickory now sought vindication for his cause, believing that he had been robbed of his rightful claim to the highest office. He immediately started scheming to take the chief executive's spot away from Adams at the next election by making a bigger push for the presidency than anyone had ever attempted before.[37]

ELECTION OF 1828

The campaign of 1828 actually began just a short time after Adams's inauguration in 1825. Jackson's supporters in Tennessee had him renominated for the presidency by the state legislature. They then set up a central committee in Nashville, headed by Old Hickory's longtime friends John Eaton and Colonel William Lewis, to start coordinating a nationwide effort. Over the next few years this group corresponded with many state and local leaders, helped raise money, and arranged for the publication of literature. At least a year before the election, a committee with similar functions was established in Washington, D.C., which would take over primary control of the operation. By that time too, many state organizations had become part of the process. Committees to elect a president may not have been new, but the expansiveness of the enterprise undertaken on Jackson's behalf was unique.[38]

The person in charge of the committee in Washington, and the one most responsible for putting together this first truly national political organization, was Martin Van Buren, senator from New York. Van Buren, soon to be called the "Little Magician," stood out as the consummate politician of his day. He had created a powerful statewide machine in New York, the Albany Regency, and now took on this bigger challenge. An unreconstructed "Old Republican" and one-time Crawford supporter, Van Buren believed that among all national figures Jackson could best restore the Jeffersonian system of limited government, which Adams and Clay were threatening to destroy. After forming the alliance with Old Hickory, the New Yorker started to contact leading politicians in a number of states, trying to get them behind the ticket. This turned out to be no easy task, for many of these men widely differed on matters of policy. Such aspects were therefore down played, with the focus being on the advantages of elevating Jackson to the White House.[39]

It was not only the efforts of national figures like Van Buren that made the new system and Jackson's subsequent victory possible. Local leaders played vital roles as well, organizing meetings, drumming up candidate support, and getting out the vote on election day. Some of these men had been involved in earlier political activities, others were recent additions to the campaign scene. Major Allen Campbell of Louisville, Kentucky, was one of those skillful newcomers in this contest who, in cooperation with "about a half a dozen, intelligent and zealous friends," created not only a central committee in Louisville, but a web of subcommittees in "every ward of the town" as well as in the countryside. He and his agents prepared regular reports, giving the names of every elector and how each would vote. They also arranged barbecues, rallies, and other events to attract the electorate. By the end of 1827 almost every city and county of importance outside of New England had a "Jackson Committee" of this sort.[40]

While many local and national leaders feverishly worked on the campaign, Jackson himself was by no means idle. Even more than in 1824 he took an active part in promoting his own election. He regularly communicated with his numerous associates, met with several state delegations, and tried to keep his name in the public eye.[41] Jackson made no campaign appearances per se but he did agree to attend the annual celebration to commemorate the Battle of New Orleans in January 1828. Supposedly nonpolitical, the journey down the Mississippi River to Louisiana and then back home to Tennessee became in fact a major campaign tour. While Old Hickory gave no speeches, he greeted crowds and received tributes in a number of locales along the way, and thus surely aided his candidacy.[42] (Similar "nonpolitical" excursions would be taken by other presidential aspirants since that time.)

In contrast to Jackson, the incumbent Adams did almost nothing. Of all presidential candidates in American history, John Quincy Adams seemed least suited to the task of open campaigning or even working behind the scenes for his own election. A gentleman of the old school, he preferred to stand solely on his record, believing that vote-getting of any kind was un- dignified. He refused any personal involvement in reelection planning and gave little encouragement to those of his followers who wished him to con- tinue for a second term.[43] Despite Adams's noninvolvement, the Coalition, or National Republicans, as their side was sometimes known, did not simply give in to defeat. Thanks to the efforts of Secretary of State Henry Clay and Senator Daniel Webster, the administration's defenders put up a cred- itable fight. They set up newspapers and disseminated literature, organized state committees, and planned rallies and meetings. Several members of the cabinet went around the country giving speeches, causing one observer to call them "the traveling Cabinet."[44] Even with all this activity, the Adams men lagged behind the Jackson forces because they lacked the fervor and know-how of their opponents.

The Jacksonians, who understood the need to rouse the public, scheduled many more rallies, barbecues, and other festive events. In Baltimore, for instance, a "Grand Barbecue" was staged ostensibly to commemorate the successful defense of the city against the British invasion during the War of 1812. After much food and drink, as well as speeches about Jackson's wartime exploits, those in attendance sang a new song entitled "Hickory Wood."[45] In fact, one of the Democrats' cleverest moves was the adoption of a symbol that would be identified with Jackson. Since he already was known as "Old Hickory," the choice was obvious. Soon the country was bombarded with hickory brooms, hickory canes, and hickory sticks. Hickory poles were erected in numerous towns and villages and placed on the corners of city streets. Many local groups even arranged to plant hickory trees in the village or town square. In response, although on a much smaller basis, supporters of John Quincy Adams used the symbol of an oak to show the sturdiness of their candidate.[46]

Probably more significant than anything else done by the Jackson forces to get their man elected was the creation of a vast chain of partisan newspapers. Upward of 300 papers ultimately spread the word about Old Hickory.[47] Beyond such praise, the Jacksonian editors filled most of their columns with attacks upon the administration and the personal character of the president. In general, they sought to portray Adams the New Englander as "a very compost of European vices" and unfit for high office. He repeatedly was condemned for having connived his way into the presidency through his "corrupt bargain" with Henry Clay. Adams also was denounced as being a spokesman for the privileged class who believed that the few should govern the many. Furthermore, he was accused of "royal extravagances" in the White House, including the use of public funds to purchase a billiard table for the East Room. Although Adams later announced that he had spent his own money for this purpose, the story was not retracted.[48]

Pro-Adams journalists retaliated by constantly imputing Jackson to be a bloodthirsty military tyrant. During the campaign they produced several items purporting to show his tyrannical behavior. Most heavily distributed was a document entitled "Some Account of Some of the Bloody Deeds of GENERAL JACKSON," later known as the "Coffin Handbill," which displayed six black coffins below the names of six militiamen Jackson had ordered to be executed for mutiny in 1815.[49] The rhetoric on both sides sank to even lower depths, containing the most vile slanders in campaign history. Charles Hammond, editor of the *Cincinnati Gazette* and a longtime foe of Jackson, charged that Andrew and Rachel Jackson lived together in adultery for two years before their marriage, that Rachel was a bigamist and Andrew her seducer. (Actually, Rachel had left her abusive husband Lewis Robards voluntarily and had married Jackson under the impression that Robards had filed for divorce. Only later was it disclosed that Robards had not done so. Two years then elapsed before the legal situation was resolved with the Jacksons officially married.)[50] On the other side, Adams was accused of being a pimp for the czar while serving as a diplomat in Russia.[51]

Aside from the number of scurrilous attacks, few substantive matters were raised by the participants. Some discussion of the tariff took place, but its impact on prospective voters was dulled by the more colorful campaign events and the barrage of news of a highly emotional nature. The rough and tumble contest of 1828 resulted in a decisive victory for General Jackson. He gained 178 electoral votes and showed strength in several sections, compared to Adams, whose total of 83 mostly came from the Northeast. Even had Adams played an active role and his supporters been better organized, it is doubtful they could have succeeded against a charismatic military hero who had not been forced to take a clear stand on the issues and who, as a resident of

Tennessee, was able to represent both the South and West. Jackson's election brought 56 percent of the eligible voters to the polls and marked the triumph of the new party organization and the new methods of electioneering. This would enable the Jacksonians to monopolize the field for the next several years.

ELECTION OF 1832

After a successful first term Jackson ran for reelection in 1832 against Henry Clay of Kentucky. Jackson's followers now tended to call themselves Democrats; Clay's backers still used the name National Republicans. The contest was notable in that the candidates were for the first time officially nominated at national party conventions.[52] The election also was far more issue oriented than its predecessor. Clay and the National Republicans believed that they had found the perfect issue by which to oust Jackson: the rechartering of the Bank of the United States. The bank, though helpful to the business community, was thought by Jackson and his friends to be both unnecessary and unconstitutional. As the opposing standard-bearer, Clay sought to bring up the recharter bill in Congress four years early, thereby forcing Jackson to accept continuance of the bank or else to destroy it. Either way, the Kentuckian felt, Old Hickory surely would alienate some of the voters.

Jackson was outraged by the move and vowed to destroy the bank. He issued a stirring veto message against the bank bill that became the rallying cry of the campaign. Jackson declared that the bank mainly benefited wealthy businessmen and that the farmers, mechanics, and laborers, "who have neither the time nor the means of securing like favors to themselves, have a right to complain of injustice."[53] These words, not unlike Jeffersonian attacks upon the elitist Federalists, struck a responsive chord. Clay and his supporters evidently had misjudged the breadth of opposition toward the bank and the way the issue could be used to stir up class antagonism. Francis Blair, an administration spokesman, denounced the bank and its president "Czar Nicholas" Biddle for creating a "hydra of corruption," which bribed congressmen and bought editors. Clay himself was pictured in the Democratic press as an immoral aristocrat.[54]

The "Nationals," as some people called them, immediately struck back, criticizing first of all Jackson's choice of the "corrupt" Martin Van Buren as his running mate. Jackson himself was denounced as an unfit ruler of a free people who, in issuing the bank veto, was imitating a foreign tyrant. But Clay and his followers mainly focused on the economic effects of the veto, claiming that chaos would engulf the country with the destruction of the bank. The National Republican campaign was fairly spirited though handicapped by its organizational shortcomings. Less than three months before election day, some major states like Virginia still lacked a functioning central committee. Also, as Lynn Marshall has written, the committee that eventually was set up there resembled the older model of party structure, "an organization of respectable 'friends' who condescended to 'bring' in the votes."[55] The Democratic operation was much more efficient and in step with public attitudes. As a result, Jackson came out ahead by a wide margin, obtaining 219 electoral votes to Clay's 49. Eighteen electoral votes went to minor candidates, including seven for William Wirt, the standard-bearer of the recently formed Anti-Masonic party.

The Anti-Masons would be the first of many third parties on the national scene. The Anti-Masonry movement had emerged in New York after the alleged murder of a former Mason, who threatened to expose the secret rituals of the group. Several astute politicians realized that they could use the incident to rally support against Van Buren and President Jackson, who was a Mason. The Masons, being popular among the well-to-do, were condemned as aristocratic. Said one critic, Freemasons were "unfit for any office of confidence." The Anti-Masonic crusade briefly caught on in the northeastern states, and its adherents captured some legislative seats for a few years before fading out. The Anti-Masons made history by holding the first national nominating convention of any party in 1831.[56] Labor or workingmen's parties also competed for votes in the Northeast. Many urban workers, believing their interests had been ignored by the major parties, formed their own political organizations. They achieved momentary success in cities like New York and Philadelphia, but soon started to decline. Part of their failure was internal, but it also stemmed from the fact that the established parties, especially the Democrats, began to push for some of the same goals. Then, too, economic conditions had not yet made the majority of workers feel the need for direct political action.[57]

By the next presidential contest, most enemies of Jackson had coalesced into a new party known as the Whigs. The Whigs took their name from the British Whig party, which had always opposed a strong monarch; here the group opposed the seemingly all-powerful "King Andrew." They favored a government that would promote industrial and commercial development and thus attracted many businessmen and merchant-planters. The Whigs, at least in the northern states, also showed an interest in humanitarian reform, winning over many evangelical Protestants to their side. They had, however, little sympathy for the immigrant, especially the Catholic Irish, and gained the backing of natives who disliked the large foreign influx. The Whigs were never as successful as the Democrats, winning only two national elections over the next sixteen years. They often had trouble shaking their image as a party of the wealthy, even though most adherents had no aristocratic pretensions. In addition, many members were uncomfortable with the concept of a party, which made it difficult to create a united front at times. Yet the Whigs provided formidable opposition for a decade and a half, and thus helped to establish the two-party system in America.[58]

ELECTION OF 1836

The Whigs faced a formidable task as they prepared to do battle with the entrenched, well organized Democrats in their first nationwide competition in 1836. The retiring Andrew Jackson had dictated the nomination of his successor, his longtime political confident Martin Van Buren. Although the choice was not satisfactory to the entire party membership, particularly in the South, most rallied to support Van Buren. The Whigs, not yet possessing a fully developed organization and unable to agree on a single standard-bearer, decided on a strategy of running three candidates, each popular in his own section: Senator Daniel Webster of Massachusetts, Senator Hugh L. White of Tennessee, and General William Henry Harrison of Ohio. They hoped that these "favorite sons" would carry enough states among them to deny Van Buren a majority in the electoral college, forcing the election into the House of Representatives, where the Whigs might prevail.

The Whigs' campaign, however, lacked the imagination and vigor of their original concept. There was little coordination among the backers of the three candidates, and the three men themselves never produced a common agenda or strategy. About the only major innovation was a tour, taken by General Harrison, of several eastern states. Although he did not deliver any partisan speeches—he simply uttered a few pleasantries when attending receptions—Harrison's journey set a precedent for future presidential aspirants. As the party was unclear about its own goals, it fell back into making a traditional assault on Jackson and the Democrats for destroying the bank and inciting corruption. Jackson himself was denounced as a tyrant and Van Buren, his successor, as a political manipulator. Van Buren frequently was portrayed, in words and in pictures, as a sly creature who secretly manipulated an increasingly senile president for his own disreputable ends.[59]

Despite the nastiness of the Whig attack, Van Buren and his followers felt little need to campaign. In fact, most of the opposition's charges were completely ignored. Administration newspapers simply reiterated the view that their candidate would pursue the same policies as Jackson. In a large sense, the election of 1836 turned on the electorate's evaluation of Andrew Jackson and his record. Given the considerable popularity of the departing president, the still fairly good times, and the Whigs' less-than-adequate effort, the Democrats were able to retain their dominant position in the government. Van Buren won a majority of states in both the North and the South, acquiring 170 electoral votes compared to 124 for his opponents. The Whigs, in their initial trial, still drew a substantial number of voters and took several key states. White finished on top in Georgia and in Jackson's own Tennessee, Webster prevailed in Masschusetts, and Harrison, the most successful of all, triumphed in seven states, including Ohio and Indiana. Overall, the Whigs combined to amass almost 49 percent of the popular vote and would prove more than a match for the Democrats the next time around in 1840.

ELECTION OF 1840

The presidential contest of 1840 was to be of monumental significance in the history of electioneering. The Democrats, starting in 1828, had introduced a brand-new vote-getting style—running a popular candidate identified with the common people, avoiding divisive issues, and playing upon the voters' emotions through an enormous outpouring of antiaristocratic rhetoric. Now the Whigs took over this approach and carried it even further, choosing a standard-bearer of questionable abilities and trying to sweep him into the White House on cheers and empty slogans. Along the way, they brought forth numerous innovations that quickly became normal procedure in American campaigning. Insofar as the use of gimmickry and ballyhoo is concerned, the 1840 campaign would be the prototype for all future elections for the presidency.[60]

At the beginning of the race the Whigs enjoyed a major advantage over the Jacksonians: the country was still feeling the effects of the financial panic of 1837 that followed the destruction of the Bank of the United States. Business failures, farm mortgage foreclosures, and unemployment were fairly widespread. Probably any well-known Whig could have beaten the renominated Martin Van Buren, whom many people blamed for the nation's economic woes. However, the Whigs wished to make victory as certain as possible, so they denied the nomination to party notables, like Henry Clay, who often had been embroiled in political controversy. They instead chose the aging General William Henry Harrison, who had made such a good showing in 1836. Former Democrat John Tyler of Virginia was named his running mate to solidify the southern vote. Even though he had minimal governmental experience, the Whigs believed that Harrison would be a far more electable candidate than Clay. Because he had never held a major office, his views on most issues were unknown and thus unlikely to offend any group. Equally important, Harrison had achieved some renown as a military commander at the Battle of Tippecanoe (1811) and in the War of 1812. Whig leaders hoped the retired general could be molded into a great popular hero as Jackson had been a dozen years earlier.

The nomination of Harrison established a strong precedent regarding presidential candidacies. Henceforth, when choosing a standard-bearer, the major parties often would look for the most "available" man, that is, someone without a controversial record or political enemies, preferably an accomplished ex-military figure. In doing so, they often rejected highly talented and politically experienced persons whose past activities, it was thought, might alienate certain segments of the electorate. Party leaders favored this approach for a second reason as well: because they believed that a newcomer to Washington would be more dependent on them for direction and less likely to pursue an independent course. This pattern, started by the Whigs and then followed by the Democrats with their "dark horse" candidates, persisted for many decades.

As they inaugurated their campaign, the Whigs published no statement on the issues, fearing that commitment on specific measures might lose them votes. Rather than presenting a detailed program, they stressed the idea of General Harrison as a man of simple frontier virtues—an early poster depicted him with plow in hand—who would come to Washington and drive away the corrupt Van Buren regime. Their cause was aided by a Democratic editor who sneered that Harrison probably would be satisfied just to live out his days with a small pension, a log cabin, and a barrel of hard cider. The Whigs happily took up the challenge, claiming they were indeed the party of log cabins and hard cider—true representations of American democracy. "The Log Cabin," said one leading Whig, "is a symbol of nothing that Van Burenism knows, feels, or can appreciate."[61]

The log cabin and hard cider, in fact, became indelible symbols of the Harrison candidacy. Whig campaign headquarters often were constructed in the form of log cabins, and hard cider abounded at all party rallies. The country soon was blanketed with Whig souvenirs containing pictures of "Old Tippecanoe" sitting in front of a log cabin with a barrel of hard cider. Campaign banners, badges, and other paraphernalia were displayed in larger quantities than ever before. Young men rolled large balls covered with Harrison slogans from town to town. At no time in the past had there been such enthusiasm in a presidential encounter or had mass meetings been so numerous, so elaborate, or so heavily attended. Tens of thousands appeared at Whig gatherings in places like Syracuse, New York. "A canvass never surpassed, never equaled in zeal was spontaneously inaugurated," declared one contemporary.[62]

One reason for the expanded numbers and enthusiasm was the widespread participation of women, who for the first time played a conspicuous role in a political campaign. While the Democrats' Francis Blair exhorted women to employ their "persuasive influence" on their menfolk to reelect Van Buren, the Whigs called on them to participate at various events—for example, to ride in parades and organize picnics—to promote the candidacy of Harrison. At a rally outside Dayton, Ohio, observers claimed that ten thousand women waved "white handkerchiefs" as the Old Hero passed by. "From Maine to New Orleans," a Whig editor declared, "our mothers, sisters, and daughters are now, as in the days of the Revolution, all Whig."[63] Although their activities still were circumscribed compared to later periods, women's presence in the campaign obviously was felt.

To run this multifaceted operation, the Whigs created the most efficient campaign organization the country had yet seen. An executive committee in Washington comprised of eight Whig legislators and their staffs coordinated the many activities. Among other things, they combined the mailing rosters of all congressional Whigs into a master list to facilitate the distribution of party literature. State organizations were no less active. They helped establish district committees, issued instructions to local leaders, and compiled reports from party workers in each area.[64] Perhaps the most important figure in the whole Whig operation was Thurlow Weed from upstate New York. A printer and journalist who long had opposed Van Buren and the Albany Regency, Weed first becme politically active in the Anti-Masonic party. Then as state leader of the Whigs he engineered the election of William Seward as governor in 1838. A modern-minded politician, he was convinced that the only way to defeat the Democrats was to abandon all traces of gentility and make a massive appeal to "His Majesty, the Voter."[65]

The amount of stump oratory sponsored by the Whigs far surpassed anything attempted in previous contests. According to one enthusiast, there were "five thousand or more speakers . . . 'on the stump' . . . from one end of the country to the other, their services everywhere . . . in demand."[66] Whig spokesmen talked a great deal about the bad economic climate brought on by the Van Buren administration and how conditions would improve under a new Harrison regime. "Matty's policy, 50 cts. a day and soup; our policy, $2.00 a day and roast beef," became a popular party slogan.[67] They also said that Harrison would be a one-term president and would not, like Jackson, seek to name his successor. But the main focus of the Whig campaign was not on issues or principles of government. More votes, they knew, could be won by slandering Van Buren personally. "King Mat" was denounced as an effete aristocrat who "laced up in corsets," beruffled and perfumed, while Old Tippecanoe, they said, dressed in the ordinary clothes of the frontiersman. Just as John Quincy Adams had been condemned in 1828 for furnishing the East Room and installing a billiard table, so Van Buren was accused of turning the White House into a palace "as richly adorned as the proudest Asiatic mansion."[68]

Despite having only lukewarm support for Van Buren among themselves, the Democrats nevertheless sought to match the wide-ranging Whig effort. They created their own party rhymes and songs. They organized "Hickory clubs" to compete with the "Tippecanoe clubs." They condemned Whiggery as federalism disguised in "people's garb." To counter the heavy thrusts against Van Buren, administration spokesmen denounced Harrison as a fraud. They claimed that he lacked all qualifications for high office and that he was hardly impoverished, having lived for years in a sizable mansion, not a log cabin. Great pains were taken to show that Harrison's military achievements in the War of 1812 had been highly overrated. He was referred to as the "petticoat general" and said to have had "cannon fever" before battle. Moreover, critics noted, he resigned his commission prior to the end of the war, when the outcome still was in doubt. Andrew Jackson, appearing at a Democratic gathering, testified that he had "never admired General Harrison as a military man."[69]

During the early stages of the race, Harrison, like Van Buren, stayed in the background. Acceding to his advisors' view that they might hurt his chances, Old Tippecanoe refrained from making any campaign statements. However, when the Democrats started questioning his mental capacity, calling him "General Mum" and "a man in an iron cage," who could not be trusted to answer his own mail, Harrison felt he no longer could remain silent. Breaking with tradition, he became the first presidential aspirant to spend a long time on the campaign trail. Over the course of a few months, he appeared at many Whig functions and delivered numerous speeches. Although he said nothing profound, primarily straddling the issues and telling stories about his military career, he convinced people that at sixty-seven he was not senile and that he could be a credible candidate. Surely, Harrison's public appearances increased his popularity. Wherever he went huge crowds flocked to see him and shake his hand.[70]

Harrison's campaigning and all the other innovations introduced by the Whig machine proved too much for Van Buren and the Democrats. In contrast to their unsuccessful debut four years earlier, the Whigs fashioned a major victory with 53 percent of the popular vote and 73 percent of the electoral vote. Harrison pulled in a total of 234 electoral votes to just 60 for Van Buren. The Whig tactics were effective almost everywhere, bringing the party a truly national triumph. Men like Weed saw that if the Whigs did not adopt their opponents' methods, they would soon die out. The Democrats had recognized at the outset what was happening. "We have taught them to conquer us!" exclaimed the *Democratic Review* that summer.[71] Unfortunately for the Whigs, the aging Harrison fell ill and died shortly after his inauguration; this put John Tyler, sometimes referred to as "His Accidency," into the White House. Tyler, an advocate of states rights and limited government, turned out to have little enthusiasm for the Whig economic program, making the whole campaign achievement of 1840 into a rather hollow success.

Often forgotten in all the hoopla of 1840 was the Democrats' adoption of the first official campaign platform. It consisted of nine resolves, most of them reiterating the party's long-standing views about limited government and individual rights. Democratic platforms in the next few races retained this basic format. The Whigs, who started embracing the concept of a platform in 1844, usually were less forthright about what they stood for and so mainly sang the praises of their party's nominee. The platform, with its approved resolutions, replaced the unofficial utterances that had appeared from time to time in the past. The platform thus became a means of pledging to the voters that the new administration would stand behind certain principles if elected. In both parties the platform initially was drawn up by convention delegates after the nomination of candidates and did not rank too high on the agenda. But by the 1850s, putting together the various planks would emerge as an important order of business, one that preceded the choice of nominees. Over the years, platform committees came to be formed, the documents grew longer, and questions involving their contents occasioned a great deal of debate. While not always fully adhered to by the candidates, the platform in most cases would provide the basis for what appeared in key statements during the campaign.[72]

One issue not addressed in the Democrats' 1840 platform was slavery. While it briefly had been raised in the press (indeed, it had been referred to as early as the 1836 campaign), both parties managed to sidestep this controversial topic. However, in the coming years the issue would be far more difficult to evade. The Liberty party, recently created by northern abolitionists, drew only 7,000 votes in its first outing, but would begin causing major candidates to take a stand on slavery. In subsequent statewide contests in the South, men on both sides started accusing their opponents of being weak defenders of the "peculiar institution." When the question of the expansion of slavery arose in connection with the proposed annexation of Texas, avoidance on the national level became impossible. Various aspects of the slavery problem would continue to permeate elections in the following decade and ultimately destroy the second party system.[73]

ELECTION OF 1844

The election of 1844 marked the first time that slavery had an impact on a presidential race and the first time since 1812 that a foreign policy question deeply affected the outcome. Although not the intention of either party at the outset, the contest would ultimately revolve around the subject of the annexation of Texas. Texas had become the Lone Star Republic in 1837 when it achieved independence from Mexico, but its future remained unclear. Both parties' chief presidential contenders, Martin Van Buren and Henry Clay, believed that annexation could cause a war with Mexico and that slavery ought to be kept out of national politics. They therefore agreed to oppose the acquisition of Texas "at this time." This stance eventually would come back to haunt them both, as annexation fever soon began to spread across the nation.[74]

At the Democratic convention, pro-annexationists and others who disliked Van Buren denied him the party nomination. They turned instead to the first "dark horse" candidate, former congressman and governor of Tennessee James K. Polk. While Polk had been in politics for a long time, he never had done anything of great distinction, causing Whig critics to ask, "Who is James K. Polk?" Polk, a disciple of Jackson and often referred to as "Young Hickory," may not have been a man of renown, but he understood the temper of the times. Catering to expansionist sentiment, he spoke out in favor of the addition of Texas "at the earliest practicable period"—meaning immediately. To attract northern backing, he also called for the takeover of the entire Oregon Territory, then under dispute with Great Britain. "The Reoccupation of Oregon and Reannexation of Texas" became Polk's chief slogan.

Clay, the Whigs' leading figure, was unanimously nominated at his party's convention. He hoped to base his campaign on traditional Whig ideas—an equitable tariff, a sound currency, distribution of money to the states from the sale of public lands, and limitations on executive power. However, the Texas issue soon came to dominate public discussion, and Clay, who had taken an anti-annexation stand, now found his support diminishing, especially in the South. Looking for a way out of his dilemma, Clay tried to soothe southern opinion by publishing what became known as the "Alabama letters," the second of which stated that annexation would be acceptable to him if it could be done honorably and without war. But this only hurt his standing with northerners, who saw him as selling out to the slaveholder class. In addition, Clay proved vulnerable to attack on several old issues. Polk partisans brought up once more the famous "corrupt bargain" story, and the Kentuckian was again condemned for immoral behavior.[75]

The Whig forces retaliated by making personal assaults on the Democratic candidate, claiming that Polk descended from a Tory grandfather and was guilty of branding his slaves. (The latter charge appeared in a number of partisan newspapers, allegedly having come from a source entitled *Travels of Baron Roorback*, in which the author, a German nobleman, stated that in passing through Tennessee he saw eighty slaves chained together with iron collars about their necks bearing the initials J K P. This type of fabrication came to be known as a "roorback.")[76] Although they could not quite match the hoopla of 1840, the Whigs went all out in organizing large demonstrations for their veteran leader. Unfortunately for Clay their efforts were not quite sufficient, as Polk captured both New York and Pennsylvania by small margins, winning an overall total of 170 electoral votes to 105 for "Harry of the West." Actually, the difference in the popular vote was very small. Of the 2,700,000 votes cast, Polk had a majority of only 38,367, receiving 49.6 percent of the total. He took New York by just 5,000 votes. Moreover, Clay would have won the election had it not been for the tiny Liberty party, which drew away enough Whig support in the Empire State to give Polk his victory.[77]

ELECTION OF 1848

Toward the end of his four years, having achieved many of his objectives and taken the country through the Mexican War, Polk kept his pledge to be a one-term president. When he refused to run for reelection in 1848, the Democrats, having no standout successor, turned to Lewis Cass of Michigan, a former military man and territorial governor, who advocated "popular sovereignty" on the slavery question. Some northern Democrats, unhappy about both the selection of Cass and popular sovereignty, bolted from the convention. Together with some Liberty party men and disgruntled Whigs, they launched the Free-Soil party, choosing Martin Van Buren, who gradually had adopted an antislavery view, as their standard-bearer. Free-Soilers supported the Wilmot Proviso, a measure designed to outlaw slavery in the territories newly acquired from Mexico. They also advocated a homestead act for free settlers in the West and federally sponsored internal improvements.

The Whigs, for their part, passed over the now aging Henry Clay. Wishing to attain another "Tippecanoe"-like victory, they nominated "Old Rough and Ready," Zachary Taylor of Louisiana, a hero of the recent Mexican War. Taylor had no previous political experience and at first had showed little interest in running for the White House, but ultimately consented to be the nominee. Like Harrison before him, Taylor's position on current issues was largely unknown, making him an asset to a political party that was becoming increasingly divided. In certain northern states such as Massachusetts, there had been a growing split into "Cotton Whigs," who favored the status quo regarding slavery, and "Conscience Whigs," who leaned toward the Free-Soilers' position. When the national convention was unable to agree on a substantive platform, they simply produced a statement extolling the virtues of General Taylor, who was described as another George Washington.[78]

Electioneering in 1848 turned out to be less spirited than in either of the two previous presidential contests. The only group that showed a high level of enthusiasm was the small band of Free-Soilers who stumped the northern states. The Whigs and Democrats sponsored rallies and held torchlight parades, but these events never produced the kind of ardor displayed in 1840 or 1844. Neither of the major candidates took an active role, though Taylor issued several statements and made a few ceremonial appearances in public. Both major parties fought sectional rather than national campaigns. The Whigs of the South argued that southern rights would be secure only if a southerner (Taylor) sat in the White House. Southern Democrats defended Cass as safe on slavery and warned that if Taylor, age sixty-three, died in office, it would put an antislavery man, Millard Fillmore, into the presidency. In the North, Democrats praised Cass as supportive of northern interests, while Whigs called Cass a "doughface," who would be dominated by southern interests.

As the campaign wore on, a good deal of character assassination took place. Taylor's lack of political experience was ridiculed, with one critic claiming that the general's main qualification for the presidency was "sleeping forty years in the woods and cultivating moss on the calves of his legs." Having been a slaveholder, he came under attack as a cruel and wicked master. Meanwhile, Cass was charged with having engaged in corrupt activities while serving as superintendant of Indian affairs. Whig writers joked about Cass's portly frame and also made fun of him by saying, "Take away the first letter of his name and what would he be?" Ultimately, two of Taylor's assets proved decisive. His being a military hero and defender of the Union made him satisfactory to a majority of northerners, and his being a slaveholder made him satisfactory to an adequate number of southerners. However, his victory was not a very large one: the tally in the electoral college stood at

163 to 127. Again a third party may have made the difference, as Van Buren's Free-Soilers took away enough votes from the Democrats in New York to enable the Whigs to carry the Empire State and gain access to the White House.[79]

One noteworthy innovation in the election of 1848 was the creation by the Democrats of the first permanent national committee. Before this time there had been a few interstate campaign committees—the Whigs and Anti-Masons as well as the Democrats had formed them. But these bodies had been loosely structured and had ceased to function following election day. The new national committee was to remain in existence even after the balloting was completed and would then be responsible for calling the next convention and arranging its physical details. The committee contained one member from each state, thus recognizing the wish for equal representation. The states named their own delegates and filled vacancies when they occurred. In regard to managing campaigns, the national committee mainly played an advisory role at first, but grew in influence as time went on.[80]

ELECTION OF 1852

The divided Whig party had secured control of the presidency in 1848 with Zachary Taylor. However, after serving sixteen months Taylor died and was replaced by the less-than-popular Millard Fillmore. Once installed, Fillmore signed the congressional measures concerning slavery known as the Compromise of 1850. The lack of any further accomplishments by his administration led the opposing Democrats to believe that they could recapture the chief executive's spot in 1852. At convention time, none of the leading lights of the party—Lewis Cass, Stephen A. Douglas of Illinois, or James Buchanan of Pennsylvania—could muster enough support to win the nomination. So the party came up with another dark horse—one even less known than Polk— Franklin Pierce of New Hampshire. Soon to be dubbed "Young Hickory of the Granite Hills," Pierce did not have a record of spectacular accomplishments. Nevertheless, he had served in Congress for several years and had been an officer in the Mexican War. "We Polked Them in '44, We'll Pierce Them in '52" became a popular Democratic slogan.

The Whigs, more divided than ever between the pro- and antislavery factions, rejected the middle-of-the-road President Fillmore and the aging Daniel Webster for another famous military figure, "Old Fuss and Feathers," General Winfield Scott, who had led the American army to victory at Mexico City in 1848. Scott, though born a Virginian, was closer to the slavery restrictionist wing of the party. Still it was hoped that his military record and nationalist attitude would unify all Whigs. This did not happen. Southerners, viewing Scott as a tool of the northerners, remained idle during the race, and some began to drift away from the fold. The Free-Soilers again played a part in the contest, with John Hale of New Hampshire serving as their standard-bearer, but they would be of less consequence this time.[81]

The campaign of 1852 was much less exciting than any in the previous two decades. As the North-South struggle had been suspended, there were no clearly defined issues. The Compromise of 1850 had cooled the subject of slavery expansion for the moment, leaving many people with little concern for national politics. Scarcely any enthusiasm accompanied the usual party demonstrations. Attendance at most events dropped sharply, even below that of 1848. The usual name-calling and other rhetoric fell on deaf ears. Scott, despite his military background, failed to arouse the kind of following that Harrison and Taylor had achieved. James Gordon Bennett in the *New York Herald* declared that never was there such a "ludicrous, ridiculous, and uninteresting Presidential campaign since the country had been emancipated from British rule."[82] In New York, he said, more interest was being displayed in the Women's Rights Convention, Fourierism, and the rivalries of two foreign concert singers.

In order to instill some spirit into their ranks and to try to overcome Scott's underdog status, Whig leaders arranged for their candidate to make an extended tour of the western states. The trip supposedly was nonpolitical, involving visits to the sites of prospective old-age homes for ex-soldiers. Scott played his role satisfactorily, but the crowds were not very large and it is doubtful the journey benefited him much. Pierce won the election by a heavy majority, especially in the South where voters had come to feel safer with the Democrats on the slavery issue. It was neither Pierce's qualifications nor his party's campaign that secured the victory, but simply the changing circumstances of the time. The Whigs were divided and increasingly apathetic, while the Democrats, acquiescent or defensive regarding slavery, came to the polls in sufficient numbers to elect their man. The gap in the popular vote was not large, but in the electoral college Pierce had 254 votes to 42 for Scott, who won just four states.[83]

Despite the lethargic Pierce-Scott encounter, campaigning by midcentury had become more exciting and more highly institutionalized than in the Federalist-Jeffersonian years. A full-fledged party system had developed (Whigs versus Democrats) with sophisticated vote-getting machinery. At each contest partisans would swing into action and employ a wide range of tactics in attempting to elect their side's ticket. A large amount of ballyhoo was now standard procedure, something necessary for stirring up potential electors. Nevertheless, the quest for votes was not as extensive as it would become in the so-called "golden age of parties" in the second half of the century. National organizations had not yet emerged as a guiding force. State parties were not truly competitive everywhere, especially in the newly settled areas of the South and West. The state of technology still limited the range of a stump speaker's efforts and curtailed the distribution of the printed word.

One also could argue that campaigns of the Jacksonian age were not as serious as they were to be later on. However, the electioneering innovations of this era set the stage for the elaborate campaigning that would come to fruition in the next.

4

The Golden Age of Parties

1854–88

The United States underwent many dramatic changes in the second half of the nineteenth century. The population rose from about 25 million in the early 1850s to more than 63 million four decades later. Several western territories achieved statehood, raising the total from 31 to 40. The economy grew rapidly with farm and industrial production reaching enormous levels. Despite some opposition, the government began expanding its role in the nation's economic and political life. As a result many individuals and interest groups, indeed entire regions, saw the advantages that could be gained from favorable governmental policies and appointments. This made them push harder than ever to elect the right persons to public office. As the late Roy F. Nichols has pointed out: "Success at elections was the more intensively sought as the rewards of power became greater. Campaign methods therefore grew more ruthless, and corruption more frequent."[1] Yet the kinds of practices employed to win votes were not altered as much as the nature and scope of the effort, which meant there were more stump speeches, bigger processions, larger organizations, and higher expenditures.

NEW PARTIES, EXPANDED EFFORTS

For many years the greater magnitude of campaigning also reflected heated party and sectional conflicts. The old national party system of Democrats and Whigs had broken down by the early 1850s because of rising North-South tensions and ethnocultural issues. After a few years of drift and indecision, it was replaced by a system that pitted the Democrats against the new northern-based Republican party, creating even sharper division along geographic lines. The Republican crusade to stop the spread of slavery brought with it a "moral fervor hitherto unknown in American politics," wrote historian Allan Nevins. "The campaign of 1840, with its hard cider, log cabins, and rolling balls, had been riotously exuberant, but its enthusiasm had been untempered by ideas or ideals. Now an exalted purpose, a clear cut set of national aims, lent strength to the ardor of the campaigners."[2] The Republicans quickly became a major party even though it hardly operated outside the northern states. They found their main support among those of Puritan stock residing in New England, rural New York, and the upper Midwest. Like the Whigs, the Republicans favored an active government that encouraged economic growth. But they went much further than the Whigs in their advocacy of social reform. During and after the Civil War, the Republicans saw themselves as the embodiment of patriotic virtue—the party that fought to preserve the Union and free the slaves.[3]

The Democrats started the era as the nation's majority party but soon lost much of their northern following after taking a pro-southern stance on the issue of slavery and its expansion. On the eve of secession their only strongholds outside the South and border states lay in the immigrant-filled cities of the Northeast. Elsewhere they became a minority and remained so for years, failing to produce any notable leaders or an appealing national program. Indeed, they would have trouble shaking their image as the party of disunion and negativism. The Democrats, from the early stages, differed with the Republicans on certain basic points. They disliked "Puritanism" in politics and their opponents' apparent concern for the Negro. The Democrats clearly stood out as a "white man's party." Also, as in earlier times, they believed in a decentralized, states-rights' conception of the Union and claimed to be the true defenders of constitutional liberty. In matters of political economy, the party showed no real enthusiasm for government aid to business. It generally opposed the chief elements of the Republican program and, for the most part, favored limits on all federal authority.[4]

The differences between the parties diminished somewhat in the postwar period. The Republicans' idealism faded as the majority seemed more interested in the spoils of office than with the problems of Reconstruction and the emerging industrial order. To maintain themselves in power, Republicans often turned to the technique of "waving the bloody shirt." This meant placing the entire blame for secession and the Civil War on the Democrats and insisting that they were still politically untrustworthy. (The term specifically referred to an incident in the House of Representatives where a northern congressman held up the bloodstained shirt of an Ohio carpetbagger who had been brutally attacked in Mississippi in 1866.) In numerous campaigns Republicans would fan partisanship by raising the specter of former Confederates regaining governmental control. As the renowned orator Robert Ingersoll exclaimed to a gathering of Union veterans: "Every man that tried to destroy this nation was a Democrat. . . . The man that assassinated Abraham Lincoln was a Democrat. . . . Soldiers, every scar you have on your heroic bodies was given you by a Democrat."[5]

The Democrats tried to combat these assaults, claiming that the war had ended and that reconciliation was in order. Their party was not "half so ferocious as the Radicals allege," they said. Classifying all its members as traitors was a serious injustice, for many had given their lives defending the Union. The Democrats viewed the loyalty issue as bogus and accused their opponents of employing the bloody shirt tactic simply to cover up their own misdeeds and ineffectual leadership. At times the Republican party toned down its war-related rhetoric and sought to build southern support by appealing to conservative whites on economic issues. But for various reasons this latter approach failed, and attacks on alleged Democratic disloyalty resumed. Waving the bloody shirt proved so effective in distracting attention from substantive matters that few Republicans could resist using it to 1890.[6]

Of course, other issues were discussed within party circles during postwar elections, the most controversial being the tariff. Most Republicans supported a high tariff, asserting that it encouraged industry and created jobs. Many Democrats, on the other hand, called for lower rates to help the farmer and the consumer, but when doing so they often were condemned as "free traders" by the opposition. The currency question stimulated much debate as well. Most Republicans favored hard money and spoke out against the expanded use of "greenbacks," which they saw as inflationary. Democrats were more likely to accept the existence of paper currency, yet they never really stood firm on the matter. In addition, there was much talk about civil service reform. Both parties criticized abuses of the spoils system, but neither one called for serious action until the 1880s.[7]

Cultural issues also took on some significance at election times. As was true before midcentury, the questions of immigrants' rights, Sabbath laws, aid to Catholic schools, and prohibition of alcohol persisted in certain areas. In fact, these matters attracted greater interest than ever, as hundreds of thousands of foreigners began to pour into the country each year. Many among the native-born saw the immigrant hordes, a high percentage of whom were Catholic, as a threat to long-standing American values and institutions. Republican candidates seeking the native vote asserted that immigrants not only lowered the wage scale but were responsible for the high increase in "crime, pauperism, disease, disorder, and immorality." In response, Democrats like Francis Grund, a German, denounced the other side as "long-faced, white livered hypocritical Yankees, who sold wooden nutmegs and cheated the honest farmers." If elected, "they would not allow a man to cook meals on the Sabbath, or kiss his wife, or take a walk for pleasure." Most of the Republicans, he added, "were temperance people and hated the Germans because they would drink beer even on Sundays and would sing and dance."[8]

Nevertheless, except for a brief period in the mid–1850s when the Know-Nothing movement arose, none of these cultural issues caused great divisiveness or became a topic for serious debate on the national level. Indeed, most national party leaders deliberately sought to avoid commitments on these matters, which they knew could destroy their broad coalition of support. As the esteemed Ohio Republican John Sherman expressed it in 1873, "Questions based upon temperance, religion, morality, in all their multiplied forms, ought not to be the basis of politics." Yet religious and ethnic appeals would affect many statewide races in the Northeast and Midwest over the years. When, for example, in the late 1880s the Republican legislature in Wisconsin passed a law that made English the predominant language in all schools, an act that seemed to discriminate against German parochial institutions, it caused a big shift of voters and resulted in a major Democratic victory in 1890.[9]

Dissatisfaction with the handling of certain issues at times led to the creation of splinter parties, whose crusade-like campaigns would take away votes from both the Democrats and the Republicans. One of the most important of these was the National Independent or Greenback party, whose chief goal was the expansion of the nation's money supply. After a slow start in the early 1870s, the Greenbackers made a significant impact in the congressional elections of 1878, amassing more than one million votes and electing fifteen of its members to the House of Representatives. However, as factional division occurred and its main issue lost force, the new party fell almost as quickly as it rose, obtaining just 3.3 percent of the presidential vote in 1880. In the long run, the Prohibition party, which worked to outlaw "demon rum," proved more damaging, especially to the Republicans. By the late 1880s it would make major inroads in the Midwest, polling as much as 6 to 7 percent in state contests in Michigan. (The Democratic party in a few instances secretly funded Prohibition candidates for the advantages that could be derived from their presence in a race.)[10]

While splinter parties occasionally tipped the balance, the essential battle always was between Republicans and Democrats. If the Greenbackers or Prohibitionists garnered a few percent, the vast majority of the voters, above 90 percent, aligned themselves with one or the other of the two main parties, and in a much stronger fashion than today. Unlike the present situation, where many voters are independent or only nominally linked to a political organization, those of the last half of the nineteenth century felt deeply committed to their side. It is estimated that anywhere from 20 to 25 percent of the electors were actively involved in campaigns. They attended numerous party functions and voted regularly, with turnout at national elections in these years averaging 70 to 80 percent and state totals not far behind. Membership in one of the major parties allowed a person to share in the glory and prestige of that group and its leaders. These loyalties were generally established around the time of the Civil War and continued for decades, often being passed on to the next generation. Party affiliation ranked on the same level as religious or family affiliation. "We love our parties as we love our churches and our families," declared a New Hampshire senator in 1885.[11]

The strength of party loyalty and the paucity of independent voters determined the nature of electioneering in this period. There was a greater effort made to stir up the voters than at any time before or since. Yet the main purpose of campaign hoopla was not to win over opponents and fence sitters, rather, all such activity aimed at reigniting the faith and enthusiasm of longtime party members. To be sure, party leaders hoped to capture waverers and gain new converts, but this never had a high priority. In an age of fierce partisanship, it did not seem worthwhile to spend time pressing individuals to relinquish long-held attachments. "It is a mistake," insisted a Wisconsin organizer, "to suppose that political successes are the results of accidents, or are brought about by a sudden change of heart on the part of people . . . during the heat of the campaign." Those in charge thought it best to concentrate on mobilizing one's own forces. President Grover Cleveland, when discussing his reelection bid in 1888, maintained that "the first duty of a party worker should be to have all his men in line and touching elbows."[12]

Under this system strong party discipline formed the basis for success. Although the Republicans won the presidency in most cases, their victories usually were obtained by small margins and did not always extend to both houses of Congress. Because only a couple of percentage points separated the parties much of the time, the cooperation of everyone at all levels was deemed essential. During national campaigns state and local candidates tried to subordinate parochial interests to those of the national ticket. This often meant focusing on national issues rather than matters relating to their own locale. Cyrus Carpenter, governor of Iowa in the 1870s, for instance, gave speeches on the tariff even though it had no political importance in his state. The party counted more than the individual. Straight-ticket voting became imperative; any hint of independence was sharply condemned. In order to assure loyalty and dedication among the rank and file, the parties rewarded large numbers of their followers with patronage. Before civil service reform began in the 1880s, many thousands of federal jobs—in the Post Office, the Treasury Department and other agencies—were available after each contest. Also, party control of the nomination apparatus compelled those seeking elective office to work hard for the organization in each campaign.

ARMY-STYLE CAMPAIGNING

Given the strong emphasis on party discipline and regularity, the campaigns of the post–Civil War years exhibited a great similarity to military contests. Each side mapped its strategy and then rallied its soldiers for the fight, often using military terms to describe various aspects of the process. As Richard Jensen has written: "Elections were treated like battles in which the two main armies (parties) concentrated on fielding the maximum number of troops (voters) on the battlefield (the polls) on election day. Party organization resembled that of an army . . . with the head of the ticket as commanding general, the lesser candidates as officers of the line, and party officials as staff officers." Jensen adds that nineteenth-century politicians, "most of whom had served in the army or in state militias, thought and acted as if their parties could be handled like real armies, but of course the fighting consisted of casting ballots, not bullets, on election day."[13]

Locally, the "armies" consisted of hundreds of regular voters who had been organized into neighborhood political clubs to serve as auxiliaries for the duration of the campaign. Much larger than similar clubs initiated earlier, they often took on the name of the party's presidential nominee—for instance, Hayes clubs or Tilden clubs. Sometimes such societies were formed according to occupation, as were the Republican Merchants' Association and the Democratic Mechanics' Club. Ethnic affiliation could also provide the basis of membership; examples of such organizations include the German Democratic Club and the Black Republican Club. Volunteer fire companies worked on behalf of the party as well. In any case, each group set up a headquarters, chose officers, and drafted its rules of operation. The members would attend regular meetings and undertake an assortment of tasks to promote the ticket, for example, being present at rallies and parades. For a long time these local clubs acted more or less independently, without any outside coordination. But in the late 1880s first the Republicans and then the Democrats established national federations, with the hope of better utilizing this important resource.[14]

To supplement the work of the campaign clubs, many towns and cities had separate uniformed marching companies. These marching companies mostly attracted eighteen to twenty-one year old men who were not yet of voting age, and helped initiate them into party activities. Like the regular clubs, marching companies had their origins in the Jacksonian era but made their greatest mark under the third party system. The Republicans created a few companies known as the "Wide Awakes" in 1856 and formed hundreds more in 1860 on behalf of Abraham Lincoln. The Wide Awakes, as they marched, carried torches and oil lamps, and wore special oilcloth capes to protect them from the dripping fuel. The Democrats, initially critical, eventually created their own military-like organizations with names like the "Douglas Guards" or "National Democratic Volunteers." After the Civil War, the Republicans, to stress their role in fighting for the Union, often called their companies the "Boys in Blue." To distinguish themselves from their opponents who had freed the slaves, the Democrats responded with "White Boys in Blue." Whatever their title, the companies generally functioned in a similar fashion, electing officers, obtaining uniforms, and then performing drills in preparation for the campaign parades and other spectacular events that lay ahead.[15]

More so than in the first half of the century, spectacular events became the hallmark of American political campaigns. Pole-raisings, flag-raisings, and banner-raisings took place in the early stages of the race, with each side attempting to put up the highest pole and the largest banner. Later, many rallies and picnics featuring famous orators were held. Brass bands provided music and the audience joined in the singing of party songs. The highlight of every contest was a giant parade scheduled shortly before election day. In small towns local marching companies and hundreds of other individuals took part; in major cities like New York up to 50,000 people turned out for the festivities. Besides the marchers, the processions would include elaborate floats carrying eye-catching displays. In addition to partisan references, some contained symbols, such as the Goddess of Liberty, or showed workmen plying their trade. Torchlight parades were frequently accompanied by the lighting of fireworks and by the burning of "red fire," which would create a colorful glow. Sympathetic residents lit up their houses as the marchers passed by. It was an awesome sight designed to keep emotions high in anticipation of the polls' opening a few days hence.[16]

The various rituals and ceremonies not only had a partisan function but served patriotic and other purposes as well. The parties had no unique logos until later, when the Republicans started using the elephant and the Democrats the donkey. Instead they used nationalistic symbols such as George Washington, the eagle, and the flag, and decorations in red, white, and blue. Rituals tended to reflect the past; speeches were delivered at monuments, and rallies were held on battlefields. The torchlight procession with its bright lights also conveyed a sense of purification. On election day the country supposedly would emerge from the darkness of the opposition's corruption and find the light of truth. The use of ritual later declined when national affirmation no longer seemed necessary and public attitudes toward politics began to change. Furthermore, urban areas in the twentieth century, equipped with electric lights, seemed less suited to torchlight processions.[17]

Although not as pronounced as in earlier days, regional variations in campaigning still persisted. In New England, vote-getting activity stayed on a lower plane than elsewhere. To be sure, the competing parties did hold picnics, clambakes, and mass meetings at times, but outside of Boston their size and number never approached the scale of gatherings in other sections.[18] In the South, large preelection barbecues remained popular. Observing such festivities in rural North Carolina in 1872, one newspaperman wrote: "At every meeting I saw a majority of the voters. . . . [A]nd when there was not an ox roast to give a free feed to the people they brought their own provisions, many coming with watermelons balanced on their heads.[19] South Carolina towns featured lengthy parades with brass bands and several hundred or more marchers. At Anderson, a crowd of 6,000 watched an elaborate Democratic procession in 1876, one stretching out over a mile with 1,600 mounted men and almost as many on foot.[20] Party organizers in the Midwest tried not to be outdone in arranging lavish spectacles. In Iowa, the Republican campaign culminated in a massive two-day affair at the capital in Des Moines, where all the leading orators "fired their last broadsides." The proceedings started Friday afternoon and went on through Saturday evening "with such an orgy of speechmaking, torchlight processions, and parades as to have satisfied the most ardent partisan."[21]

Western cities like San Francisco and Denver also witnessed fairly large demonstrations and rousing speeches. But in some of the recently settled areas of the West, electioneering was carried out on a more personal basis, and the candidate would look to socialize with his constituents. An episode involving the colorful Rollin M. Daggett, a former miner and businessman who sought election to Congress from Nevada in 1878 was probably typical. Entering a saloon in a small mining town where he once resided, Daggett threw down four or five dollars on the bar and shouted: "Come on boys, and have a drink." Subsequently, Daggett said hello and shook hands with all the patrons, some of them old friends. "How do you do, Mike? Well, God bless you, old fellow. Haven't seen you for fifteen years." "Pat, what the devil are you doing here? and Corny, you old rambler, where have you been?" These greetings were answered by such expressions as, "Well, he's the same old Daggett still," and "He's a fine fellow." The men shared jokes and anecdotes of the early days in the territory. When Daggett finally left the proprietor exclaimed: "Be jabers, I'll vote for Daggett." Many of the others present echoed him.[22]

In virtually every part of the country, stump speaking continued to be one of the best ways to rouse potential voters. Before each election the parties sent out a host of stump speakers to inform and, at the same time, entertain their audiences, which sometimes numbered several thousand. Speakers generally prepared one basic speech but could add or delete material to suit a particular crowd. Along with current issues, they dwelled heavily on long-held party principles. The more learned campaigners also included quotations from antiquity and scripture plus rhetoric about America's glorious achievements. People of that day, enthusiastic about politics and used to hearing lengthy sermons, listened intently to an orator's discourse, which might go on for two to three hours. Carl Schurz, the noted German-American advocate for the Republican party, remembered an instance when, with the temperature in the high nineties, he sought to conclude his address after one hour but heard shouting voices protest, "No, no; go on; go on!" He talked for an hour longer, "and even then the people did not seem to have enough."[23]

Further improvements in transportation allowed candidates to arrange long speaking tours in order to reach as many voters as possible. During the famous Illinois senatorial battle in 1858, Abraham Lincoln delivered 63 major speeches and many minor ones, as he covered 4,300 miles by train, carriage, and riverboat. His opponent Stephen Douglas made over 100 appearances, traveling more than 5,200 miles around the state. As time passed, campaign tours covered even longer distances. James Garfield journeyed 7,500 miles over the course of the 1866 congressional contest, giving 65 speeches and attending countless party functions. That the lot of a campaigner was not an easy one is attested to in a letter Garfield sent his wife while out on the hustings in 1874. "I have had two hard days work since I left you," he wrote. "A cold ride of eleven miles from Baconsburg, a two hour speech at Gustavus. Yesterday morning in the rain, an ugly wagon ride of 17 miles—a speech at Andover—and then a colder wagon ride of 16 miles to this place, and a speech of two hours among enemies, in reply to an ugly two hours attack made here the night before by Judge Tuttle of Painesville and a cold cheerless night at the hotel. This brings me to morning, and near to the train time to go to Conneaut to speak again among enemies."[24]

Among those traveling on the campaign trail in this era were an increasing number of women. Women had joined in parades and rallies beginning with the election of 1840, and by the next decade certain candidates' spouses such as Adele Cutts Douglas, wife of the Illinois senator, would accompany their husbands on tour and sit on the platform during their speeches. But in the 1860s and 1870s a handful of women actually spoke at gatherings of pro-spective voters. The first famous female stump orator was Anna Dickinson, a young Quaker girl from Pennsylvania. After having become a recognized figure in the prewar abolitionist movement, Dickinson was sent by Repub-lican leaders to enhance the party's effort in state elections in Connecticut and New Hampshire in 1863. Audiences everywhere showed great enthu-siasm. Commenting upon her address in Hartford, the Connecticut state chairman declared: "She has no equal." Although Dickinson moved on to the Chautauqua circuit and gave few political speeches in subsequent years, other women became active campaigners starting in 1872, when the Repub-licans expressed at least some sympathy for a woman's suffrage amendment. That same year the notorious Victoria Woodhull, condemned as an advocate of "free love," proposed a wide range of reforms in her bid as the first woman to seek the presidency.[25]

PRESIDENTIAL CAMPAIGNING

Presidential candidates from the major parties still did not campaign much. They did not even attend their party's nominating convention or make an in-person acceptance speech. Instead, they waited at home for a select com-mittee to come notify them of their choice as nominee. After a brief statement of thanks, they generally did not utter another word to the public until the election had concluded. Their only communication with voters was through a written "letter of acceptance," in which they endorsed as best they could the main tenets of the party platform. Starting with Stephen Douglas in 1860, a few nominees, who trailed badly from the outset, broke with tradition and went on extended speaking tours. Nevertheless most candidates rejected this option, fearing they might say something to damage their position. For men like Ulysses S. Grant who lacked oratorical prowess, remaining silent probably made good sense. As Grant wrote candidly to Senator Roscoe Conkling of New York in 1872: "My judgment is that it will be better that I should not attend any convention or political meeting during the campaign. It has been done, so far as I remember, by but two Presidential candidates heretofore, and both of them were public speakers, and both were beaten. I am no speaker, and don't want to be beaten."[26]

By 1880, however, the public seemed to have developed a desire for more personal contact with a presidential candidate. Moreover, a man like James Garfield, who had spent much of his political life on the campaign trail, found it difficult to remain in total seclusion. One alternative, with which he experimented, later became known as the "front-porch" method. As election day approached, Garfield offered a few well-chosen words to some of the many groups of visitors who journeyed by rail to his home in Mentor, Ohio.[27] In 1888 Benjamin Harrison, who resided in Indianapolis, Indiana, built his whole campaign around these pilgrimages to his doorstep. Carefully planning his appearances in advance and always making them appropriate to the occasion, Harrison made a total of seventy-nine public statements in this manner. To those who thought it better to go on tour, Harrison said, "I have great risk of meeting a fool at home but the candidate who travels cannot escape him."[28]

Presidential aspirants continued to be promoted in numerous ways. One format that attracted increasing attention was the use of material objects. This period saw a great profusion of paraphernalia advertising White House hopefuls. Surpassing the variety of items produced for the "log-cabin campaign," the major parties on almost every occasion put forth a wide array of silk and cotton ribbons or elaborate handkerchiefs and bandannas, which sometimes contained the candidate's portrait, a slogan, or both. One ribbon in 1864 bore a picture of Abraham Lincoln with the caption, "Lincoln and Johnson, Union and Liberty." Later, small ribbons with pins were worn as badges on lapels. In addition to cloth, dozens of medals and tokens with the candidate's likeness were struck in brass, copper, or bronze. After 1860 small ferrotype portraits lodged in brass shells proved very popular, ferrotypes and photographs having replaced paintings. At rallies and parades local groups often created huge banners or posters featuring the name and picture of the nominee and his running mate. Many included an American flag, an eagle, a goddess of liberty, or other patriotic symbols in the background.[29]

PRINTED MATTER

Printed matter—pamphlets, handbills—was distributed in ever larger quantities. Within the print medium, however, newspapers continued to be the chief means of reaching the voter and in many ways created the voter's political world. The number of papers grew enormously, the biggest rise being in small country papers. Overall, 12,000 sheets were published in 1890 compared to 2,300 in 1850. Most were highly partisan and contained heavy doses of political news, particularly at election time. As editors depended on the party for patronage and printing contracts, their commitment to the ticket did not waver. To demonstrate their loyalty they carried the names of the party standard-bearers on the paper's masthead. They constantly wrote editorials criticizing the opposing side and praising their own. Even news stories were sometimes slanted or falsified for partisan purposes. Indeed, it was difficult to find objective accounts of any event amidst a campaign. Beginning in the 1870s and 1880s, some newspapers showed a slight tendency toward editorial independence. Higher standards of journalism were adopted, leading to a more objective approach to the news. Also, due to a greater amount of nonpolitical advertising, editors did not have to be so concerned about always following the party line. Nevertheless, for the majority, close party affiliation remained the norm.[30]

One form of journalism that had a great impact on voters in these years was the political cartoon. Although some election-related cartoons appeared in the Jackson era, only around the time of the Civil War did they proliferate. Many noteworthy drawings were found in such magazines as *Harper's Weekly*, *Frank Leslie's Weekly*, *Puck*, and *Judge*. *Harper's* carried the powerful and imaginative creations of Thomas Nast, surely the foremost cartoonist of his day. Nast's antiappeasement cartoons enhanced Lincoln's reelection bid in 1864, his swipes at Greeley aided Grant in 1872, and his attacks on Tammany Hall helped destroy the Tweed Ring (a corrupt band of New York politicians led by "Boss" William Tweed) and elevate Samuel Tilden. By 1884 campaign cartoons flourished not only in magazines but in daily newspapers. The most sensational one that year, "The Royal Feast of Belshazzar" by Walt McDougall, which appeared in the *New York World*, ridiculed Republican James G. Blaine's attendance at a dinner for millionaires. The wealthy plutocrats were shown consuming "monopoly pudding" and "lobby pie," while a poor man begged for a piece of crust. From that time onward candidates increasingly had to cope with criticism in pen-and-ink pictures as well as in words.[31]

Many different kinds of election literature—including newspaper editorials and cartoons—were brought together in a more expansive format in this period: the campaign textbook. These books, published by the major parties at the start of the race, were designed to give the reader, and particularly party activists, a full-blown view of the party's position on a wide range of subjects. Not a work by a single author, but a compilation of many items, the textbook contained the party platform, a biographical sketch of the candidate and his letter of acceptance, various congressional reports and important speeches, and perhaps the lyrics of some party songs. Each volume sought to convey an overall theme. The Republican textbook for 1876, for example, emphasized the positive achievements of the recent administrations while denouncing the Democrats as still untrustworthy. The Democratic counterpart that year dwelled almost entirely on its opponents' shortcomings, carrying every conceivable charge of Republican corruption during the previous decade.[32]

STATE AND NATIONAL CAMPAIGNS

In this era there was still no standard date for all major elections. According to law, beginning in 1848 presidential elections and some state votes were to occur on the first Tuesday after the first Monday in November. Many state and congressional contests, however, still took place at different times of the year, particularly in late summer or early autumn. The state elections that had the greatest national impact were those in Maine each September (leading to the phrase, "As Maine goes, so goes the nation") and the ones in Indiana, Ohio, and Pennsylvania in October. The "October states," because of their size and balanced party divisions, became hotbeds of conflict. Big-name speakers and barrels of money were often shipped in when the race was tight. Party leaders knew that clear-cut victories in these encounters would bode well for the national balloting in November, so they went all out trying to win them. By the mid–1880s, however, charges of corruption and other pressure led the "October states" to give up their separate contests. Only Maine and a few other small states continued the practice after 1885.[33]

National campaigns started slowly after the party conventions in early summer and then proceeded at a quickened pace right up to election day. During the initial stages the national committees would inaugurate their fund-raising efforts. Preparation and distribution of literature would commence as well. At this time, too, many local communities held "ratification" rallies at which party enthusiasts registered their approval of the presidential ticket. This was followed some weeks later by a large ratification rally at the state capital, where dozens of party dignitaries and thousands of the rank and file came to honor the nominees and pledge their support. Campaigning would then accelerate especially in the half dozen or so "doubtful states," usually Connecticut, New York, New Jersey, Ohio, Illinois, and Indiana. In the towns and cities of these six states, mass meetings were scheduled almost every night. (The importance of the doubtful states also can be seen by the fact that the parties generally selected the presidential and vice presidential candidates from them. The Republicans most often chose someone as standard-bearer from the three above-mentioned midwestern states; the Democrats frequently named a New Yorker.)[34]

In the doubtful states, and sometimes elsewhere, it became common for the parties to improve their campaign effectiveness by taking extensive polls. Although no scientific sampling took place, the results probably were as accurate as those of today's polls, since they involved a thorough survey of every voter in a specific locale. In a majority of cases, the poll focused on one "swing" county or district that contained numerous fence sitters. But for elections of crucial importance—the presidential contest in Indiana in 1876, for example—party leaders always commissioned a poll of the entire state. In such instances, each county chairman asked all the party workers available—editors, postmasters, other civil servants—to visit every elector in their village, town, or precinct and record their response. The whole project took an enormous amount of time and effort to coordinate, but in the extremely competitive politics of that era it was considered vital. Through a full survey political leaders were able to determine the areas that remained questionable and choose where to concentrate their resources.[35]

In their quest for votes the parties usually followed their platform quite closely. In contrast to previous platforms, which mentioned certain principles but were rather brief and vague, those of the new era were at least a few pages in length and fairly specific concerning the issues. In platforms and other statements, however, the major parties abandoned many of the rhetorical appeals of the past. It became far less common to accuse one's opponent of being an aristocrat (before the Civil War the Republicans condemned the power of the "slaveocracy" of the South). It was now almost impossible to charge anyone with having been a Federalist—except for the aging James Buchanan in 1856. Candidates from both parties nevertheless continued to invoke the names of the nation's founders in many of their public statements. Lincoln and Douglas both claimed they were following Jefferson in their positions on slavery, and in 1876, Democrat Samuel Tilden asserted in his acceptance letter that "the reformatory work of Mr. Jefferson in 1800 must now be repeated."[36]

National campaigns tended to be better organized than in the previous era. This was largely due to the expanding role of the national committees. Each party's national committee contained thirty or more members—normally one from each state—and was headed by a small executive board. The board, especially its chairman and secretary, played a significant part in assigning speakers, publishing documents, and raising money. The national chairman usually was an important banker or businessman with close ties to the New York financial community—such as Edwin D. Morgan (Republican) and August Belmont (Democrat)—who knew how to elicit widespread monetary support and at the same time work effectively with state and congressional leaders. The national committees by no means controlled the entire operation. Their main function was to advise not to supervise. As historian James Rawley has put it: "national headquarters was a clearing house rather than a seat of authority, a bond rather than bondage."[37] For the most part, the direction of the canvass in each state remained in the hands of local politicians. They actually dispersed the funds, arranged dates for speakers, and distributed the literature. Down to the late 1880s the national committee intervened mostly in an indirect manner, supplying aid but not dictating how it should be used.

In addition to the national committees' handling of the presidential contests came the creation of party congressional committees to oversee congressional campaigns. As the Republican National Committee in the mid–1860s fell under the influence of a hostile chief executive (Andrew Johnson), some congressional leaders decided to establish a separate organization to help conduct the 1866 House campaign. Although set up at first on a temporary basis, it soon became a permanent part of the election apparatus. By 1868 a similar group had been formed by the Democrats. (The Democratic Congressional Committee at the time was composed of two senators, five representatives, and four other major party figures.) From that point onward the congressional committee would work together with the regular national committee to aid the campaigns of members of Congress, assist in fund-raising, and designate speakers. It would be in complete charge of off-year elections when the main committee was not in operation. Early in the next century, when the Constitution was amended to permit the direct election of senators, separate senatorial committees were established.[38]

As in the past, the grass-roots campaigning was conducted by state and local committees. Every district and county, and even smaller units had party committees to oversee their affairs. All the affiliates in a particular state functioned under the nominal authority of a statewide executive committee that distributed the resources and decided on basic strategy, although local leaders still exercised a good deal of autonomy. In the larger cities elaborate political organizations known as "machines" ran the operation. Machines, such as Tammany Hall in New York City, consisted of loosely knit neighborhood groups each headed by a ward boss, who often owed his allegiance to a single figure—the citywide boss. As election time neared, the ward boss, who had often provided aid of various kinds to his constituents, sought to have them return the favor by participating in rallies and especially by voting. The bosses were assisted by local precinct captains or committeemen whose main job was to get out the vote and distribute ballots. (Before the introduction of standard ballots in the 1890s, each party prepared its own, in a distinctive color, to keep track of its adherents.) Wooden booths were set up near the polls, in front of which party workers handed out the tickets and sometimes collared those seemingly headed for the opposition's booth. The effectiveness of these men could sometimes mean the difference between victory and defeat.[39]

CAMPAIGN FINANCE

A major difference between campaigns in this period and earlier ones was the enormous increase in the amount of money involved. Large financial outlays gradually became indispensable, and the prospect of winning or losing frequently was described in terms of dollars and cents. During the presidential contest of 1860, Lincoln's managers insisted that with $10,000 more the state of Indiana "can be carried" by the Republicans, but "without 'foreign aid' they are in trouble."[40] Even though most party members worked as unpaid volunteers, some performed services that required remuneration. Money, declared Oliver Morton of Indiana, was needed "to pay men to travel and organize—to print and circulate documents."[41] It also had to cover various kinds of incidental expenditures. As Henry H. Sibley, Democratic committeeman from Minnesota, told the Stephen Douglas organization when requesting funds: "The people are very poor. Many voters living at a distance from the polls must be transferred thither by teams, and a thousand other legitimate expenses must be defrayed."[42] As a result the cost of a national campaign rose from about $150,000 in 1860 ($100,000 for Lincoln, $50,000 for Douglas) to over $2,000,000 by the 1880s. Generally, the Republicans raised and spent much more than the Democrats, although in the 1876 and 1884 races the resources employed by each side stood about equal.[43]

The higher cost of campaigns naturally meant an acceleration of fundraising activities. In the pre–Civil War years money came from three main sources—assessments made on each congressional district (about ten percent of the total), funds contributed by the financial community in the major cities of New York, Philadelphia, and Boston (about twenty-five percent), and the remainder from individuals, primarily businessmen and contractors.[44] Following the war a considerable proportion still came from business and financial leaders. However, as the spoils system had greatly expanded, party heads looked to state and local officeholders for a large part of their revenue. Before each contest state committees sent out form letters to party appointees requesting a certain percentage of their salary; the committees repeated the process if no response was forthcoming. A letter from the state Republican organization in Pennsylvania in 1876 began: "Our books show that you have paid no heed to either of the requests of the Committee for funds. We look to you, as one of the Federal beneficiaries, to help bear the burden. Two percent of your salary is ——. Please remit promptly. At the close of the campaign we shall place a list of those who have not paid in the hands of the head of the bureau you are in."[45]

After the passage of the Civil Service Act in 1883, which forbade direct assessments on federal employees, officeholders' contributions declined. Consequently, political managers turned more and more to big business for campaign financing. Raising funds among businessmen often was referred to as "frying the fat." As James P. Foster of the Republican League of America stated: "I would put the manufacturers of Pennsylvania under the fire and fry the fat out of them."[46] In pleading for money party officials tried to show industrialists how much they would benefit from tariff increases and other probusiness policies. Most corporate leaders came to favor the Republicans, but some, especially those involved in importing, backed the Democrats. A few magnates followed the practice of the notorious Jay Gould and gave to both sides. "I was a Republican in Republican districts, a Democrat in Democratic districts," he once said.[47]

The rapid increase in campaign funding made possible a high degree of fraud and bribery. Indeed, more than at any other time in U.S. history, the vote-getting process in the Gilded Age was known for its flagrant corruption. In Indiana, where almost every contest was a close one, payoffs to electors grew exceedingly common. "Election frauds have become as notorious as divorce cases," exclaimed the *Indianapolis Journal*.[48] Floaters—men who voted according to the highest bidder—were paid anywhere from $5 to $20 and then guided to the polls. Colonel W. W. Dudley, the treasurer of the Republican National Committee in 1888, ordered local Hoosier leaders to "Divide the floaters into blocks of five and put a trusted man in charge of these five and make him responsible that none get away and that all vote our ticket."[49] Tammany Hall bosses in New York City brought in men from New Jersey and Pennsylvania to vote early and often in crucial races. Actually, according to Richard Jensen, the greatest number of such incidents occurred in the South. "Nearly every closely contested election in the rural South in the late nineteenth century was besmirched by frauds, irregularities, coercion, or even violence," he claims.[50]

Despite the widespread attention given to the subject, Jensen insists that the amount of electoral corruption in these years has been grossly exaggerated. Many of the charges of "dirty politics," he says, have not been substantiated. Also, it would appear that much preelection talk about fraud consisted of "mere rumor, designed to shock respectable voters and encourage local supporters to work harder for their own side."[51] In quite a few cases, both parties carefully looked at their opponents' activities, hoping for a chance to expose even the slightest impropriety on the eve of the balloting. Of course a good deal of fraud and bribery did take place in this period. Republican financier John Wanamaker, describing his secret distribution of money in 1888, declared that it happened so quickly, "The Democrats never knew anything about it. They had their spies out supposing we were going to do something, but before they knew what it was we had them beaten."[52]

PARTY REALIGNMENT

The era began with the old parties—especially the Whigs—in disarray. The issues that kept the second party system flourishing were no longer relevant, and the new sectional questions seemed less and less possible to resolve. The Compromise of 1850 soon broke down, and the situation went from bad to worse. The Kansas–Nebraska Act, pushed through Congress in 1854 by Senator Stephen Douglas and his southern allies, repealed the Missouri Compromise and opened the new Kansas Territory to the possibility of slavery. This alienated northerners of all political persuasions, who were appalled at what they believed was capitulation to the dominant southern influence in the federal government (which they referred to as the "slave power". Numerous northern Democrats began to leave their party, weakening it considerably. An even greater number of northern Whigs fled from their organization, hurting it to such a degree that it practically disintegrated as a national entity within the next couple of years.

Not everyone was immediately caught up in the sectional fray. Many people, frustrated by the slavery controversy, rapid economic change, and the large influx of European (especially Catholic) immigrants, at first joined the new American, or Know-Nothing, party. (Originally a secret order, the group's password had been, "I know nothing.") The Know-Nothings appealed to anti-Catholic, anti-immigrant prejudices, claiming that popery would soon take over America. They demanded that the residency requirement for newcomers who wished to be citizens be raised from seven to twenty-one years. They also opposed the election of Catholics to office and in some areas backed the prohibition of alcohol. The Know-Nothings enjoyed quick success in several ethnically divided eastern states, capturing six governorships and electing seventy-five congressmen. But this attraction to the nativists was short-lived. Where they won, they generally were ineffective, and the party's leaders turned out to be no purer than other politicians. Moreover, their failure to take a strong stand on sectional issues alienated potential followers who opposed the power of the slaveholding class just as much as they disliked the influx of immigrants.[53]

Gradually, the majority of northerners were won over to a new, more broadly based party, the Republicans. Even though its appeal was sectional, it had a wide range of support. Comprising former Whigs, Free-Soilers, Know-Nothings, and "Anti-Nebraska" Democrats, Republican groups spontaneously sprang up in a few northwestern states such as Michigan and Wisconsin, and soon reached out over the entire North. The Republicans insisted that something had to be done to stop the growing "slave power" and prevent the continued expansion of slavery. Although not every member was abolitionist in outlook, all agreed that slavery must be completely prohibited in the new western territories. For America to remain the land of opportunity, they said, the West must be open solely to freedom and not be a place for slaveholders to bring their chattel. They hoped to carry the free-soil concept further than the former Free-Soil party did.[54]

It was not easy to build the new party into an effective vote-getting operation. As abolitionist Henry Stanton, now a Republican, wrote to Thurlow Weed, who also had joined the bandwagon shortly before the New York state election of 1855: "Everything in the shape of *organization* is in utter chaos—I mean the kind of minute and detailed organization having for its chief object the bringing of votes to the polls. All the old *Whig* committees are of course disabled and their substitutes are to a large extent yet to be appointed." There also existed the problem of convincing a confused electorate that the issue of slavery expansion was more pressing than the question of Catholic power. George E. Baker, one of the New York leaders, told Senator William Seward, "If we fail this fall it will be because the people have read more about the Pope and Bishop Hughes than about Slavery and Equal Rights."[55] The new party did not fare well in 1855, but by the following year the Republicans were able to compete with the Democrats not only in New York but on a national level.

ELECTION OF 1856

The presidential election of 1856 was the most hard-fought since 1840. The Republicans, embarking upon their first national campaign, brought to the contest a great deal of energy and fervor. They selected as their standard-bearer John C. Frémont, the bold and adventurous "Pathfinder," who had spent many years exploring the American West. Frémont had no previous political record, but his strong opposition to the expansion of slavery made him acceptable to the party leadership. If Frémont lacked political training, he did have, at age forty-three, youth and vigor. Another asset was his charming and intelligent wife Jessie, daughter of Senator Benton of Missouri. This would mark the first time that a candidate's spouse would play a role in the campaign—issuing statements about her husband's controversial past and helping to prepare his campaign biography. Her name would also be widely mentioned in slogan and song. "Frémont and Jessie" was heard as often as "Frémont and Dayton." (William L. Dayton of New Jersey was Frémont's actual running mate.)[56]

The Democrats, despite signs of strain, still possessed a formidable party. They chose sixty-five year old James Buchanan of Pennsylvania, a loyal party man and foreign diplomat, as their nominee. While Buchanan lacked dramatic flair, he was quite experienced and, as an opponent of sectional politics, could attract many conservative voters, including former Whigs. The Know-Nothing party, rapidly losing popularity, split its allegiance; many northern members supported Frémont, whereas the southerners backed longtime Whig Millard Fillmore. Know-Nothings in the South tried to appeal to the populace as the party of true nationalism, but their campaign had little impact outside the border states. The fading Whig party nominated Fillmore, although nationally the Whigs would have no greater impact than the Know-Nothings.

The campaign was to be fiercely ideological, perhaps the most ideological since the election of 1800. The Republican party, while casually mentioning the need for internal improvements and a transcontinental railroad, primarily focused on the question of slavery in the territories. Their platform condemned the repeal of the Missouri Compromise, attacked the Pierce administration for opening the possibility of slavery expansion, and called for the immediate admission of Kansas as a free state. The Republicans insisted that

Congress had sovereign power over the government of the territories and should use that power to keep it free. In fact, "Free soil, free labor, free speech, and Frémont," became the party's most popular slogan.[57] In response, the Democrats maintained that Congress could not interfere with slavery in the territories and warned of the danger to the Union that their new antislavery opponents represented. "The Black Republicans," wrote Buchanan, "must be boldly assailed as disunionists, and this charge must be reiterated again and again."[58]

Despite the Republicans' underdog status, their initial canvass elicited great excitement. "The mass meetings," declared George W. Julian of Indiana, "were not only immense in numbers, but seemed to come together spontaneously and wholly independent of machinery. The processions, banners, and devices were admirable in all their appointments, and no campaign has ever been inspired by such charming and soul-stirring music."[59] At rallies everywhere, Republican speakers hit upon the failings of the incumbent Democratic administration. Their cause was aided by news of further disorders in Kansas as well as by letters from the ailing antislavery spokesman Charles Sumner of Massachusetts, who had been brutally beaten in the Senate chamber by South Carolinian Preston Brooks. While personal criticism of Buchanan did not go too far, a few writers called "Old Buck" a superannuated bachelor or referred to him as "Ten Cent Jimmy," because he allegedly had said American workingmen ought to be paid at the European level of ten cents an hour.

The Democrats, having a well-established, widespread organization, took their adversaries lightly at first. They foresaw no problems in the southern states because the Republicans usually did not enter tickets, and Fillmore's Know-Nothing party offered but limited opposition. Victory in most of the North was expected too. Yet after losing the state election in Maine by a big margin, the party realized that a more aggressive campaign was needed if it wished to remain in power. Large amounts of money and a flock of speakers were sent to rescue both Indiana and Pennsylvania from their opponents' grasp. Democratic presses stepped up their assaults on Frémont's military record, his financial dealings, his illegitimate birth, and particularly his alleged Catholicism. Although Frémont was an Episcopalian, the fact that he had been married by a Catholic priest and had sent his niece to a Catholic school made refutation difficult. Also difficult to refute was the charge of a Republican link with Know-Nothingism, which hurt the party's chances for the immigrant vote.

The late Democratic drive proved successful. After his side won the Pennsylvania state election in October, it became clear that Buchanan would triumph nationally in November, and he did. He garnered 174 electoral votes compared to Frémont's 114, with just eight going to Fillmore. Buchanan swept the entire South and several major states in the North, including New York and his own Pennsylvania. Overall, he had a numerical superiority in three-fourths of the nation's county units, but he only accumulated 45 percent of the total popular vote, far below Pierce's 53 percent in 1852. Moreover, Frémont took eleven of sixteen northern states and came closer to winning than many experts had predicted in this initial Republican presidential effort. Most important, the fact that nearly all of Frémont's votes had come from the North showed that nothing less than a revolution was taking place in American politics, although this was not sufficiently recognized at the time.

The trend toward greater polarization and increasing Republican strength became clearer in the congressional election of 1858. The Buchanan administration's support for the fraudulent, proslavery Lecompton Constitution in Kansas and its sympathy for the Supreme Court's Dred Scott decision, repelled ever-larger numbers of northern voters. Even some Democrats like Senator Douglas began to question Buchanan's pro-South policies. Perhaps the most crucial state contest took place in Illinois, where in the Senate race, the incumbent Stephen Douglas was challenged by a Springfield lawyer named Abraham Lincoln. Generally, there had been little campaigning for this office in the past, as senators were appointed by the winning party after the vote for state legislators. But the Republicans thought they somehow could influence the outcome by having their nominee speak out on the main issue and force Douglas to do the same. Soon the two men were going about giving dozens of speeches and engaging in a series of joint debates, with Lincoln stressing the restriction of slavery and Douglas championing his concept of "popular sovereignty." Because Douglas's political future stood on the line, newspapermen covered these encounters more closely than any previous political event. Douglas eventually won the election, but only because the legislative districts were apportioned in the Democrats' favor, not because of a superior performance. In fact, many observers believed that Lincoln had got the better of him, and in the state as a whole the Republicans had the higher popular vote. Nationwide, the Democrats lost eighteen congressional seats, and the administration's political influence seemed to be waning.[60]

ELECTION OF 1860

The presidential election of 1860 clearly was the most consequential in American history, for upon its result hung the fate of the Union. The Democrats, if they had remained united, might have been able to win the election and prevent the subsequent breakdown of the system. But rifts within the once close-knit organization widened and any hope of a cooperative effort soon became impossible. The southern wing of the party walked out of the national convention, disturbed about a proposed platform that did not fully endorse slavery and about the prospective candidacy of Stephen Douglas. Later on, after a second convention had failed, the northern Democrats, now without opposition, nominated Douglas. The bolting southern Democrats then met and selected John C. Breckinridge of Kentucky, along with a plat-form protecting slavery. Many former southern Whigs and Know-Nothings, hoping to find a compromise candidate, created the Constitutional Union party and chose longtime congressman and senator John Bell of Ten-nessee. Claiming that elaborate platforms only served to "mislead and deceive the people," the new group resolved merely "to uphold the Constitution and the union of the states." Meanwhile, the Republicans, buoyed by the division among their opponents, proposed as their candidate Abraham Lincoln, who had given Douglas so much trouble in the Illinois senatorial race.

In their platform and in all public statements, the Republicans displayed more practicality and moderation than in 1856. Although they still firmly opposed slavery expansion, it did not become such a dominant theme. Nor was much said about such recent events as John Brown's raid on Harpers Ferry or the threat of southern secession. Party spokesmen mainly stressed economic issues such as the tariff, free homesteads, and the transcontinental railroad. The growing corruption within the Buchanan administration was also heavily dwelled on. In contrast, the other parties' leaders ignored what they considered minor issues and devoted all their energies to exposing the threat to the Union that the antislavery Republicans represented. But the division and sniping among the three groups made their criticism far less effective than had it been uttered with a single voice.[61]

Despite the urgency of the situation, the campaign itself lacked some of the excitement and competitiveness shown in 1856. For one thing, debate was often one-sided. No clear-cut practical issue was discussed, no frank dialogue took place about the possibility of secession. The Republicans ducked the question in the North, and realistic forms of compromise could not be aired in the South. Also, the split among the Democrats and the addition of the Constitutional Unionists made many people believe that a Republican victory was inevitable. Moreover, the fact that four parties had entered the field may have created a certain amount of confusion for tradi-tional voters. Indeed, two separate contests developed—one between Lincoln and Douglas in the North, and one between Breckinridge and Bell in the South—with neither Breckinridge nor Bell having much of a chance of achiev-ing an overall popular majority. Of course the absence of a strong, united opposition did not prevent local Republicans from stirring up the party faithful. Charles Francis Adams, Jr., of Massachusetts described the goings-on around his home as a "canvass of rockets, illuminations, and torchlight processions. Every night was marked by its tumult, shouting, marching and counter-marching."[62]

In addition to all the hoopla, Lincoln's managers sent out tremendous amounts of literature about the life of the candidate. Several full-length biographies were prepared—one by the soon-to-be famous writer William Dean Howells—as well as many shorter sketches. All tried to promote certain basic ideas: that Lincoln was born in a log cabin, raised in a poor family, and worked hard as a youth to improve his condition. To underline his common origins each of the authors mentioned the fact that Abe had once been a "railsplitter." This latter image soon caught on with the public beyond anyone's expectation. Posters and banners displayed the symbol everywhere. A campaign newspaper called *The Railsplitter* began to be published in Chicago. Rails or replicas of rails allegedly split by Lincoln as a young man were carried in every Republican procession. In Lincoln's home town of Springfield, a few persons developed a thriving trade, selling beat up old rails to sightseers as souvenirs.[63]

Lincoln himself did not play a visible role in the campaign. He complied with the wishes of party leaders to "make no speeches, write no open letters as a candidate." He stayed close to Springfield and took part in only one public event. Yet he came to be quite active behind the scenes—consulting close associates at home, corresponding with officials in other states, trying to iron out differences among the Republican factions. Lincoln demonstrated a great deal of ability in handling such matters, though opposition writers ignored this as well as his legal and legislative career in calling him a third-rate politician whose public life was as obscure as it was "unmeritorious." One Illinois Democratic editorialist saw the nomination of "Honest Old Abe" as a complete farce. "He is honest! Yes, we concede that. Who is not? 'He is old!' So are thousands. 'He has mauled rails!' What backwoods farmer has not? But what has he ever done for his country?"[64] Lincoln's supporters saw no real need to answer such attacks, preferring instead to emphasize the goals the Republicans would pursue once elected.

Activity on behalf of the other candidates was much less pronounced. Breckinridge's campaign, as one historian has written, tended to be "mediocre" and "noncommittal."[65] It had the support of President Buchanan and the regular party organization in many states, but the failure to launch a serious effort in the North foreshadowed defeat. Breckinridge himself made only one personal appearance—at a barbecue in Ashland, Kentucky—where he reaffirmed his loyalty to the Union but did not reveal at what price. Many Breckinridge Democrats, deeply wedded to their principles, seemed to prefer inaction and probable defeat than to pursue a strategy that might include compromise. They simply dwelled on the threat of the "Black Republicans" and ignored other possibilities. John Bell's campaign effort was even more lackluster than Breckinridge's. Even though Bell had a good deal of backing from former southern Whigs and a middle-of-the-road position that could have been the basis for a larger following, he and his friends generally sat back and failed to exploit their strengths.

The Douglas campaign, while more advanced than those of Bell and Breckinridge, was slow in getting off the ground. A pro-Douglas newspaper editor complained: "The enthusiasm for our candidate is intense. . . . But we want something more. We must have organization—a thorough organization. General enthusiasm will not supply its place."[66] Groups of "Little Giants" and

"Little Dougs" began to be formed, but they scarcely matched the numbers and exuberance of the Republican "Wide Awakes." Moreover, with his party divided and victory doubtful, Douglas found it much harder to raise money than previous Democratic standard-bearers. The attempt by national chairman August Belmont to assess state committees for funds brought only a limited response.

Lacking adequate finances and an effective party organization, Douglas took the unprecedented step of openly campaigning on his own behalf. He was convinced that Lincoln's election would spell disaster and that he alone could keep the nation from dissolving. To get his message to the public, Douglas embarked on a long cross-country tour, often speaking several times a day from railway platforms or hotel balconies, making a fervent plea for the Union and for his concept of popular sovereignty. While the huge crowds who gathered to hear and see him generally were pleased, opponents belittled this new departure of direct vote-seeking by a presidential candidate. An Illinois Republican newspaper scoffed: "Douglas is going about peddling his opinions as a tin man peddles his ware. The only excuse for him is that he is a small man, he has the right to be engaged in small business; and small business it is for a candidate for the Presidency to be strolling around the country begging for votes like a town constable."[67]

Despite the criticism, Douglas continued his arduous journey. Speaking in the South he insisted on the duty of everyone "to submit to the verdict of the people and to maintain the Union." When asked what a president should do if the southern states seceded, he said it was the chief executive's duty to enforce the laws of the United States. If he himself were in charge he would do everything in his power to prevent resistance from whatever quarter it might come. At Raleigh, North Carolina, he declared that he favored hanging anyone who forcibly resisted the Constitution. Even when it became clear that Lincoln would be elected, Douglas returned to the South preaching compromise and appealing for national unity. He probably understood the danger of secession better than any of the other candidates. But if most southerners patiently listened to his speeches—only a few incidents marred his trip—they showed little inclination to accept his ideas. One electioneering banner in Mississippi typified the growing anti-Union sentiment: "Death rather than submission to a Black Republican government."[68]

At the ballot box Lincoln received only 40 percent of the popular vote, but with his voters concentrated in the North he had a large majority in the electoral college. The final tally gave Lincoln 173, Breckinridge 72, Bell 39, and Douglas 12. Lincoln won every northern state except New Jersey, Breckinridge every southern state except Tennessee. This showed that taking the more extreme view on the slavery question was the way to attract the sectional vote. (Of course, it can be argued that Lincoln and his followers did not believe they were taking an extreme position and that they honestly thought the South was bluffing on the matter of secession.) It is interesting that

Douglas and Bell, who took moderate stances, together accumulated more popular votes than Lincoln and had more evenly distributed support around the country than "Old Abe." But as American presidents are elected on the basis of state totals, Lincoln and the Republicans triumphed. Within the next few months several southern states departed from the Union and formed the Confederacy. Less than a month after Lincoln took office the Civil War began.[69]

ELECTION OF 1864

Electioneering largely declined with the onset of the Civil War. Regular elections continued to be held—unique for a country engaged in bloody internal conflict—but the somber wartime atmosphere was not conducive to all the usual hoopla. Moreover, the Democrats, devastated by defeat and secession, were at first hardly in a competitive position; many people considered them disloyal. The Democrats did make a partial comeback in 1862 and 1863, and their expectations rose once again as the nation moved closer toward the presidential election of 1864.[70] Despite major Union military victories the previous year, the war had not come to an end. The public gradually was losing its confidence in Lincoln and his administration. Some Republicans hoped to replace him with Secretary of the Treasury Salmon P. Chase, and others backed John C. Frémont. Although Lincoln won renomination on the first ballot and strengthened his position by selecting Andrew Johnson of Tennessee, a War Democrat, as his running mate, he still faced much internal opposition.[71] Seeing his own party divided and war-weariness on the rise, even Lincoln himself doubted his chances. During the summer he wrote in a private memorandum: "This morning, as for some days past, it seems exceedingly probable that this Administration will not be reelected."[72]

Wishing to capitalize on the growing peace sentiment, the Democrats postponed their convention until late August. After some hesitation they chose as their nominee controversial General George B. McClellan, who, regardless of his inability to defeat the South, was still much admired. The platform written by the extreme peace faction stressed the "four years of failure to restore the Union by the experiment of war." It called for an immediate armistice with the hope of returning to constitutional relationships as they had existed prior to 1861. McClellan soon realized that advocating such a position would be ruinous and repudiated the peace plank, emphasizing instead the need for restoring the Union. He tried to show that the Lincoln administration had failed not in its intentions but in its goal of winning the war. Democrats pleaded with disgruntled conservatives inside their party and out to forget the past and to remember that "the last hope of the Union—and for Constitutional liberty—will be destroyed if Lincoln is elected."[73]

The Republicans, acutely aware of the Democratic threat, began to close ranks and to retaliate. They denounced their opponents in stronger language than ever before, going so far as to paint them as traitors. Each spokesman at the Democratic convention, said Horace Greeley, "seemed to try his best to outdo the last in going to the furthest limits of treasonable speech."[74] Republican editorialists pointed out that the McClellanites did not utter one word in condemnation of the Confederacy. The peace platform, they claimed, was written at the behest of southern agents and represented but one phase in an overall conspiracy against the government. In addition, Republicans played up stories of "Copperhead" plots in the West, which linked the conspirators to the Democratic party. Even though only a small number of true Democrats were involved in such activities, party leaders had a hard time responding to charges of disloyalty. Indeed, the wartime treason issue would continue to hurt their election chances over the next quarter of a century.

Other than a bitter exchange in the newspapers, the race started rather slowly. Neither candidate made himself visible, and their supporters were not much engaged. But by mid-September everything stood in full swing. The *New York Times* reported: "The apathy that was so marked a month ago, has merged into activity and eagerness."[75] One Pennsylvania Republican later recalled: "The campaign soon became one of great acrimony on both sides. Night and day, without cessation, young men like myself, in halls, upon street corners, and from cart-tails, were haranging [sic], pleading, sermonizing, orating, arguing, and extolling our cause and our candidate, and denouncing our opponents. A great deal of oratory, elocution, rhetoric, declamation, and eloquence was hurled into the troubled air by speakers on both sides."[76]

To make possible the financing of speakers and a broad distribution of literature, a larger amount of money was raised and spent than in 1860. The Republicans found it easier to solicit funds this time, tapping army contractors and government suppliers who had made huge profits during the war. Furthermore, the party did not need private sources to cover all expenses. According to the opposition press, a certain percentage came directly out of the taxpayers' pockets. Over one hundred government clerks were said to be addressing documents full-time for the Republican National Committee. On the whole, complained the *New York World*: "The Democrats [operated] under the great disadvantage of having to contend with the greatest patronage and the greatest money-power ever wielded in a presidential election. An administration in power has always money in hand as well as swarms of well drilled office-holders to conduct the canvass: but the Lincolnites . . . control a thousand dollars where former administrations could not raise ten."[77]

One unique aspect of electioneering in this contest was the massive drive for the soldier vote. Believing that ballots cast by the men in arms could be crucial, each side mentioned the soldiers in their respective platforms and each made a concerted effort to gain their support. The Democrats, seeking to contradict the belief that all soldiers backed Lincoln, established a veterans organization known as the McClellan Legion, while the Republicans formed the Veterans Union Club to promote its cause. In addition, each party's newspapers published letters from soldiers claiming that whole regiments backed their candidate. The Republicans ultimately proved themselves more effective. They sent greater amounts of literature to the men at the front and in some cases prevented the distribution of pro-Democratic material. Also, Lincoln and Grant arranged for thousands of troops to obtain furloughs coinciding with election day or made it possible for them to vote in the field by absentee ballot.[78]

Although deemed crucial at first, the soldier vote turned out to be unnecessary. For if Lincoln's reelection looked doubtful in the summer, the situation rapidly changed. News of General Sherman's taking of Atlanta and other Union successes made northerners feel that the end of the war was finally near. Pessimism shifted to optimism, assuring the Republicans of victory; it was the first time a presidential administration had been reelected in thirty-two years. Lincoln triumphed over McClellan by a majority of more than 400,000 popular votes and achieved an overwhelming proportion of the electoral tally, 212 to 21. Only the three states of New Jersey, Delaware, and Kentucky gave their vote to the former general. Lincoln, looking forward to peace and reconciliation, unfortunately served just a few weeks of his second term, becoming a victim of assassination shortly after the war ended.

The Civil War solved certain problems—the Union was preserved, slavery was abolished—but it brought about new ones, particularly with regard to the status of the former Confederate states and the recently freed slaves. Within a year the electorate would have a chance to make its influence felt on these matters, when partisan division manifested itself in the first major election in the postwar period: the congressional contest in 1866. Andrew Johnson, who succeeded Lincoln, soon collided with the Republican Congress over many aspects of reconstruction policy. A Tennessean and War Democrat, Johnson vigorously opposed the Fourteenth Amendment and parts of the new civil rights legislation. He hoped to block "radical" measures in Congress by uniting conservative Republicans and Democrats into a National Union party. However, the new organization did not get very far. Although Johnson personally campaigned on behalf of National Union candidates in his famous "swing-around-the-circle" through the Middle West, he antagonized many of his listeners by insulting blacks and debating hecklers. The regular Republicans, condemning Johnson's policies, won easy victories in most states.[79]

Just as they had sought the soldiers' vote in 1864, the Republicans beginning in 1866 attempted to cultivate the veterans' vote, feeling that the ex-soldiers' assistance was "as necessary to combat the forces of treason in the political arena as it had been on the field." Veterans were encouraged to join the new organization known as the Grand Army of the Republic (the forerunner of the American Legion). Party spokesmen frequently addressed veterans' conventions, proclaiming support for generous pension legislation and waving the bloody shirt against the Democrats, so that the "great prizes" won in the battle would not be "shamefully and blindly" surrendered at the ballot box.[80] While working on the veterans' vote in the North, the Republicans endeavored to use the freedman's vote to retain political control of the South. A partisan organization known as the Union League operated in several southern states to encourage the black voter. Where blacks felt physically threatened, League members often succeeded in marching them to the polls in armed, tight-knit groups. Union military forces stationed in the region sometimes provided protection as well. But protection was not always available, and southern whites stepped up economic pressure and intimidation to keep some blacks away from the ballot box. By the late 1870s many instances of violence and skullduggery had occurred, further reducing black participation. Nevertheless, in certain areas they continued to be a political factor down through the 1880s.[81]

ELECTION OF 1868

The presidential election of 1868 was the first one following the Civil War's outcome and to a large degree hinged on voter reaction to the war and reconstruction. Andrew Johnson's policies and subsequent impeachment trial had eliminated him as a viable candidate. The Republicans, therefore, turned to General Ulysses S. Grant, a popular military hero and to many "the saviour of the nation." General Grant had no formal political experience, but because he had done well running the Union army, it was thought he could do the same with the federal government. Although he did not question congressional reconstruction efforts, the concluding words in his letter of acceptance, "Let us have peace," led most people to believe that he would pursue a moderate course. Grant's Democratic opponent was Horatio Seymour, an able politician who had been the wartime governor of New York, but who would have difficulty handling Republican charges of wartime disloyalty.[82]

The Democratic platform, endorsed by Seymour, declared that slavery and secession were closed questions. It denounced Republican reconstruction, calling for the restoration of all southern states and amnesty for ex-Confederates. Negro suffrage, it said, was a question that should be left to the states. For their part the Republicans believed that while suffrage for blacks in the North should be left to the people to decide, it should be guaranteed in the South as a matter of justice and public safety. They also insisted that the South was again "seeking domination of the government through the Democratic party," which was "the same in character and spirit as when it sympathized with treason."[83] Indeed, how much the former rebels could be trusted and how far to extend black political rights formed the crux of the campaign. Going further than in 1864 and 1866, the Republicans eagerly waved the bloody shirt. "Scratch a Democrat and you find a rebel under his skin," became a popular rallying cry.

Republican campaigners showed much more spirit than their Democratic counterparts. "Tanner Clubs" feverishly worked to stir up the voters throughout the North. (Grant had been a tanner as a young man.) Marching companies and veterans' groups also were extremely active. Republican mass meetings usually featured major military figures. A huge two-day gathering in Philadelphia in October, for example, spotlighted former General Burnside. General Grant made no speeches, but he did appear in public on a few occasions, most notably together with generals Sherman and Sheridan at a well-attended reception in Denver, Colorado. On the Democratic side, some impassioned campaigning took place, especially in the South, though speeches by former Confederates probably hurt as much as helped their cause when excerpts were printed in northern newspapers. In the late stages of the race, Governor Seymour, hoping to overcome the Republican lead, went on a speaking tour of major cities, but it did not change the result.

When the ballots were counted, Grant and the Republicans emerged triumphant. The reasons for their victory were clear enough: they occupied a stronger moral and psychological position, and they also had a stronger ticket and a stronger platform. Seymour's gubernatorial record could not compete with the wartime achievements of General Grant. Moreover, the Democrats did not sufficiently play up economic issues—particularly the Republicans' hard-money and high-tariff policy. Grant dominated the vote in the electoral college, 214 to 80, carrying the entire North except for New York and New Jersey. Yet he received only 52.7 percent of the popular vote, winning nationally by just 300,000 in a total of 5.7 million. In fact, without the support of blacks in six southern states, Grant would have lost.

ELECTION OF 1872

Grant's presidency started with high expectations, but after a while many even within his own party concluded that his administration was a failure. Upset by growing corruption, indifference toward reform, and the continuing problems of reconstruction, many reform-minded Republicans refused to support Grant for a second term. They bolted from the regular organization to form a separate Liberal Republican party to compete in the election of 1872. The new group chose as its nominee Horace Greeley, the outspoken and somewhat eccentric editor of the *New York Tribune*, and created a platform that emphasized civil service and tariff reform. The Democrats, having no attractive alternative, reluctantly decided to make Greeley, a longtime adversary, their candidate as well. The Republicans stayed with Grant, hoping that his popular image as a war hero would overshadow any doubt about him as a political leader. To counter the progressive stance of their opponents, the party made a few gestures toward civil service reform and women's rights in the platform.[84]

While the Liberal Republicans wanted a campaign based on ideas, it rapidly degenerated into a campaign of mudslinging. More name-calling probably went on than in any contest since 1840. Reform spokesmen denounced Grant as corrupt and incompetent; regular Republicans jumped on Greeley for his offbeat ways. The latter's strange appearance—in white coat and hat, carrying an umbrella—soon became the object of ridicule. All the radical schemes he had ever hinted at in editorials, such as vegetarianism and free love, were held against him. The Republicans also vigorously waved the bloody shirt. Without any basis in fact, they charged Greeley with having favored the southern cause and advocating pensions for rebel soldiers. It was said that if he were elected he quickly would become a tool of the Democrats and appoint ex-Confederates to his cabinet. The Republicans furthermore claimed responsibility for the existing economic prosperity, implying that it would come to an end if the other side took over.

The hastily established Liberal Republicans, having little adequate organization or funding, faced an uphill struggle competing against the regular Republicans. After party losses in the state contests in September, Greeley felt his only chance would be to go on a massive speaking tour. Therefore, he went out on the stump and gave over two hundred speeches, stressing the damage caused by Grant's misrule and the need for sectional reconciliation. Many of his statements had a positive impact, but Greeley committed several blunders, especially in criticizing blacks and Union veterans. In the end, the Democrat–Liberal Republican coalition was destroyed, and Greeley suffered a disastrous defeat. Grant won in the electoral college 286 to 66, capturing 55.6 percent of the popular vote to his adversary's 43.9 percent— the biggest margin in the last third of the nineteenth century. The president saw the result as an endorsement of his political leadership. Most impartial observers recognized, however, that it stemmed from other factors, particularly the weakness of his adversary.

ELECTION OF 1876

Although Grant easily won in 1872, scandals in his administration, continued factionalism, disputes over reconstruction, and a sharp economic downturn hurt the Republicans' position after that. The Democrats took control of the House of Representatives in 1874 and looked forward to capturing the White House for the first time in two decades during the centennial year of 1876. They selected as their standard-bearer Samuel J. Tilden, reform governor of New York, who had helped initiate the prosecution of the corrupt Tweed Ring. The Democratic platform emphasized civil service reform, a low tariff, and an end to reconstruction. The Republicans, sensitive to the concern about party corruption, passed over the charismatic but tainted James

G. Blaine and chose as their nominee Rutherford B. Hayes, the governor of
Ohio, who was known as a man of integrity. The Republican platform
implied a commitment to the rights of all citizens (supposedly including
blacks), a protective tariff, and a hard-money policy. The National Independent, or Greenback, party, which advocated an alternative soft-money
program, nominated the eighty-five-year-old industrialist Peter Cooper, although his candidacy would have no bearing on the outcome in any state.[85]

Tilden and the Democrats embarked on a new kind of campaign, attempting to educate voters rather than appeal to their emotions. Instead of concentrating on spectacular events, Tilden and his campaign manager Abram
Hewitt worked at raising large amounts of money, setting up a well-staffed
"literary bureau," and then flooding the nation with party literature. Hewitt
and his associates produced a variety of pamphlets plus a campaign textbook
that contained more information than any previous one. In key states such
as New York and Indiana, a heavier canvass than usual took place. "By use
of this system," said Hewitt, "we will secure every vote to which we are
entitled."[86] Speakers condemned the eight years of Grantism and explained
that Tilden's election would usher in an era of reform. Indeed, "Tilden and
Reform" became the party's chief slogan. Even though the educational approach was not effective everywhere (many local leaders felt reluctant about
changing tactics), the Democrats triumphed in the statewide contest in Indiana in October and seemed headed for a national victory in November.

The Republicans, reeling from all the criticism, found it difficult to get
untracked. But having thousands of placemen and the resources of the federal
government at their command, they eventually fought back in a hard-nosed
fashion. As in the past, the best campaign tactic involved leveling the charge
of continuing Democratic disloyalty. As candidate Hayes reminded Congressman James Garfield: "Our main issue must be 'It is not safe to allow
the Rebellion to come into power.' "[87] Garfield and others made countless
speeches claiming that a democratic triumph would lead to former Confederates holding government posts and paying off Confederate debts. Meanwhile, partisan editors praised the honesty of Hayes and attacked Tilden, a
former corporate lawyer, regarding questionable business deals and alleged
tax evasion. (This was the first time that a presidential candidate's wealth
had become an election issue.)

One unique effort on behalf of the Republican cause was undertaken by
John I. Davenport, the chief federal elections supervisor for New York City.
In order to counter the widespread illegal voting encouraged by Tammany
Hall, Davenport and his staff engaged in some extraordinary and time-
consuming work. They drew up several large-scale street maps and compiled
four thousand registration books—one for each block—giving the name, address, and other pertinent information about every voter. A multivolume
alphabetical index for this series was prepared as well. During the weeks of
registration, Davenport's men checked the list of prospective voters against

those names recorded in their books, enabling them to pinpoint doubtful registrants. Davenport also had warnings printed in the newspapers that threatened fraudulent voters with arrest. Although the entire project cost the Grant administraton $80,000, many Republicans felt that any outlay that could help stop Tilden was worth it.[88]

When the ballots were cast in November, it appeared certain that Tilden would win. The popular vote seemed to be in his favor. He defeated Hayes in New York, New Jersey, Connecticut, Indiana, and all the "redeemed" southern states. However, the Republicans, in charge of the election machinery in the three 'unredeemed" states of Louisiana, Florida, and South Carolina, announced that Tilden lacked one electoral vote and held up the returns. In subsequent days they insisted that Hayes had won in all three states, making him the overall winner (185 electoral votes to 184). Angry Democrats immediately shouted fraud and for a time there was immense confusion about how to proceed. Eventually, a fifteen-member electoral commission was chosen to investigate the situation. Then, after weeks of deliberation, the commission—with its eight Republicans forming a majority—ruled that Hayes had been elected. If the election was stolen from Tilden—and it seems to have been, at least in the case of Florida—it is clear that many southern Democrats were not too unhappy with the result. During informal talks Republicans had promised that they would withdraw the remaining federal troops and allow "home rule" in the South, appoint a southerner to the cabinet, and support government aid for the still war-torn section. As Tilden and other Democratic leaders acquiesced in these developments, the so-called "compromise of 1877" was allowed to stand, and Hayes became the nineteenth president.[89]

ELECTION OF 1880

Hayes could point to several achievements during his years in office, especially improved North–South relations, but many people felt he could have accomplished more. When he did not stand for reelection in 1880, the two main Republican factions, now known as Stalwarts and Half-Breeds, each sought to designate Hayes's successor. The Stalwarts wanted Grant for a third term, the Half-Breeds favored James G. Blaine. As neither could get a majority, the party ultimately named popular Ohio congressman James Garfield to head the ticket. Because Garfield leaned somewhat toward the Half-Breeds, Chester Arthur of New York, a Stalwart, came to be nominated for the vice president's spot. To oppose Garfield, the Democrats, hoping to bury the bloody shirt theme, chose General Winfield Scott Hancock of Pennsylvania, who had won renown at the Battle of Gettysburg. Hancock had no political experience, but his backers believed that his military record would make him attractive to the voters. Hancock, however, did not capitalize on his experience and, compared to Garfield, did little to promote his own candidacy. Garfield, a seasoned politician, worked hard on his own behalf, healing factional disputes, advising subordinates, and making many public appearances.[90]

Although the two parties differed on a number of points, the campaign lacked discussion of substantive issues. The Democrats primarily focused on the election fraud of four years before and on Garfield's alleged connection with the Crédit Mobilier scandal of the early 1870s. As Garfield supposedly had profited by $329, that figure often was painted on billboards and fences by Hancock partisans. The Republicans started out waving the bloody shirt, but found a better issue in the tariff, especially when Hancock, asked to explain the Democratic concept of a tariff for revenue only, replied that "the tariff question is a local question."[91] While in many ways true, the statement gave many people the impression of political indifference or ineptitude. Hancock, whose campaign had been on the upswing following a Democratic victory in Maine in September, now began to flounder, and Garfield seemed headed for the White House. Nevertheless, an attempted last-minute smear threatened to reverse things. A letter, apparently written in Garfield's hand and, dealing with the sensitive subject of Chinese immigration, said that an employer had the right to obtain labor as cheaply as possible. Pro-Garfield workingmen, particularly along the west coast, began to reconsider their loyalties. But after some delay the Republicans succeeded in demonstrating that the so-called "Morey letter" was a Democratic forgery.

In the nationwide popular vote count, this stood as the closest presidential election in American history. Garfield received 4,454,416 ballots to Hancock's 4,444,952, less than a 10,000 vote differential. Yet the margin in the electoral college was much larger—214 to 155—and in general the Republicans outcampaigned the Democrats, winning the key undecided states of Indiana, Ohio, and New York. On the whole it represented a considerable triumph, as the party gained control of both houses of Congress for the first time in half a dozen years. Garfield's success, however, was short-lived, for three months after he assumed the presidency, he was assassinated by a crazed office seeker. Vice president Chester A. Arthur took over the chief executive's post.

ELECTION OF 1884

As president, Chester Arthur did not accomplish much. Moreover, factional rifts within his administration seemed to get worse not better as time passed. Thus the Republican convention in 1884 rejected the renomination of Arthur and turned to James G. Blaine, senator from Maine. Blaine, known as the "Plumed Knight," had long been the most celebrated figure in Republican ranks, but had never gained the presidential nod because of his alleged ties to past business scandals. By this time party leaders presumed that such matters were largely forgotten and that Blaine could now be elected. Still many liberal Republicans, popularly known as Mugwumps, had not forgotten and bolted to the opposing side, especially when the Democrats decided to nominate Grover Cleveland, reform governor of New York, as their standard-bearer. Cleveland, who only recently had come into the limelight, was noted for being honest and hard-working. Having an attractive candidate at a time when their opponents lacked unity seemed to give the Democrats their best chance of winning the presidency since the Civil War.[92]

The campaign did not start out in a heated fashion, as the attempt by reformers to rouse the public by stressing economic issues was not too successful. The differences between the parties were narrowing on such matters, minimizing the possibilities for conflict. However, as public attention focused on the private life and personal morality of the candidates, the battle intensified. The Democrats took the lead by reviving charges contained in the so-called "Mulligan letters" of Blaine's complicity in railroad stock swindles. In addition, they published new evidence, including a letter drafted by Blaine exonerating himself from any wrongdoing, which had been sent to a friend for a signature with a covering note containing the instruction, "Burn this letter!" Those words were soon converted into an endless taunt, and, in general, Democratic newspapers would refer to Blaine as a dishonorable schemer and falsifier.[93]

In retaliation, the Republicans began delving into Cleveland's past, seeking something damaging to pin on him. They eventually discovered that years earlier he had been intimate with a Buffalo, New York, widow who then bore an illegitimate son. Although Cleveland had taken responsibility for the child, the Republican press looked upon the Democratic nominee as an infamous adulterer compared to Blaine, a thoroughly proper family man. For many weeks partisans would chant over and over, "Ma! Ma! Where's my pa?—Gone to the White House, Ha! Ha! Ha!" Yet for all the capital that the Republicans gained from this revelation, Cleveland's admission of the truth showed many voters that he was a man of integrity. This sharply contrasted with the conduct of Blaine who continually denied any former corrupt business ties.

Cleveland remained fairly isolated from the campaign, making but few appearances and devoting most of his time to his duties as governor. Blaine, on the other hand, took to the stump, hoping to overcome the barrage of negative words being said and written about him. His efforts helped solidify party support in much of the Midwest. But in New York, the most crucial state, he made two serious blunders shortly before election day, which severely hurt his chances. At a gathering of clergymen, when a Protestant minister, Samuel Burchard, referred to the Democrats as the party of "rum, Romanism, and rebellion," Blaine failed to repudiate the remark, eventually costing him a number of Irish-Catholic votes. Then, when he attended a banquet with wealthy businessmen in order to raise some last-minute funds,

Democratic newspapers widely publicized the event, reinforcing the idea of Blaine as a friend of the rich and an enemy of the poor.

The exact impact of these occurrences is impossible to measure. Yet Blaine lost New York by 1,149 votes and with it the election. Perhaps the "rum, Romanism, and rebellion" remark was not so critical as believed, since Blaine's tally in Irish-Catholic districts surpassed that of previous Republicans. Even so, one can argue that he might have done still better had the statement never been uttered. Blaine probably lost votes in two other ways: in defections to the Prohibition party and through nonparticipation because of rain in upstate counties. In any case, Cleveland won narrow victories not only in New York, but in Connecticut, New Jersey, and Indiana as well. Overall, Cleveland triumphed in the electoral college by 219 to 182, though he had just a 30,000 majority in the popular vote among the ten million cast. In fact, Blaine, whose campaigning efforts have often been criticized, ended up with a higher percentage than his victorious Republican successor four years later.

ELECTION OF 1888

Grover Cleveland's first term in the presidency was not overly successful. Although hardworking, courageous, and strongly wedded to principles, his executive actions, such as vetoing pension bills and measures to aid struggling farmers, alienated considerable portions of the electorate. Still his party had little choice but to renominate him at the Democratic convention in 1888. His Republican opponent, once Blaine dropped out, was Benjamin Harrison of Indiana, a prosperous lawyer and former Civil War general. Harrison attracted support partly as a representative from a doubtful state and also for being the grandson of "Old Tippecanoe," William Henry Harrison. In addition, it was hoped that as a man with a compromising nature, he might be able to heal the wounds that separated the different Republican factions.[94]

Whether it resulted from Harrison's influence or the leadership provided by national chairman Matthew Quay of Pennsylvania or simply the fact that they were the "out party," the Republicans put together a well-ordered campaign. A businessman's advisory board headed by department store tycoon John Wanamaker raised large sums of money and spent lavishly on literature and speakers. "To one Democratic speech . . . the Republicans made ten . . . and their organization and activity in that respect was wonderful," noted one observer.[95] An important element in the Harrison campaign was, undoubtedly, the front-porch style exhibited by the candidate himself. Harrison, though not charismatic, proved to be an adept spokesman. He was careful not to commit the kind of last-minute blunders that had ruined his predecessor. The Democratic campaign, by contrast, contained neither a high degree of unity nor much enthusiasm. Part of the problem was the president himself who did little to encourage his own reelection. He made

few appearances, leaving much of the work to others. The national committee's effort suffered from mismanagement and sluggishness, and the party
had trouble solving numerous factional disputes. In addition, funds were not
as plentiful as in the previous campaign. Perhaps, too, the Democrats felt
uncomfortable being on the defensive. All in all, they would have difficulty
meeting the Republican challenge.

Though the race was close and involved many charges of vote buying
against the GOP, Harrison won. While Cleveland registered a slight plurality
in the popular vote, Harrison carried several key industrial states, including
New York, by narrow margins, giving him a considerable majority in the
electoral college, 233 to 168. Actually the gap of sixty-five electoral votes is
deceiving, for a switch of about 6,000 votes in New York, perhaps less than
the number purchased, would have meant Republican defeat. Afterwards,
Harrison told Matthew Quay that "Providence has given us victory." Quay
later wrote to a friend, "He ought to know that Providence hadn't a damn
thing to do with it. . . . He would never learn how close a number of men
were compelled to approach the gates of the penitentiary to make him President."[96]

The election of 1888 would represent the high point of the "army-style"
campaign. It marked the culmination of an era of disciplined parties mar-
shalling the troops and readying them for the big battle at the polls. Torchlight parades and massive rallies remained the essence of campaigning; all of
it was aimed at whipping up enthusiasm among the rank and file and getting
them to march to the ballot box in greater numbers than their adversaries.
American elections in this period, remarked English commentator Lord
Bryce, were "largely a matter of booming."[97] But within a short time some
of the noise would begin to diminish, the lights would die out, and in general
there would be a retreat from the flamboyant "army style."

5

The Merchandised Style of Campaigning

1892–1920

In the years after 1890 campaigning once again underwent an enormous transformation. The "army-style" encounters, in which two military-like organizations engaged one another by means of competing spectacular events, started to decline. In their place, a quieter pattern gradually evolved, one based to a greater extent on educating the populace, which Richard Jensen has called the "merchandising style." As noted in chapter four, an educational emphasis had first been introduced nationally in the Tilden campaign of 1876 and had been tried on occasion in the 1880s, but not until the 1890s did it come to prevail. The acceptance of the new mode was partially connected to the rise of complex issues like "free silver," which required considerable explanation. It also stemmed from the growth of a more independent-minded electorate. Under these circumstances the parties realized that "it was necessary to appeal to voters on a higher plane than a colorful rally would permit." They began to focus on the intellect and went about describing their positions much as competing businesses described their wares. In this manner each side hoped to obtain a larger share of the "market," or popular vote, than it had held before. In their desire to corner the voting market, the merchandisers eventually felt the need to combine the educational approach with that of modern advertising. This would modify campaigning even further, pushing it toward an exercise in salesmanship.

The emergence of the new style represented not only a response to changing issues and voter predilections but a reaction against older campaign ways. The public had become somewhat tired of all the noisy fireworks and elaborate display that had long been associated with nineteenth-century election contests. "Spectacular campaigning," according to Michael McGerr, "no longer seemed a vital part of political life." "As memories of the Civil War faded," says McGerr, "people lost the martial spirit" that had comprised a major aspect of campaign spectacle.[1] Marching companies seemed out of place as the nation moved into the new century. In addition, the upper classes who in the past had encouraged mass participation in the political sphere were not as inclined to do so, believing that reduced involvement might help bring about a less corrupt system and one less likely to become radicalized. Given little encouragement to remain politically involved, the mass of people began to find alternative outlets in the new leisure-time activities available—vaudeville, amusement parks, spectator sports. The old political theater soon had trouble competing with these modern diversions. Henceforth, the public's connection with politics would not be on the same communal or emotional basis as before.

EDUCATIONAL CAMPAIGNING

The new style, as Jensen has pointed out, necessitated a major "redistribution of party resources and rhetorical emphasis." Rather than spending money on brass bands, banners, and torches, party officials now allotted the bulk of their funds to preparing and distributing printed matter. They also started holding large numbers of "educational meetings" to explain party positions to their constituents. By the mid–1890s fewer people marched in the street, and more listened to intricate discussions of the tariff, currency, and other issues. James Clarkson, editor of the *Des Moines Register* and a leading figure in the transformation, had founded the National Republican League, one of whose functions was to establish a meeting place in every community where individuals could learn the substance of party views. The Democrats would undertake similar measures; Wisconsin state chairman William Vilas, for example, called for a heavy dose of "school district speaking."[2] Under this revised format, the parties, instead of concentrating only on their regular membership, devoted more energy toward capturing independents and convincing opponents to switch allegiance.

In addition to reflecting new attitudes, the altered campaign style partly resulted from modifications in the party system that took place in these years. The economic and political upheavals of the mid–1890s broke the virtual deadlock between the two main parties, ultimately giving the Republicans a clear majority on the national level. Sectional patterns became more pronounced, as the GOP largely dominated the Northeast and Midwest, while the Democrats controlled the entire South. Competition fell drastically where the opposing side saw little chance of winning. This soon led to a substantial drop-off at the polls. Whereas approximately 80 percent of the eligible voters had cast ballots in national contests in the 1880s, only 60 to 65 percent did so two and three decades later. The diminished participation was accompanied by a slight erosion of party loyalty and a growing feeling of political apathy. The merchandising style itself seemed somewhat to blame, for its strategy of appealing to independents meant there was not as much interest paid to longtime supporters. Also, as educating voters became the primary task, stirring them into action naturally lost its preeminence.[3]

At the same time electioneering would be affected by a series of "progressive" legal changes aimed at regulating the conduct of elections and the role of parties in the process. Nonpartisan contests, established in many localities, curtailed party involvement and generally slowed the bid for votes. The standard "Australian ballot," which had replaced those provided by partisan groups, enhanced secret voting and limited the amount of politicking around the polls. Stronger voter-registration laws, enacted in thirty-one non-southern states by 1920, forced the parties to focus as much on registering individuals as on activating them. Tighter registration tended to reduce the size of the electorate. Moreover, the southern states effectively disfranchised blacks through such measures as the poll tax, literacy test, and grandfather clause. This virtually assured the existence of a one-party South and made campaigning for many offices unnecessary. The only vote-getting activity remaining there occurred in the newly created intraparty primaries, yet a majority of these races were probably uncontested. National presidential primaries, instituted after 1901 to bring about popular control of candidate selection, did not create much competition either.[4]

Whatever the causes, the movement toward a less rousing style already was underway by the presidential election of 1892. The *New York Herald* found an "exceptional calmness" and "an unprecedented absence of noisy demonstrations, popular excitement and that high pressure enthusiasm which used to find vent in brass bands, drum and trumpet fanfaronade, boisterous parades by day and torchlight processions by night, vociferous hurrahs, campaign songs, barbecues and what not."[5] While some resurgence of hoopla could be observed in the "battle of the standards" in 1896, the next few national contests seemed conspicuously lacking in noise and ritualistic display. "I have never known a Presidential campaign so quiet," remarked Senator Henry Cabot Lodge of Massachusetts in 1900.[6] The races in 1904 and 1908 brought forth similar comments, as party leaders no longer organized marching companies or arranged many spectacular events. At the end of the decade, the editor of *Outlook Magazine* compared contemporary electioneering practices to those of a quarter century earlier and commented that one accustomed to the past encounters "in which Mr. Blaine was a prominent figure might have considerable difficulty finding himself as much exercised emotionally as he was then." The country, he said, has passed "from the emotional side of campaigning to the more generally educative method."[7]

To be sure, the old-style ballyhoo did not completely disappear. In some northern towns shortly before election day, groups of young men continued to march in fancy uniforms, while "girl brigades" waved their handkerchiefs as the "troops" passed by. Lively barbecues featuring food and drink as well as colorful speeches still prevailed in many parts of the South and West.

Mammoth parades remained an attraction in some big cities, especially those run by the still-powerful machines. Democrats in New York City in the year 1900 arranged several outdoor rallies and filled the sky with large kites and streamers bearing inscriptions from the William Jennings Bryan campaign. Chicagoans organized huge demonstrations and a "blaze of fireworks" to highlight Bryan's appearance there in 1908. As late as 1920 New York Republicans staged an elaborate torchlight procession with 75,000 persons, including vice presidential nominee Calvin Coolidge, taking part. However, the *New York Times*, in reviewing the latter event, noted that it was something that recalled a bygone era rather than evoking the present one.[8]

While these political gatherings had as their goal the arousal of partisan enthusiasm, many of the get-togethers now held were smaller and more informational. One new form characteristic of this concept was the tent meeting. Popularized by Tom Johnson, the longtime progressive mayor of Cleveland, the tent meeting had a number of advantages over an open-air rally or hall meeting. Tents could be set up at a moment's notice and did not require a heavy rental fee. Despite the fact that no chairs were available— just a few boxes for seats—such an event could bring out hundreds of spectators, and not simply partisans. As Johnson himself pointed out: "In a tent there is a freedom from restraint that is seldom present in halls. The audience seems to feel that it has been invited there for the purpose of finding out the position of the various speakers. There is a greater freedom in asking questions, too." Sometimes this could lead to serious heckling, but, said Johnson, that provided a "valuable form of political education." Actually, in certain cases party leaders would deliberately plant a heckler to allow the candidate to answer any previous charges brought against him.[9]

Among the major changes in campaigning at this time was the gradual decline of oratory. According to the early-twentieth-century political scientist Moise Ostrogorski, the new political atmosphere and the emergence of complicated economic issues were "not very favourable to a lofty and aspiring style of eloquence."[10] Such spellbinders as William Jennings Bryan and Theodore Roosevelt could still attract huge crowds as they toured the country, but fewer campaigners felt inspired to master the art of moving an audience from the speaker's platform. The lessening emphasis on colorful oratory practically eliminated the phenomenon of the joint debate, which had had a long and honored tradition. In fact, such debates had been slowly disappearing from the scene ever since the Civil War. It still remained the custom in some southern states, where primaries had developed, for the candidates to appear together at joint meetings. During the gubernatorial primary in Mississippi in 1899, several "speakings" were scheduled with each of the aspirants given an hour to present his views and then a twenty-minute rebuttal at the conclusion.[11]

Even if latter-day stump speakers proved less dynamic than earlier ones, the parties still employed great numbers of them, particularly during national campaigns. Speakers' bureaus, under the auspices of the national committees, would send out senators, congressmen, governors, cabinet members, lawyers, journalists, businessmen, and even clergymen to advocate their party's cause. Some of the better speakers received as much as one hundred dollars a night plus expenses. But the speeches they delivered were comparatively short and not looked upon as high-level entertainment. Audiences no longer expected or desired the two- and three-hour flamboyant harangues so commonplace several decades before. A stump speech often was delivered so that the text could later appear in print and be read by thousands more than those who had heard it spoken. Surely, campaign speaking did not retain the same vitality and importance that it had in former times. As the journalist Alexander McClure observed in 1902: "When railroads, telegraphs and newspapers became accessible to nearly every home the hustings became secondary to the school and the press."[12]

EXPANDED USE OF PRINTED MATTER

As the "army style" gave way to a more educational approach in the 1890s, publishing and distributing the printed word emerged as the dominant form of electioneering. The parties produced literally millions of documents at each national election, reaching the point where Republican presses in 1896 ran off ten to fifteen items for each eligible voter, under a wide variety of titles. In this instance and others a large "literary bureau" staffed by professional writers was assigned the task of drawing up these documents. As in past eras the literature mainly consisted of pamphlets, leaflets, and handbills, plus the longer textbooks and biographies. Early in the new century, however, the quantity and variety of material would start to diminish. Party leaders, after devoting a great deal of money and effort to the enterprise, came to believe that generating this massive amount of educational literature was not the most effective way to use their resources. Instead, they turned more to newspapers as the best means of reaching the voter by the print medium.[13]

Newspapers always had been the main source of political reading matter for the general public. By the early twentieth century roughly 2,200 dailies and 10,000 weeklies were being published, most of them retaining some form of party ties. Party press bureaus frequently supplied them with "plate matter," that is, ready-made news stories. Yet the newspaper was not quite the same electioneering tool that it had been in the past. Independent journalism continued to grow. There was a stronger desire to present the news more accurately and impartially. This was helped along by the introduction of wire-service stories, which increasingly neutralized national news. At this point too, many editors, inspired by the efforts of Joseph Pulitzer and William Randolph Hearst, began promoting sensationalism and downplaying party politics. Campaigns received far less coverage than in the earlier party organs. Of course, Hearst, Pulitzer, and their disciples were interested in reporting

on dramatic political events, such as those surrounding the origins of the
Spanish-American War. But as Michael McGerr points out, the Hearstian
style "offered readers no sustained perspective on political life comparable
to the viewpoint provided by the old party press." Practicing what was called
"yellow journalism" to attract reader attention, its advocates could not afford
to dwell too long on a single subject. In these years neither independent
journalism nor the sensationalist approach monopolized the newspaper business, but they did force the majority of papers to take heed of their styles
and become less like the partisan sheets of previous times.[14]

Newspapers and other printed material always retained an educational
function—discussing issues and policy positions—but as time passed party
leaders came to see that they also could be employed simply to advertise the
candidates and make them better known. Indeed, by the time of World War
I, there was a growing realization that the best way to get individuals elected
was through the use of recently developed advertising techniques. Highly
innovative advertising had crept into American business life in the late nineteenth century. Cartoons, colorful illustrations, and catchy slogans had been
introduced by the newly formed advertising agencies to help sell household
products. Soon many political leaders came to see that the same methods
could be used to sell candidates. Even before 1900 the Republicans had placed
a few ads on streetcars in New York City. Early in the new century both
parties started reprinting old cartoons and creating a mass of originals for
distribution. They also sent out enormous quantities of lithographed portraits
of their presidential nominees and had pictures of them placed on billboards,
fences, and other structures. Likenesses of William Howard Taft appeared
on 23,000 billboards in 1912, and an even greater number would be displayed
for Woodrow Wilson in 1916 and Warren Harding in 1920. By this point
mass advertising would clearly overshadow the educational approach.[15]

NEW TECHNOLOGY AND MATERIAL OBJECTS

Certain forms of advanced technology furthered the advertising of candidates for high office. The invention of the phonograph, followed shortly
thereafter by the development of motion pictures, enabled those running to
be heard and seen by countless people with whom they could not come into
direct contact. The phonograph's rising popularity resulted in nominees preparing "canned speeches," records of which could be bought by the public
or played at party meetings. The first presidential aspirant to have his words
put on a record was William Jennings Bryan in 1900. His managers hoped
that the voice of the "silver-tongued orator" would impress those who had
no chance to hear him in person. Bryan also became the first White House
hopeful to appear in a brief campaign movie. Certain parts of the Nebraskan's
Labor Day visit to Chicago in 1908 were captured on film. He was seen
riding from the railroad station to a large auditorium where he delivered an

address. (There would be sound but without any synchronization.)[16] In subsequent years moving pictures of such candidates as Taft, Wilson, and Harding would be widely displayed in theaters around the country. Preserved clips show Taft and Wilson at work in Washington, while Harding was presented at home in a more personal fashion. The quality of these productions, however, left something to be desired, and it is hard to know what effect, if any, they may have had on their respective races.[17]

As they adopted a more conspicuous merchandising style, the parties also made greater use of buttons and badges. Miniature likenesses of the nominees, though somewhat less elaborate than earlier ones, were distributed in huge quantities. Starting with the presidential campaigns of 1896 and 1900, both sides produced millions of party emblems, especially the newly developed celluloid button bearing a portrait of the standard-bearer and sometimes his name and a motto. People from all walks of life adorned their lapels with these circular objects, which carried inscriptions such as: "I Am For McKinley. Are You?" or simply, "Wilson for President."[18] Aspirants for local office sometimes used buttons and badges to advertise their candidacy, but most often they sent out various sized cards containing their name and picture with perhaps a slogan such as "a proven leader" or "the man for the times." Some offered a twist of humor. One Missourian running for circuit judge placed the words, "I Want the Office" under his portrait. On the reverse side was a picture of his six children with the caption, "We Want the Salary."[19]

Newer practices notwithstanding, a significant part of the vote-getting process still was carried out by the old-fashioned method of direct contact. In some sections, particularly in the South and West, buttons and printed materials meant much less than a close personal connection. To achieve this it was necessary for an office seeker to meet with his prospective constituents, show an interest in their affairs, and impress upon them certain likeable qualities. In many towns the candidate would spend a good deal of time knocking on doors or greeting people in various public places, for example, train stations, eating establishments, saloons, street corners. One congressional aspirant from Nebraska would stand all day "at a corner near the bank . . . shaking hands with everyone not once but every time he met him."[20] Canvassing in rural areas was not so easily accomplished. The nominee generally was restricted to seeing prospective voters at crossroads stores and post offices or at grange meetings. Yet politicians in some midwestern districts went to much greater lengths to reach the electorate. Claude Bowers, a well-known Democratic activist and historian, has described what rural campaigning was like at the turn of the century in Indiana:

We set out from the county seats in a cavalcade of buggies the first of every week, sleeping wherever the night meeting might be held. During the day the procession would move slowly through the countryside, pausing at each farmhouse to solicit the farmer's vote personally. If he was working in a distant field some of our party would join him at his work and others would talk to the farmer's wife and daughter, and if he was at the churn the candidate would take his turn. The elector would be quizzed discretely about the other candidates, and the information as to preference and prejudice would be passed on. . . . In the evening we could count on a country dinner at the farmhouse of one of the faithful. . . . After eating we would draw up our chairs before the blazing hearth until time to go to the evening meeting at some neighboring town. When there was no such town, the meeting would be in some country schoolhouse. . . . The room would be packed with farmers in their workclothes, and these meetings were the most intimate of all, since the speaker could reach over and touch the shoulders of those in the front row.[21]

By the second decade of the new century, many candidates, particularly in large rural districts, would make similar journeys in a new mode of transportation. The automobile or "motor car," as it was sometimes called, enabled an office seeker to greet more people and deliver many more speeches than was previously possible. Young Franklin Roosevelt, seeking his first elective position as a member of the New York state legislature, did most of his campaigning by car, driving hundreds of miles and visiting numerous hamlets along the Hudson River.[22] Another youthful candidate who depended on the automobile was Roosevelt's future nemesis Huey Long of Louisiana. When he sought his first political post as state railroad commissioner, Long found his opponent in control of most votes from the larger towns. To counter this Long drove to the smaller towns and villages, and even to isolated farmhouses, to speak to farm families. Some politicians claimed that campaigning by car among country people was counterproductive, because the people would resent it as a pretense of superiority. Long realized, however, that the masses might vote for a man who owned an automobile, as it showed the man was something of a success.[23]

Among the campaigners traveling around at this time were increasing numbers of women. Minor parties such as the Prohibitionists and Populists employed several female orators on their behalf. Beginning in 1896 a few women affiliated with the major parties went on the stump in those western states where female suffrage already was in force. Soon afterwards women also became active in the eastern states. One New York Republican in 1904 mentioned that, in the last campaign, women canvassers helped reduce the Democratic margin in Brooklyn by 2,000 votes. In 1916 the Republicans took the unprecedented step of sending a group of New York "society ladies" from coast to coast on behalf of presidential candidate Charles Evans Hughes. Despite the effectiveness of some of the speakers, the trip probably cost Hughes more support than he won, for it came to be identified with Wall Street wealth. By 1920, when the suffrage amendment finally was approved, both parties quickly expanded their use of women in all phases of the vote-getting process.[24]

PRESIDENTIAL CAMPAIGNING

Presidential aspirants began to play a more active and visible role in this period. Campaigns had grown more candidate-oriented, putting the nominee's personality and leadership potential under closer scrutiny. Thus it became necessary for him to be in the public eye to some degree. Gone were the days when men like Lincoln and Grant remained silent and acted only behind the scenes. At the very minimum, party standard-bearers, beginning with Grover Cleveland in 1892, would appear at a public notification ceremony to deliver an acceptance speech. To be sure, certain candidates, particularly incumbents, did not go much beyond this one appearance. Even William Howard Taft, clearly the underdog in 1912, felt it improper to go out on the stump. Still, more than in the previous era, challengers in desperate circumstances were apt to undertake long speaking tours. The best example is William Jennings Bryan, the three-time Democratic nominee (1896, 1900, 1908), who, having limited funds and organization, sought to win over voters through his great oratorical skills. Those in a more favored position like William McKinley and Warren Harding preferred the front-porch style developed by Garfield and Harrison, further refining it to suit their needs. It allowed the candidate to stay at home and operate in a controlled environment, yet keep a high profile in the process.[25]

Not only did the presidential nominee more frequently appear before the populace, but his vice presidential running mate increasingly was expected to campaign as well. A few vice presidential candidates had gone out on the stump in earlier years, for instance, John Logan, who was on the Blaine ticket in 1884, and Allen Thurman, who ran with Cleveland in 1888. But over the next three decades or so the practice became more habitual. Some like Adlai Stevenson and Whitelaw Reid in 1892, and most notably Theodore Roosevelt in 1900, would carry out the brunt of the public speaking while the head of the ticket said relatively little. Not all vice presidential hopefuls took an active role. The wealthy, eighty-two-year-old Henry Gassaway Davis of West Virginia, chosen by the Democrats in 1904, seems to have contributed to his party's cause mainly in a financial way. James Sherman, Taft's Republican running mate in 1912, was unable to campaign because of illness. By 1920, however, both parties' second-spot choices, Franklin Roosevelt for the Democrats and Calvin Coolidge for the Republicans, wound up spending much of their time out among the people.[26]

The increase in long-distance traveling by presidential and vice presidential nominees was largely made possible by improvements in rail transportation. The expansion of railroads ushered in the golden age of whistle-stop campaigning, where the candidate would deliver short speeches from the back of his private car at many points—small and large—along the route. Such men virtually lived on the train for weeks at a time, following an irregular schedule and taking naps before emerging to address a waiting crowd. The most famous whistle-stop campaigner was William Jennings Bryan, who in 1896 made a record 569 speeches as he journeyed over 18,000 miles. As amazing as Bryan's feats were, his totals would soon be surpassed by Theodore Roosevelt, who in 1900 as McKinley's stand-in covered 21,209 miles and gave 673 speeches. Roosevelt, as the Progressive candidate in 1912, and Democrat James Cox in 1920 also would engage in extensive whistle-stopping. Speaking from a train had its drawbacks, of course, especially when having to compete with other noise at the railway station. "It was a common saying," Cox noted, "that we could tell the politics of the man who was running the switch engine near by. He was quiet with his locomotive or not, according to his partisanship."[27]

NATIONAL CAMPAIGNS

National campaigns in this era began with the traditional nominating conventions in early summer. After the usual wrangling, the candidates were chosen and the platform approved. Platforms had become more detailed, and greater care was taken in their preparation. Following the conventions, each side's national headquarters would be established. Once the national chairmen were selected and the staffs put together, the national committees started their fund-raising and document distribution. The public notification ceremony for each candidate, usually scheduled a few weeks after the convention, became the first big moment of the campaign and attracted much publicity. Besides the notification ceremony, very few other events took place in July and August. Not until September did anything of major consequence occur (including many state primaries). Only Maine and (until 1913) Vermont continued to have regular statewide elections some weeks in advance of the federal balloting. But as they offered clues about the relative strengths of the competing sides, they received close attention.[28]

The parties' national committees, which mainly had played an advisory role in previous presidential races, now assumed more authority and functioned with greater efficiency than before. While there had been some movement toward better coordination in the 1880s, especially in the reign of Republican Matthew Quay in 1888, subsequent national chairmen went a good deal further. Under the direction of such men as Mark Hanna, who ran both of McKinley's campaigns (1896 and 1900), George Cortelyou, Roosevelt's manager in 1904, and Frank Hitchcock, who guided Taft's successful attempt in 1908, everything became more highly systematic. They and others sought to apply the principles of modern business enterprise to the job of acquiring votes. More seasoned and professional workers began to be employed at party headquarters. Up-to-date bookkeeping methods and other new office procedures were introduced. Beginning in 1896, the telephone was used in order to keep track of goings' on around the country. Preelection canvassing was heavily expanded—some areas were polled two or three times.

While the thoroughness of the operation varied from one election to the next, and by no means approached today's standards, it represented a marked improvement over earlier experiences.[29]

The national committee was now a much larger and more complex organization than in the past. Various subcommittees were appointed and a number of bureaus created to carry on different phases of campaign work. They included the finance committee, which took charge of the most important task of raising money; the publicity or "literary" bureau, under whose direction printed matter was prepared and distributed; the speakers' bureau, which obtained and assigned speakers and sometimes even handled their travel arrangements; the campaign club committee, to promote association among groups who had some common interest; the organization bureau, to keep in touch with all the state, county, and municipal organizations; and numerous other subordinate bureaus, who carried on specialized work—the farmers' bureau, the labor bureau, the foreign-born voters' bureau, and the women's bureau. While each bureau had its specific role to perform, the national chairman and the rest of the executive committee would have the final word on all major decisions.[30]

Campaigning on the state and local level remained under the auspices of the state and county committees. Each committee had its hierarchy of officers, who made the key decisions, and its rank and file, who carried them out. Machines in the larger cities handled the operation in more or less the same manner as before. In addition to the party regulars, temporary campaign clubs continued to supply a considerable number of workers. Campaign clubs still organized themselves primarily according to ethnic and occupational lines, though in the 1890s they also began to appear on college campuses. However, the attempts to utilize these clubs on a more systematic basis under the National Republican League and the Democratic Association did not work out very well in practice. Indeed, party leaders gradually came to see campaign clubs, like marching companies, as having less and less importance in the overall scheme of things.[31]

CAMPAIGN FINANCE

As the merchandising style began to take hold, campaign financing inevitably reached higher and higher levels. It turned out to be enormously costly to produce and distribute the huge quantities of documents, buttons, and other paraphernalia prepared by the competing parties. The money spent on national campaigns by each side, which had never gone above $1.5 million before 1890, often went far beyond that figure. While some of the older sources of funding dried up, notably the assessments on federal officeholders, new corporate sources were secured. The emergence of railroad and trust problems plus the free-silver issue caused big business leaders to start making larger contributions than they had given in the past. The man who first succeeded in tapping these sources was Marcus Alonzo (Mark) Hanna, a master at political finance. A wealthy Ohio steel magnate, Hanna, had entered Republican politics in the 1880s and eventually came to the forefront as the campaign manager for William McKinley. He proved to be a deft fund-raiser and, despite cartoons portraying him as greedy and corrupt—the most famous drawing pictured him in a gaudy checkered suit with a dollar sign on each checker—he probably was one of the more honest political figures of the day.[32]

Under the chairmanship of Mark Hanna, the Republican National Committee raised anywhere from 3.5 to 7 million dollars for the presidential contest in 1896—perhaps three times the amount of any previous effort—and in doing so set the trend for the future. Hanna did not create any new techniques; rather, he used the established ones in a more orderly and thorough fashion than his predecessors. Contributions were determined on the basis of ability to pay, with quotas set on certain institutions. The rate for banks was one-quarter of one percent of their capital.) Some major corporations were assessed fixed amounts: Standard Oil, for example, paid $250,000 starting in 1896. Hanna, states his chief biographer, "always did his best to convert the practice from a matter of political begging on one side and donating on the other, into a systematic assessment according to the means of the individual and institution."[33] Hanna took pains to avoid situations where favors were implied in return for contributions. To keep his candidate McKinley from becoming tainted, Hanna, during the election of 1900, returned a $10,000 gift to a Wall Street firm that seemed to be making a political demand.[34]

The Democrats never developed an efficient fund-raising system the way Hanna did, and most of their presidential candidates had a tough time obtaining money. Although Grover Cleveland, someone not unfriendly to business, was adequately financed, his successors usually operated at a big disadvantage. Bryan in 1896 was said to have obtained no more than $300,000 to $675,000—one-fifth to one-tenth of the sum available to McKinley. He experienced the same problem in 1900, accumulating only $425,000 compared to the $3,000,000 collected by the other side. In 1904 the Republicans again outspent the Democrats, though it proved harder for Theodore Roosevelt to attract corporate money than for his predecessor, because many businessmen were appalled at TR's trust-busting activities. The president, however, did get support from a few wealthy friends, such as George Perkins and Republican National Committee treasurer Cornelius Bliss. The Democratic candidate, Alton B. Parker, untainted with free-silverism, reportedly received contributions totalling $700,000 from longtime Democratic "angels," August Belmont, Jr., and Thomas Fortune Ryan.[35]

By this time public opinion had become highly critical of campaign financing by big business, prompting government action. Investigators soon discovered many improprieties involving corporate donations to the Republican party over the previous decade. Such revelations eventually led Congress in 1907 to approve the Tillman Act, making it illegal for national banks and corporations to contribute to election funds. In 1910 the first candidate disclosure laws were passed, and in 1911 limits were placed on expenditures in congressional contests. Yet this legislation was not well enforced, and laws prohibiting direct contributions from corporations did not prevent officers and stockholders from making private contributions as individuals. Nevertheless, from then on, the national parties felt compelled to solicit funds from small contributors so as not to appear too heavily tied to the wealthy. In 1912 the Wilson campaign instituted "dollar drives" and took in almost a third of its income ($1.1 million) in sums under $100. The Republicans, beginning in 1916, made any donor of ten dollars a "contributing member" of the party and sent the person an engraved certificate to that effect. Although big donations still comprised the bulk of the money received, small contributions definitely were on the rise.

Of course, minor parties were completely dependent on small contributions. "Passing the hat" at meetings was the manner in which General James Weaver, the Populist nominee in 1892, financed his entire campaign. On one occasion in Denver after Weaver had finished his speech, a woman supporter suggested to the audience that anyone desiring to contribute might throw silver dollars directly at her. "Instantly there came a rain of dollars from every part of the hall in such number and force as to threaten injury to the occupants of the platform," it was reported.[36] Statewide Populist organizations sometimes tried to raise money by selling party literature, though this did not prove too lucrative. Selling literature was the chief method by which the later Socialist party acquired funds. In addition, the Socialists charged admission to their meetings and sold copies of Eugene Debs's autograph as well as little squares of red cloth that could be waved as flags.[37]

In state and local campaigns, a good deal of money continued to be raised through assessments on officeholders. While various statutes had made it illegal for party and government officials to assess workers, the civil service laws did not prevent "voluntary subscriptions" from taking place. Thus the subscriptions went on in many areas in defiance of the spirit if not the letter of the law. In Philadelphia, for example, it was common for the Republican machine to assess people on a graduated scale: those with salaries between $600 and $1,199 were assessed at three percent; between $1,200 and $1,999, four and one-half percent; between $2,000 and $2,999, six percent; between $3,000 and $5,999, nine percent; and above $6,000, twelve percent. It was said that 94 percent of all employees regularly paid these assessments and that those who failed to comply were faced with dismissal. A former director of public works testified in 1913 that in no single year of the last ten had the amount contributed to the Republican campaign been less than a quarter of a million dollars, and in 1910, "almost half a million was so collected."[38]

Besides assessments on those already in office, it became common in many areas for parties to call on the candidates for contributions to the campaign fund. Since the nominees benefited from the party connection, it seemed only natural that they should assist the party in its fund drive. The amounts varied—sometimes it was at the discretion of the individual, sometimes it was based on the anticipated salary of the particular post. In Ohio it generally was agreed that a person should be assessed at ten percent of the expected annual pay. In Florida the asked-for amount was just one percent—perhaps due to the limited level of vote-seeking in that state. In addition to officeholders and candidates, certain individuals or businesses who received favors from a city or state—construction contractors, gambling-house operators—might be assessed during political campaigns.[39] Overall, this era saw a wide variety of fund-raising methods introduced as the demand for funds increased.

THE PARTIES

At the beginning of the 1890s, each of the major parties more or less maintained their traditional appeals to the voters. Having their base of support in New England and the Midwest, the Republicans continued to present themselves as the party that preserved the Union, ended slavery, and brought about Reconstruction. They also claimed responsibility for the growth of industry and agriculture in the postwar period. As before, the Republicans emphasized the need for a strong and active government, declaring that the tariff and other probusiness measures would promote national prosperity. Not yet committed on the currency issue, the GOP eventually supported the gold standard and opposed the coinage of free silver. Toward the end of the century, the party would adopt an aggressive foreign policy, fight a war against Spain, and seek to acquire territorial possessions. Though perhaps to a smaller degree than before, the Republicans still showed concern for the moral welfare of Americans, and some in the party favored legislation prohibiting alcohol and restricting immigration as a way to retain old-time values.

The Democrats, on the other hand, continued to be the party of states' rights, decentralization, and limited government. They sought retrenchment in federal programs, reduction in expenditures, and noninterference in personal matters. This laissez-faire attitude found widespread backing in the South, which disliked any effort by the national administration to intervene in its affairs, particularly with regard to the Negro. It also remained popular in the North among those religious groups, like Roman Catholics and German Lutherans, who hated the idea of prohibition and other government controls. On foreign policy matters, the party would take an anti-imperialist stance and oppose adding new territories. The Democrats and their limited-government philosophy soon faced immense strains as the economic crisis of the mid–1890s caused many in the party to reconsider their position. A majority ultimately supported William Jennings Bryan and a reformist view, demanding that federal action be taken to expand the currency and regulate the trusts.[40]

Two new parties that caused a stir in this period were the People's, or Populist, party and the Socialist party, though because of the nation's winner-take-all political system neither one ultimately succeeded. Populism had its roots in the agrarian discontent that had been developing for two decades. Farmers joined the Populist party in hopes of achieving reform, especially the unlimited coinage of silver to solve the currency shortage. But internal and external difficulties, plus the return of prosperity in the late 1890s, prevented the Populists from attracting sufficient numbers.[41] After Populism failed, some who sought radical solutions to America's's long-term economic problems were drawn to the new Socialist party, formed in 1901. Although it favored public control of the means of production, it hoped to achieve its goal through evolutionary means. The party obtained a certain degree of support from immigrant workers in the eastern states who were familiar with socialism in Europe. However, socialism had its greatest attraction among western miners, lumberjacks, and other laborers who had joined the radical union known as the I.W.W. (the International Workers of the World), and among disgruntled farmers in places like Oklahoma. Nationally, the Socialists never received more than six percent of the total vote.[42]

It was during this period that organized labor first became a key factor in national elections. Of course, the major parties in earlier times had made appeals to workingmen and tried to show that their policies (the tariff, and so on) helped the wage earner. Yet it was only in the decades after 1900, when the urban population surpassed that in rural areas, that the labor vote came to be seen as critical. Each party sent speakers to union meetings and put prolabor symbols like the arm and hammer on its literature. While the parties sought out workers, workers' organizations sought out the parties. Groups such as the American Federation of Labor (AFL), now began to engage in political action beyond just lobbying. Initially, there was no commitment to a single party, but in 1908 the prolabor planks in the Democratic platform influenced the AFL leadership publicly to endorse Bryan's candidacy. Again in 1912 the union backed the Democratic ticket, now headed by Woodrow Wilson, rejecting the Progressives because of Theodore Roosevelt's ties to financier George Perkins. In 1916 labor groups were even stronger in their support of Wilson due to his advocacy of the Clayton Antitrust Act and other legislation to aid workers.[43]

Many workers who were newcomers to America also would be wooed as members of their ethnic group, for the parties made a great effort to capture the increasingly heavy immigrant vote. Foreign-language newspapers regularly were provided with material from party headquarters. McKinley's acceptance speech in 1900, for example, was printed in German, Norwegian, Swedish, Bohemian, Polish, Italian, and Dutch. The Republican National Committee that year employed over one hundred foreign-language speakers, including six Finns. Parties preparing for state and municipal elections had to exhibit great care in selecting an ethnically balanced slate of candidates and later in campaigning among all the various groups. For example, in Detroit in the 1890s, Irishmen, Germans, and Poles were placed on the ticket, and Mayor Hazen Pingree drank "red-eye" whiskey with the Irish voters, addressed several German societies, and made flattering statements about the Poles in order to maintain himself in office.[44]

Some urban bosses believed that the way to appeal to the immigrant voter was not by political means, but through a personal touch. George Washington Plunkitt, a second-generation Irish leader connected with Tammany Hall in New York City, was for many years a master of the game. "What tells in holdin' your grip on your district is to go right down among the poor families and help them in the different ways they need help," he said. "If there is a family in my district in want, I know it before the charitable societies do, and me and my men are the first on the ground. . . . The consequence is that the poor look up to George W. Plunkitt as a father, come to him in trouble—and don't forget him on election day. Another thing, I can always get a job for a deservin' man. I make it a point to keep on the track of jobs, and it seldom happens that I don't have a few up my sleeve ready for use." If a young man could sing, Plunkitt got him a spot in a glee club, and one who could play baseball was put on a local ball club. "That fixes him. You'll find him workin' for my ticket at the polls next election day," he added. "I don't trouble them with political arguments, I just study human nature and act accordin'."[45]

On a somewhat smaller scale than with the immigrants, certain candidates, primarily Republicans, sought to appeal to black voters in the northern states. (Because of disfranchisement there were almost no black voters left in the southern states.) Claiming to represent the "party of Lincoln," Republicans said they were the only party to have done something for blacks—appointing them to federal jobs.[46] In the South, blacks may have played a negligible role as participants, but the Negro, as an issue, would come to dominate many campaigns. Beginning in the 1890s white fears of the black alliance with the Populists led some politicians to seize on the anti-Negro question. Speeches stressing the dangers of Negro influence became commonplace. It was soon apparent that the easiest way to build voter support was to "out-Negro" one's opponent. Demagogues such as Tom Watson of Georgia, Jeff Davis of Arkansas, and James Vardaman in Mississippi sometimes carried this to extremes, referring to blacks as "coons" and calling for a "lily-white" South. Running for governor in 1903, Vardaman traveled in a whitewashed wagon drawn by white oxen and wore a white linen suit to symbolize his goal of white supremacy. The impact of these efforts could be seen in the harsher treatment of southern blacks and the passage of Jim Crow legislation.[47]

ELECTION OF 1892

The new era began with the two major parties still dominant but now facing formidable outside challenges. Although not as popular as he had been with either the public or the party bosses, Benjamin Harrison was renominated by the Republicans in 1892. The Democrats turned to former president Grover Cleveland, who still was thought of as a man of integrity and was pleasing to the conservatives who controlled the party. The platforms of both sides looked fairly similar; neither took a strong stand on the silver question, a matter that was becoming increasingly controversial. The only issue on which a serious difference existed was the tariff: the Republicans championed protectionism, and the Democrats called for big reductions in tariff rates. Taking a stronger reformist stance than the main political organizations, the new Populist party and its standard-bearer General James Weaver advocated many programs of government ownership and regulation.[48]

The Populists, though lacking money and organization, conducted an energetic campaign. Making the most of their limited resources, they concentrated on trying to win over the common people of the South and West through attacks on big business and demands for reform. General Weaver and other leaders, such as Ignatius Donnelly and Mary Lease, told farmers to "raise less corn and more hell" and delivered hundreds of speeches on the evils of the existing system. Their words found many sympathetic ears in places like Kansas and Colorado. But in the South, long-held sectional attitudes caused problems. Weaver, a former Union officer, sometimes had trouble even getting a hearing. On one occasion in Georgia, abuse became so heavy that he was made a "regular walking omelet." Also, numerous poor whites, while favoring Populist ideas, succumbed to racist propaganda and kept their old party ties.[49] Compared to the Populists' campaign, those carried on by the two major parties were rather restrained. Neither presidential candidate made many public appearances nor delivered inflammatory remarks. The few public statements issued by each man emphasized past party doctrine and did not include any personal attacks.[50]

While they might have been more high-minded than usual, the Republicans did not display the kind of enthusiasm they had in previous campaigns. Organization and fund-raising were not up to par. Moreover, the party had trouble finding any attention-getting issue. They ultimately fell back on the tariff, but had difficulty explaining why retail prices had risen in the past two years. The Democrats insisted that the tariff did not protect the worker; in reality, they said, it held him down. A series of strikes, particularly one by steelworkers at Homestead, Pennsylvania, lent credence to their argument. The Republicans also had a hard time defending the Sherman Silver Purchase Act and the Force Bill, two measures that had harmed them in the 1890 congressional campaign. The GOP also lost votes in the Midwest among certain ethnic groups as it veered toward a prohibitionist stance.

It was not simply their own weaknesses that caused the Republicans' eventual defeat, but Democratic strengths as well. The latter side displayed greater harmony than four years earlier, thanks in large part to the work of National Committee Chairman William Whitney, who managed to get Grover Cleveland and the Tammany Hall bosses to reconcile long-standing differences. Furthermore, the Democrats, due to Cleveland's increasing conservatism and friendliness toward business leaders, succeeded in raising more money than the Republicans—one of the few instances when this has occurred. This allowed them to conduct more of an educational campaign and distribute heavy amounts of literature. They also undertook a broader canvass than normal, enabling them to reach across party lines. By election day everything seemed to fall into place for Cleveland, assuring him of a big victory.

Cleveland did better than in his two previous attempts, polling 5.5 million popular votes to Harrison's 5.18 million, and 277 electoral votes to 145 for his opponent. (The Populists acquired about a million popular votes, taking four western states and a total of twenty-two electoral votes.) In winning, the Democrats carried not just the doubtful states, but many normally Republican strongholds as well. It was the most decisive victory for either party in twenty years. The Democrats now controlled the White House and both branches of Congress. Yet the shift in support proved to be temporary when economic conditions began to deteriorate soon after Cleveland took office. The Republicans and Populists both would pick up strength in the midterm elections of 1894, as the Democrats showed themselves unable to cope with the unemployment, labor strife, and farmer discontent brought on by the so-called Panic of 1893. By the time of the next national election, the entire Democratic organization would split apart.[51]

ELECTION OF 1896

The presidential contest of 1896 would be one of the most intensely fought in American history. It would also lead to significant political realignments and have a profound effect on campaigning practices for the future. The Republicans, hoping to capitalize on the failures of the Cleveland administration, chose William McKinley, longtime congressman and former governor of Ohio, as their candidate. McKinley's nomination was secured largely through the efforts of his friend and manager, Mark Hanna, who had skillfully rounded up the necessary delegates before the convention. On the big issue of the day, the Republican platform rejected bimetallism and came out squarely for the gold standard. "We are unalterably opposed to every measure calculated to debase our country," and "are therefore opposed to the free coinage of silver," it stated.

The Democrats at their convention found themselves sharply divided on the money question. Many easterners and former Cleveland supporters pleaded to retain the gold standard, but the prosilver forces from the South and the West were in the ascendancy. The greatest spokesman for the silver cause turned out to be a thirty-six-year-old Nebraska congressman named William Jennings Bryan. Bryan, known as the "boy orator of the Platte," had been pressing the silver issue for several years. In what would become the most notable convention speech ever, Bryan proclaimed that if the business class insisted on a gold standard, the silverites, backed by the "producing masses" and the "toilers everywhere," would "fight them to the end." He finished with the powerful peroration: "You shall not press down upon the brow of labor this crown of thorns, you shall not crucify mankind upon a cross of gold." Immediately thereafter the majority of delegates rose to their feet and adopted a platform calling for "the free and unlimited coinage of both silver and gold at the present ratio of sixteen to one." The next day Bryan was enthusiastically nominated as the Democratic standard-bearer.[52]

Bryan's nomination, however, caused problems for hard-money Democrats and also for the Populists. The so-called Gold Democrats refused to accept Bryan, declaring that they would take no part in the campaign. Typical was Governor David B. Hill of New York, who stated: "I am a Democrat still—very still." Some extreme "goldbugs" later organized a splinter group—known as the National Democrats—and nominated their own candidate, Senator John M. Palmer of Illinois. But Palmer did not become a serious alternative, offering only token opposition in most states. For the Populists the question was whether to support Bryan and possibly lose their separate identity or to select their own nominee and probably assure McKinley's success. While certain leaders opposed fusion, the majority felt that with Bryan they had their greatest chance of achieving their goals and that he, after all, had ardently championed free silver. The Populist party did, nevertheless, endorse their own vice presidential candidate and never became fully integrated in the Bryan-Democratic camp.

The lack of unity was compounded by the lack of organizational backing. Those around Bryan had little experience in running a large campaign. The Democratic National Committee, under the leadership of Senator James K. Jones of Arkansas, was weakly staffed and inadequately financed. The committee did send out some literature on the silver question and set up a speakers' bureau, but its efforts were hampered by a paucity of funds. Pleas for contributions among the "plain people" brought but a limited response, and only a few wealthy men like William Randolph Hearst donated any considerable sums. Another handicap was meager press support. In New York City only one major newspaper, Hearst's *Journal*, backed Bryan. Throughout the East and Midwest, most of the important dailies opposed him. One Philadelphia paper stated that with Bryan and his allies, "the Jacobins are in full control."[53] Over the course of the campaign, Bryan constantly would be vilified as a dangerous radical—a socialist, an anarchist, a revolutionist, a "Popocrat."

Having little money or newspaper backing, Bryan soon realized that his only chance lay in bringing his message directly to the people. Going far beyond any previous presidential candidate, even Douglas in 1860, Bryan took to the stump and virtually remained there until election day. In all, he traveled through twenty-seven states, speaking before an estimated five million people. Everywhere he went huge crowds gathered to see and hear him. Even in small towns hundreds of persons came from miles away and lined the railroad tracks to catch a glimpse of the man. Wherever he spoke Bryan mentioned a broad range of issues, although he mainly concentrated on the money question, stating that this held the key to the future. Free silver, he said, would restore prosperity and stimulate the creation of jobs. Bryan's campaign went beyond the usual political quest—it became a moral crusade. Many of his rallies sounded like religious revival meetings and included the singing of hymns. To Bryan, free silver embodied not merely an economic position: it also implied virtue and justice. At the same time gold represented not simply the metal of the creditor class: it stood as the cause of evil and injustice.[54]

Bryan's powerful one-man effort created much uncertainty for the Republicans. By distancing himself from the Cleveland administration and making emotional, class-based appeals, Bryan was turning what should have been an easy Republican victory into a difficult struggle. In order to dispel the doubt, GOP chairman Mark Hanna put together the most elaborate election-year organization formed up to that time. Special new bureaus with large staffs were set up to handle each phase of the campaign. Huge sums of money were raised to help finance over 1,400 speakers plus an unheard-of amount of campaign literature—approximately 250 million pieces. Hanna believed that a thorough "campaign of education" was necessary to counteract the free-silver crusade. The majority of printed items dealt with the currency issue, and many were published in foreign languages. Moreover, a number of striking posters of McKinley were produced, the most popular one bearing the inscription "The Advance Agent of Prosperity." According to Theodore Roosevelt, Hanna seemed to be advertising McKinley "as if he were a patent medicine."

In addition to Hanna's efforts, McKinley played his own part in combating Bryan. Unwilling to compete with the "boy orator" on the stump, the GOP nominee undertook a carefully orchestrated front-porch campaign. Over the summer and fall, numerous delegations of loyal Republicans—sometimes containing over a thousand people—were invited to McKinley's home in Canton, Ohio, to pay their respects. Brass bands escorted each one from the railroad station right up to the doorstep. The head of each group then delivered a short speech, and the candidate would answer in an appropriate manner. Every aspect of these occasions was planned in advance to limit the possibility of a damaging remark. "The general procedure," according to Hanna's biographer Herbert Croly, was as follows:

A letter would be sent to the National Committee or to Canton, stating that a delegation of farmers, railroad employees, cigar-makers, wholesale merchants, Presbyterians or what not would, if convenient, call on Mr. McKinley on such a day. An answer would immediately be returned expressing pleasure at the idea, but requesting that the head of the delegation make a preliminary visit to the candidate. When he appeared, Mr. McKinley would greet him warmly and ask: 'You are going to present the delegation and make some remarks. What are you going to say?' The reply would usually be: 'Oh! I don't know. Anything that occurs to me.' Then Mr. McKinley would point out the inconveniences of such a course and request that a copy of the address be sent to him in advance, and he usually warned his interlocutor that he might make certain suggestions looking towards the revision of the speech.[55]

In his few formal addresses McKinley emphasized both the silver menace and the importance of a protective tariff. The Ohioan tried to point out that free silver would hurt, not help, farmers and laborers. Debasing the currency would cause inflation, and this would increase food costs. Workers needed jobs, he said, and this would come with the restoration of the protective tariff. Contrary to Bryan, who argued that industrial prosperity depended on agrarian prosperity, McKinley claimed that good times in the farm belt would result from expanding industry, and this would occur only through protectionism. Along with these themes McKinley sought to convey a strong spirit of nationalism. He denounced Bryan's sectional appeals and his talk of class conflict—labor against capital, farmers against bankers. The idea of class distinctions, he insisted, was "repugnant to our form of government." Also, he refrained from the usual Republican rhetoric on cultural issues, thereby putting himself in a stronger position among ethnic groups.

On election day a greater number of Americans went to the polls than in any previous presidential contest. Almost fourteen million votes were cast, with McKinley capturing 51 percent to Bryan's 46 percent. (Three percent went to minor candidates.) More successful than any of his immediate predecessors, McKinley swept the entire East and the Midwest, running up a ninety-five vote victory (271 to 176) in the electoral college. Bryan's support was limited to the South, the Plains states, and the Rocky Mountain area. In analyzing the returns it is clear that the silver crusade failed to have much impact on the farm and labor vote beyond those sections. The Republicans managed to convince a majority that their program better served the needs of the rapidly industrializing society. It has sometimes been claimed that the McKinley victory resulted from the intimidation of voters, for example, businessmen threatening to cancel contracts or telling employees not to report to work if Bryan won. While incidents of this type did occur, their number probably was not very large, surely not large enough to have affected the outcome.

ELECTION OF 1900

Once in the White House William McKinley enjoyed a successful four-year term. Indeed, the return of economic prosperity coupled with military victory in the Spanish-American War (1898) placed him and his party in a favorable position to be reelected in 1900. At the convention that year McKinley easily won renomination as the Republican standard-bearer. His running mate was Theodore Roosevelt, the popular and unpredictable war hero then serving as governor of New York. McKinley did not particularly want Roosevelt, but succumbed to the pleas of eastern "bosses" Thomas Platt of New York and Matthew Quay of Pennsylvania, who wished to have the "Rough Rider" politically "out of the way." The Republican platform emphasized traditional themes like the gold standard and the tariff, though it did make slight gestures toward reform. The Democrats designated Bryan for the second time and created an unabashedly reformist platform in both foreign and domestic affairs. Denouncing the postwar acquisition of the Philippines, they declared that imperialism was the "paramount" issue, stating that no nation can endure "half-republic and half-empire." The party also condemned monopoly as "intolerable," and, at Bryan's insistence, touted free silver.[56]

Without heavy funding or organizational strength, Bryan again was the underdog. Although he planned not to conduct the same kind of whirlwind campaign he had undertaken in 1896, circumstances forced him to go back on the stump. His early speeches contained a great deal of anti-imperialist rhetoric, but as this did not catch on well, he increasingly focused on the antitrust issue and on "special privilege." A common Bryan slogan became "Equal Rights to All—Special Privilege to None." The candidate also talked about government ineptitude during the Spanish-American War and, in an appeal for German and Irish votes, criticized the British for their involvement in the Boer War. Toward the end he propounded the idea of free silver once more. But no matter which issue was stressed, Bryan found it difficult to make much headway, especially in the enemy strongholds of the East and the Midwest.

The Republican effort in 1900 was not as fervent as in 1896, though it really did not have to be. Displaying the same kind of efficiency as four years earlier, Mark Hanna took charge of McKinley's second campaign. He again raised large amounts of money in the business community—not as much as in the previous race, but, at two-and-one-half million dollars, five times the Democrats' total. There was less campaign literature, both in variety and number, but again far more than the opposition produced. As President, McKinley did not engage in much campaigning; he did, however, issue a few policy statements defending his record. To counter Bryan the Republicans sent Theodore Roosevelt on a long speaking tour, particularly through the West, where his "Rough Rider" image attracted enthusiastic crowds. Roosevelt ably recounted his party's accomplishments over the years and asserted that Bryan, if elected, would destroy the existing prosperity.

When the final tabulation was made, McKinley had defeated Bryan by a bigger amount than in 1896, acquiring twenty-one additional electoral votes for an overall total of 292 to his opponent's 155. Bryan again lost the entire East and Midwest; he even lost his home state of Nebraska and several states in the Rocky Mountain region. Anti-imperialism and the other issues raised by Bryan obviously had fallen on deaf ears, though to turn things around, it is difficult to argue that in voting for McKinley, the majority of Americans had taken a pro-imperialist stance. Prosperity was the key factor for most voters—they wanted "Four Years More of the Full Dinner Pail." McKinley began his second term with a greater mandate than before. However, a few months into the new administration, the president was killed by a deranged man, who was perhaps an anarchist. As a consequence, Theodore Roosevelt, whom the bosses had tried to eliminate politically by pushing him into the vice presidency, became top man in the White House.

The emergence of Theodore Roosevelt as president coincided with the rise of the Progressive movement in American politics. Progressives were reformers who felt that the industrial growth of the country had been achieved at a terrrible cost in human values. They believed that big business had stifled economic competition and gained excessive political power. Influenced to some degree by the Populists, but more urban in orientation, the Progressives sought a variety of reforms—regulation of trusts, tariff revision, the graduated income tax, improvement of labor conditions, an end to municipal corruption, and more popular control of politics (including direct election of senators, woman suffrage, initiative, referendum, and recall). Soon quite a few members of both parties began campaigning on the basis of the progressive agenda as the movement spread from the cities to the states, especially in the West. The new spirit also influenced President Roosevelt who, though somewhat conservative, gradually supported this program of change.[57]

ELECTION OF 1904

In mid–1904, looking at his first three years in office, "Teddy" Roosevelt could point to a solid record of accomplishment. His antitrust activity, his conservation program, his labor policy, and his acquisition of the Canal Zone, all received high marks. Moreover, Roosevelt's colorful manner made him a very popular national figure and assured his renomination by the Republicans. The platform was fairly conventional so as not to offend the "Old Guard," though TR, as he sometimes was called, promised a "square deal" for all Americans. The Democrats, still heavily divided, this time rejected Bryan as their candidate. Sensing the problem it would be to attract the liberal voter, they instead chose an eastern conservative, Judge Alton B. Parker of New York, in hopes of winning support in the business community and among traditional-minded Americans. The Democratic platform generally avoided controversial issues, even though Parker in his acceptance speech criticized the administration's antitrust policy and also its actions in the Philippines.[58]

The campaign began as the most lackluster in memory—the most apathetic since James Monroe's second election, someone said. Roosevelt, acting presidential, did not speak out much. When he did, he usually assumed a safe position, not wishing to stir up dissension within his own ranks. The GOP raised only two-thirds the amount of money that it did in 1900 and produced fewer pieces of literature. However, under the leadership of national chairman George Cortelyou, a major effort was undertaken through the press. Articles sent to thousands of newspapers emphasized the increased prosperity and strengthened national position that the McKinley and Roosevelt administrations had brought about. The Republicans also expanded their appeal to ethnic groups, publicizing Roosevelt's appointment of individuals of many nationalities to high-level posts.

While better financed than with Bryan and able to produce more literature, the Democrats, were not well organized or very active. Parker himself remained on his farm except for a brief speaking tour in October. Of course, regardless of what Parker and the Democrats had done, it would have been difficult to make any dent in the popularity of the president. The race heated up somewhat toward the end when Parker desperately sought to make an issue of corruption involving Republican campaign funds. He charged that Cortelyou, former secretary of commerce, had virtually blackmailed corporations into donating large sums for Roosevelt's election bid. As the attacks continued, TR came out and denied the accusation as "unqualifiedly and atrociously false." He demanded that Parker supply proof of his charges, and because the Democrats had no access to any financial records, the matter died—and with it Parker's hopes for any success.

Whether it was due to his personality, his policies, his opponent's shortcomings, or a combination of the three, TR won the election in the biggest landslide since Grant's defeat of Greeley in 1872. He received 57.4 percent of the popular vote to Parker's 37.6 percent, and 336 electoral votes to his opponent's 140. Roosevelt even carried several border states, as Parker took only the Solid South. Many Bryan Democrats obviously stayed away from the polls, as Parker's overall total was one million behind Bryan's figure. Republican strength in Congress was greater than at any time since the Civil War. About the sole positive sign for the opposition was the choice of a few progressive Democrats for governorships in northern states.

ELECTION OF 1908

Even though he had a fairly successful second term and could have probably been reelected, Roosevelt decided not to run again. He did, however, wish to have a close disciple follow him into the White House. His choice was William Howard Taft of Ohio, the secretary of war and former governor general of the Philippines. Roosevelt believed that Taft would continue his policies and, thanks to the president's support, Taft easily achieved the Republican nomination. The platform probably echoed the status-quo more than either man wished, yet it did endorse a few reforms. The Democrats, having been overwhelmed with the conservative Parker in 1904, once again turned to Bryan, who claimed he was the true heir to Roosevelt's progressivism. The Democratic platform, influenced by the Bryanites, was more progressive than its Republican counterpart, insisting on greater corporate regulations; but other proposals were not as far-reaching as those of 1896 and 1900.[59]

Bryan at first operated cautiously, hoping that greater party unity and fewer intemperate remarks might get him elected this time. But he eventually went out on the stump and began a vigorous attack on the trusts as well as urging federal ownership of large interstate railroads. His antibusiness, prolabor stance helped bring him some union backing, but it is not clear how much of an impact this made. No longer a novelty, Bryan generally failed to excite crowds to the extent he had on former occasions. Despite the usual shortage of funds, the national organization did try to step up their news distribution effort, establishing a press committee of leading Democratic newspapermen. However, the group was not overly successful in getting its message out to the public, leaving most of the burden to Bryan.

The Taft-Republican effort started slowly, but then began to gather steam. The national organization under chairman Frank Hitchcock, while operating with less money than in the three previous races, still ran a fairly efficient, business-like campaign. The candidate said little at the outset, but later went on a long speaking tour. If he did not mesmerize his audiences, Taft did give a good account of himself, promising when elected to carry out certain reforms. He was aided by President Roosevelt, who issued statements claiming Taft had "wisdom and moral courage, and embodied what is best and highest in our American citizenship." The combination of the Republican organization, Taft's participation, and TR's endorsement helped turn what might have been a close race into a rout. While the size of his victory was smaller than Roosevelt's in 1904, Taft won election in 1908 by a considerable margin. He received 7.6 million popular votes to Bryan's 6.4 million and almost doubled Bryan's electoral count, 321 to 162. Bryan did better than Parker had done, carrying sixteen states; but he was still able to win only in the South and in parts of the West. Voters may have been more anti-Bryan than pro-Taft, but Taft was headed for the White House.

ELECTION OF 1912

Although Roosevelt supported Taft at the beginning of his presidency, he gradually grew unhappy with his successor, whose policies seemed to veer toward those of the "Old Guard." At the same time progressives in the Republican party, under the leadership of Senator Robert La Follette of Wisconsin, had begun to revolt. La Follette, in fact, appeared ready to compete against Taft for the next presidential nomination. As anti-Taft sentiment mounted, Roosevelt, who previously had stated his opposition to a third term, now felt a strong urge to break with tradition and cast his hat into the ring. In early 1912 he wrote to several governors, announcing his intention to run. Pushing La Follette aside, Roosevelt seized the progressive standard and entered several primaries, winning a considerable bloc of delegates. But at the Republican convention, the Old Guard, disliking the Rough Rider's tactics and his increasingly radical pronouncements, blocked his efforts to dislodge the president. They made Taft the nominee once more, and forced him to run on a conservative platform.[60]

Even before Taft became the official GOP designee, many progressives had walked out of the proceedings and, along with Roosevelt, formed the new Progressive, or Bull Moose, party. Over 2,000 delegates, including numerous women, met at the quickly arranged Progressive convention and nominated TR as the standard-bearer. The Progressive platform constituted a massive program of reform. Beyond a desire for democratic political changes—direct election of senators, woman suffrage, and even recall of state judicial decisions—there was a whole list of social-welfare goals—restriction of child labor, minimum wages for women workers, workmen's compensation, and old-age insurance. The Progressive convention had the atmosphere of a revival meeting, as delegates sang "Onward Christian Soldiers" and "The Battle Hymn of the Republic." In a rousing address known as the "Confession of Faith," Roosevelt told his eager followers: "We stand at Armageddon, and we battle for the Lord!"

The Democrats, meanwhile, had selected New Jersey governor Woodrow Wilson, a one-time conservative but now a moderate progressive, as their nominee. A decade earlier the austere Wilson would have seemed a rather unlikely figure in national politics. A respected author and academician, he had served as head of Princeton University without showing any inclination to run for high political office. Thrust into the governorship of New Jersey in 1910 by the state Democratic party's need for a respectable leader, Wilson surprised everyone by acting in a strong fashion. Breaking with the party bosses who helped elect him and also with some of his conservative views, he introduced several reform measures. So successful was his administration that he soon was being touted as a candidate for president. After forty-six ballots at the national convention, Wilson finally was chosen. Even though he previously had been at odds with Bryan and his ideas, it was Bryan who ultimately helped Wilson win enough delegates to clinch the nomination.[61]

Starting out as a three-way contest, it soon became clear that the real race was between Wilson and Roosevelt. Taft fell far behind and did little to try to overcome his disadvantage. Unwilling to break with tradition, the president did no more than give his acceptance speech, leaving the rest of the electioneering duties to other party officials. "I have been told that I ought to do this, ought to do that . . . that I do not keep myself in the headlines. I know it, but I can't do it," he admitted to a newspaperman.[62] Besides the president's inactivity, the Republican National Committee under Charles D. Hilles had trouble forging a large-scale effort due to the Progressive defections and a lack of money. Hilles tried to make the most of his scarce resources by heavily advertising in newspapers, magazines, and on billboards. He also had movies of Taft shown in 1,200 theaters. But all the advertising in the world could not have saved Taft, given the unremediable split in Republican ranks.

In contrast, the Wilson campaign was well organized and, except for a couple of minor incidents, not plagued by factional division. Both progressive and other Democrats eagerly supported the candidate, and Wilson took special care to please all segments of the party. (Perhaps being out of office for a long period and now sensing victory encouraged this unity.) Strong appeals were made to immigrant and labor groups in the East as well as to farmers in the South and West. Bryan proved extremely helpful in the western states, campaigning vigorously there for Wilson. Unlike past Democratic election struggles, where money stood in short supply, this time enough existed to provide for numerous speakers and plenty of literature. Lawyer William G. McAdoo, who had become a close associate of Wilson, ran the whole operation with energy and effectiveness on taking over from the ailing William L. McCombs.

Wilson, to be sure, played an important part in his own campaign. Although at first reluctant to go on tour, the candidate eventually spent a number of weeks out on the hustings. In his speeches he tried to emphasize the differences between his "New Freedom" and Roosevelt's "New Nationalism." Most critically, he advocated elimination of large corporate trusts rather than government regulation of them, which Roosevelt wanted. Roosevelt's system, he said, would destroy individual freedom and ultimately subordinate the people to many government controls.[63] Roosevelt, in response, dismissed Wilson's ideas as "rural toryism," a policy that might have worked fifty years earlier, but could never succeed in the increasingly industrialized twentieth century. He declared it unrealistic to think of breaking up modern corporations; they were inevitable. Instead of limiting government it was necessary to strengthen government to promote the welfare of the individual. Not only did the Bull Moose criticize Wilson and the Democrats, but he also took swipes at Taft and the "corrupt" Republicans, who had denied him the regular party nomination.[64]

To spread his message Roosevelt stayed out on the campaign trail far longer than Wilson, traveling thousands of miles from coast to coast, and even going into the South. Tremendous crowds came to see him wherever he appeared. Like Bryan's campaign in 1896, TR's foray resembled a crusade, as his appeals were made to the voters in strident, emotional terms. Even when his throat bothered him and he felt weary, he pushed on. Perhaps the dramatic highlight of his journey happened in mid-October when before a speaking engagement in Milwaukee, TR received a gunshot wound from a crazed assassin. Refusing immediate medical attention, Roosevelt went to the auditorium and delivered his speech while the crowd gasped at his blood-stained apparel. "I have just been shot," he said, "but it takes more than that to kill a Bull Moose." Then, after a brief stay in the hospital and a couple of weeks' rest, he went back to seeking votes.[65] However, Roosevelt lacked a solid supporting cast; the hastily put together Progressive party had little in the way of organization. In many states the Progressives were not even able to arrange a full slate of candidates. Then, too, many regular Republicans who privately favored Roosevelt refused to jump to the Progressive ticket, fearing probable defeat.

The split in the Republican party coupled with Wilson's moderate progressivism and reassuring tone made Roosevelt's quest impossible. As election day appeared, Wilson was the obvious winner. He received only a plurality of the popular vote (41 percent), obtaining 6.29 million to Roosevelt's 4.22 million (27 percent) and Taft's 3.48 million (23 percent). But in the electoral college he gained an overwhelming majority with 435 to Roosevelt's 88 and Taft's 8, the latter being the worst showing by a major party candidate up to that time. Most voters obviously were unhappy with stand-pat Republicanism and in favor of some form of change. Besides the ten-and-one-half million votes for Wilson and Roosevelt, roughly 900,000 ballots were cast for Socialist Eugene V. Debs. Afterward, the Progressive party would begin to disintegrate, not having any offices to provide their followers; but the movement would continue to be felt in the Wilson administration and at the next election.

ELECTION OF 1916

Woodrow Wilson's general popularity during his first term created problems for the Republicans as they approached the election of 1916. What they needed was a candidate who was liberal enough to bring the Progressives back into the party and yet conservative enough to satisfy the Old Guard. They thought they found the right man in Charles Evans Hughes, a Supreme Court justice and one-time reform governor of New York. Although he favored some progressive political measures, his more traditional views on economic questions made him acceptable to most party leaders. The Republican platform, showing little interest in reform, attacked the Democrats' ultraprogressive (antibusiness) domestic record and also what they claimed was Wilson's weak foreign policy toward Germany and the continuing European war. Wilson naturally was renominated at the Democratic convention. The platform emphasized a continuance of progressive measures. While Wilson hoped to run on the themes of progressivism and prosperity, the peace issue increasingly occupied center stage. This could be seen as early as the party convention itself when the keynote speaker mentioned several foreign crises and noted that in each case, thanks to Wilson, the country did not go to war. Soon, "He Kept Us Out Of War" became the Democrats' most effective slogan.[66]

The Democratic campaign was very well managed. Under the leadership of national chairman Vance McCormick of Pennsylvania, the various elements of the Democratic party worked smoothly together. Associations were formed to attract Progressives and independents. The party developed an effective strategy, writing off the Northeast and concentrating on the Midwest and the Far West, where strong progressive sentiment existed. The Democrats also made good use of available money, with publicity director Robert Woolley substituting short brochures for lengthy pamphlets and sending quality plate matter to many newspapers. Perhaps more than in previous Democratic canvasses, the party targeted specific interest groups—farmers, businessmen, labor, and women. In addition, Democratic editorialists around the country repeatedly challenged Hughes on the issues, referring to him as "Charles E-vasive Hughes."

The Republican campaign organization, in contrast, proved less effective. The National Committee did not provide adequate direction. The ample funds raised were not efficiently used. The advertising ventures and material for newspapers did not measure up to the quality of their opponents'. To be sure, those in charge had a difficult time finding the proper grounds on which to attack Wilson. Moreover, the party remained heavily split, and the factional divisions in certain states would prove very costly to Hughes. Nowhere was this more true than in California when the candidate, in the company of party regulars, wound up snubbing progressive governor Hiram Johnson and went on to lose the state by a small margin. (This incident long would be remembered as the "forgotten handshake.")

Hughes, although an attractive and dignified figure, was not a crowd-pleaser on the stump. He clearly lacked the common touch. Besides this liability, Hughes had trouble responding to Wilson's progressive achievements and explaining alternative policies that he would pursue. He also stumbled badly on the major issue of war and peace. At first he displayed a cautious attitude, not much different from that of Wilson. Then, influenced by Theodore Roosevelt's harsh criticism of the president and his call for a tougher stand against Germany, Hughes's statements grew increasingly bellicose, leading people to believe that if he were elected, he would lead the country into war. Indeed, one of the most effective pieces of propaganda against Hughes was a large newspaper ad toward the end of the campaign that read, "Wilson and Peace with Honor? or Hughes with Roosevelt and War?"[67]

Wilson did not campaign as much as Hughes; however, he did deliver a number of front-porch addresses from his summer home in New Jersey. Later in the fall he went on a few campaign swings, traveling as far west as Denver on one occasion. In his acceptance speech and other appearances, Wilson stressed the achievements of his first term and claimed that all Americans had benefited from his Democratic administration. Painting the Republicans as conservatives, he asserted that the GOP could not meet the new conditions of the new age. Although he made no specific promises regarding involvement in the European conflict, he tried to show that some Republican leaders wanted war, whereas he did not.

Even though Wilson campaigned more effectively than Hughes, the race remained in doubt right up to the end. With no Progressive party to siphon off votes, Republicans stood in a better position than in 1912, and Hughes seemed certain of victory in most of the East and Midwest. As the figures began coming in on election night, it looked as if he would go to the White House. But then late returns from the West gave Wilson a narrow victory in California, and with it, reelection to a second term—the first Democrat to accomplish that goal since Andrew Jackson. The final tally showed Wilson with 49.4 percent of the popular vote to Hughes's 46.2 percent and 277 electoral votes to his opponent's 254. Wilson's popularity in rural America enabled him to hold the South and nearly the entire West. Overall, his reform program and his image as the peace candidate kept many progressives from returning to the Republican party.

Wilson was inaugurated for his second term in March 1917. A month later, the United States, faced with unlimited submarine attacks by Germany, entered the European war. Although most Americans supported the government's decision, isolationists, plus those unhappy about wartime restrictions and Wilsonian financial policies, helped cause the Democrats to lose control of both houses of Congress in 1918. This loss, shortly before the fighting ended, would hamper Wilson's efforts at negotiating an effective peace in Versailles and at gaining Senate approval of the proposed League of Nations. Hoping to swing public opinion in favor of the League, Wilson undertook an extended speaking tour, but he soon suffered a physical breakdown. Thus his cause and his party were left leaderless. The Democrats also had to contend with a major postwar economic downturn. At the same time incidents of radical agitation occurred, which then were suppressed heavy-handedly by Wilson's attorney general, A. Mitchell Palmer. All in all, the Democratic outlook for the next presidential election was not very bright.[68]

ELECTION OF 1920

The Republicans, confident of victory in 1920, met in Chicago for their convention. Former general Leonard Wood, Senator Hiram Johnson of California, and Governor Frank Lowden of Illinois were the top contenders for the nomination. Yet as each of these men bumped off one another, party professionals (supposedly sitting in a smoke-filled hotel room) decided on a less-qualified but more congenial figure, freshman senator Warren G. Harding of Ohio. Harding, while a man of few accomplishments, was someone who could be counted on as a party loyalist. A handsome, pleasant, easygoing individual, he seemed like a person with whom the average American clearly could identify. Governor Calvin Coolidge of Massachusetts, who projected similar qualities, was nominated for the vice presidential spot. The Republican platform condemned the Democrats' economic policies and especially their efforts at conducting the war and negotiating the peace. It also supported the Prohibition amendment.[69]

The Democrats had trouble finding a successor to Woodrow Wilson. William G. McAdoo, the secretary of the treasury, was perhaps the most qualified candidate, but as Wilson's son-in-law, he was too closely identified with the now unpopular and ailing president. The party eventually chose Governor James M. Cox of Ohio, a known vote-getter and a man of some ability, though hardly in the class of the incumbent. A thirty-eight-year-old New Yorker, Franklin D. Roosevelt, former Assistant Secretary of the navy and a cousin of the late Rough Rider, was designated as the vice presidential nominee. The Democratic platform naturally favored entry into the League of Nations but was silent on the matter of Prohibition.

The Republican campaign was better organized and better financed than the Democrats', having three to four times as much money to spend. The National Committee, under the energetic Will Hays of Indiana, put out huge numbers of posters and brochures. The party also hired advertiser Albert Lasker, who had sold Wrigley's gum and Lucky Strike cigarettes, to help sell Harding. A strong effort was made to create a folksy, home-loving image similar to that of the late President McKinley. Many stories and pictures of Harding and his family were circulated to the press. Like McKinley, Harding conducted a closely controlled front-porch campaign from his home in Marion, Ohio. Delegations from all over the country came to visit. There were special days planned for similar kinds of groups: a women's day, a foreign voters' day, a colored people's day, a traveling salesmen's day. Harding, at the advice of his managers, said little of substance in his remarks. Regarding the most controversial issue, the League of Nations, Harding stated that he did not want the League as currently proposed, but hinted that he might accept some other international association in the future. This vagueness helped him gain support from pro-League Republicans as well as from isolationists.[70]

With the odds strongly favoring the Republicans, the Democrats had their work cut out for them. Despite the existence of an incumbent administration, their party organization was weak. Many Democrats, unhappy with Wilson, had little enthusiasm to work for his potential successor. The lack of money was another problem. As in the case of Bryan years earlier, Cox sought to overcome the situation by spending a lot of time out on the stump. (His running mate, Roosevelt, also went on an extended speaking tour; the pair logged more miles—about 40,000—and gave more speeches than any twosome up to that time.) Unlike Harding who tried to duck anything controversial, Cox deliberately spoke out on the issues, particularly the League. He criticized Harding's vague, negative position, hoping to force him clearly to commit himself and perhaps make a fatal blunder. However, it was Cox himself who wound up making several inconsistent and intemperate statements that probably lost him votes. Besides the League, he had trouble defending Wilson's other policies and dealing with the Prohibition question. Even had he said all the correct things, it is doubtful whether he had much of a chance. By election day the odds were ten to one against him.

In the balloting, now substantially augmented by the women's vote, Harding received 61 percent of the overall tally, carrying every state outside the South and even one inside—Tennessee. The electoral college totals were 404 to 127. Republicans also rolled up large majorities in both houses of Congress. It was more than a landslide; it was an "earthquake," as one Democrat exclaimed. In general, the vote was a rejection of Wilson and many of the policies he stood for, especially progressivism and internationalism. Yet it is difficult to argue that the vote can be equated with a referendum on the League of Nations. Many people were undecided on the issue, and, even if Harding had favored approval of the League (with reservations), he still would have won.[71] Harding's image makers had succeeded in portraying him as the personification of traditional American values. They had crafted the most sophisticated merchandising effort up to that time, although the techniques used soon would be improved on in the decades to come.

6

The Merchandised Style—Continued

1920–48

The period between 1920 and 1948 saw mainly an acceleration of the merchandising style of electioneering established in the three previous decades. Modern advertising techniques were more heavily applied in this era as publicity became the key element in campaigning. Inventions like the radio were quickly put to use by those trying to "sell" candidates. At the same time, elaborate parades and other tactics of the old army style declined even further. While numerous mass meetings still were scheduled, crowds at such events tended to be smaller. Former New York governor and presidential candidate Al Smith wrote in his 1929 autobiography: "I cannot help but feel that there was greater interest in elections in my early days than there is now."[1] Fewer and fewer men stayed around the polling place while the ballots were being cast. On election night, he added, throngs of people no longer stood outside newspaper offices eagerly awaiting the results. In general, the campaigns of these years were more efficient, utilizing the latest forms of technology and expertise, but politicians found it hard to kindle the type of spirit manifested in Smith's youth, a half century earlier.

The fall in participation and enthusiasm partly reflected certain ongoing changes in American political life. Communal involvement continued to shrink as national committees increasingly oversaw the management of campaigns. Also, state and local parties lost influence as further reforms had reduced their control of the electoral process. Even in places that withstood the effects of "progressive" legislation, party organizations exhibited less potency. The amount of patronage available to them diminished as government agencies took over many social welfare functions. In states lacking political competitiveness, the internal structure started to deteriorate. Even the entrenched city machines were affected. The curtailment of immigration following World War I meant a smaller pool of newcomers for the bosses to mobilize. Newly enfranchised women did not take up enough of the slack. (This was most evident in the generally downward trend of voter turnout from the 1920s to the 1940s.) In addition, politics now had an even greater problem competing with various kinds of leisure activity. The modern entertainment industry provided more enjoyable diversions than normally could be found at party meetings. Indeed, to assure good attendance at major gatherings, those in charge felt it necessary to put on a show to supplement the speechmaking.[2]

PUBLIC RELATIONS METHODS

Even had a fall in participation not occurred, campaign leaders already were moving toward wider use of political propaganda and public relations methods. There had been, to be sure, considerable devotion to image making since the time of Andrew Jackson, and innovative advertising techniques had come into play by the early 1900s. But starting in the 1920s the process went far beyond previous levels. As advertising grew by leaps and bounds in the commercial sphere, it also permeated much of the political sphere. The political party became more of a broker of public opinion, seeking to capitalize on people's emotions. Earlier merchandisers' attempts at education increasingly were replaced by efforts at manipulation, with greater concern paid to political symbols. Posters and billboards commonly displayed the candidate in front of the American flag. Each party's heroes and historic achievements were glorified as never before, and celebrity endorsements acquired new importance. Current issues were not ignored but came to be discussed in simplified terms, with the focus rarely shifting from the name of the party, the name of the candidate, and some catchy slogan picked for the race.[3]

To keep their man in the public eye, party publicists tried to stage events that would attract heavy attention in the press and maybe get into the newsreels. They had him visit historic sites, such as Lincoln's birthplace, as well as attend numerous pageants, fairs, and sporting contests, always accompanied by a group of reporters and photographers. Seeking a common touch, they had the candidate pose for the camera in various folksy activities. Thus Calvin Coolidge was shown milking cows or cavorting in western attire. Franklin Roosevelt was pictured holding his fishing rod or talking to factory workers or sitting at family gatherings. Wendell Willkie, Roosevelt's adversary in 1940, although not a farmer, was photographed husking corn with rolled-up sleeves and hair falling over his brow. In addition, Alf Landon and Frank Knox, Republican standard-bearers in 1936, were portrayed on a poster as two-fisted horseback riders, in a pose reminiscent of Theodore Roosevelt. (Actually, Knox had been a Rough Rider in the Spanish-American War.)[4]

A good illustration of the trend toward maximizing publicity can be seen in a comparison of the campaign tour undertaken by William Jennings Bryan in 1896 with that of Al Smith thirty-two years later. Bryan, as he crossed the country, traveled in regular day coaches with only a small entourage and rarely anyone from the national press. He usually had to depend on newspeople in the places he visited to report his activities. In contrast, Governor Smith's journey west in 1928 occurred on a specially designed eleven-car train accompanied by a large staff of advisers, secretaries, and publicity men. The assemblage also included forty reporters, several cameramen and "still" photographers, plus three expert stenographers. One car was equipped for press conferences, another for typing and mimeographing and with space for a "dark room," which enabled pictures to be developed immediately after they were taken. Herbert Hoover's long-distance train trips that year and those of succeeding presidential candidates in this era would offer similar facilities and personnel.[5]

The 1928 presidential contest marked a turning point in the upgrading of propaganda efforts, as both parties greatly expanded their publicity divisions. Then, in 1929, following their landslide defeat, the Democrats set up the first permanent publicity bureau, headed by experienced newspaperman Charles Michelson, formerly of the *New York World*, to keep up the attack on their opponents. The apparent success of this venture soon led the Republicans to establish a comparable organization. By the mid–1930s publicity men exerted a tremendous influence over the entire flow of information from party headquarters. Although journalists served as the mainstays, an increasing number of public relations persons—many of them skilled in advertising—worked on campaign staffs offering their expertise. In 1936 Republican Alf Landon became the first presidential aspirant to employ a regular advertising agency—Blackett, Sample, and Hummert, Inc., of Chicago—to enhance his appeal. Blackett's involvement would lead to charges of Landon being "sold" according to a "well-conceived marketing plan."[6]

Nevertheless, the role of public relations people in campaigns at this point remained restricted to certain publicity phases. They did not handle the entire operation. Moreover, as one political scientist observed, practitioners of the new style had yet to develop some of "the more subtle ways of manipulating public opinion." There was a notable exception, however. In the state of California in 1933, two Bay area public relations experts, Clem Whitaker and Leone Baxter, founded Campaigns, Inc., the first political management firm in the country. Over the next two decades the husband-wife team of Whitaker and Baxter served clients in a wide variety of contests—local and statewide, including referenda—always insisting on complete control. In each case the twosome worked out a detailed strategy and then put their plan into action. Overall they compiled a better than 90 percent success record (70 victories in 75 attempts) and introduced many of the public relations gimmicks and media techniques common today. Yet not until the 1950s and 1960s did this full-scale public relations approach spread through the political system nationwide. Before that time candidates and party leaders showed great reluctance toward giving up any authority over their affairs. They wanted to run their own campaigns and to rely on well-established publicity methods.[7]

While the overall use of material objects for publicity would decline in importance, some forms such as campaign buttons continued to be popular. Buttons often were more cheaply made—stamped from lithographed tin sheets—but were distributed in the millions during presidential races. The high point occurred in 1940 amid the Roosevelt-Willkie contest, when an estimated 54 million buttons found their way into people's possesssion. The year 1940 also marked a high point for satirical comment, usually in reference to Roosevelt seeking a third term. Opponents sported buttons that said "Two Times Is Enough For Any Man"; supporters answered with "A Third Termer Is Better Than A Third Rater." Besides buttons, campaign posters made of thin, inexpensive paper became more plentiful and adorned fences and telephone poles throughout the land. Stamps, stickers, and decals gradually emerged as propaganda items as did automobile license plate attachments of various kinds, which included narrow metal strips to be put on top of the license plate and larger, rectangular, plate-like objects for the front bumper.[8]

PRINTED MATTER

Printed matter remained in vogue, though its style was streamlined to fit the times. On the presidential level, short sketches superseded lengthy biographies as the chief means of fashioning a candidate's image. These works usually focused on a specific theme and exaggerated certain qualities to mythical proportions. In 1928 Herbert Hoover was portrayed as an almost superhuman individual, whose skills could meet any challenge. One booklet began: "Into a brief span of 54 years, this leader of men and thought has crowded a score of achievements any one of which would assure his lasting fame."[9] Meanwhile, statements on behalf of Al Smith stressed his friendly, personal manner rather than his record. The sketch printed in the Democratic Textbook declared: "Al Smith is above all else a human being. . . . His is the strength of a man, warm with the love of his kind, touched by the sorrows of ordinary people, sharing their joys, knowing their hearts."[10] After reading through such material, one critic remarked: "The American people will elect as President a nonexistent person—and defeat likewise a mythical identity. They will vote for and against a picture that has been painted for them by protagonists and antagonists in a myriad of publications, a picture that must be either a caricature or an idealization."[11]

The amount of negative, often defamatory, propaganda grew substantially in this era, perhaps because of perceived threats to the existing culture and economic system as well as fears surrounding the outbreak of World War II. The religious issue raised by Smith's candidacy in 1928 inspired a torrent of anti-Catholic literature. The New Deal's social and economic experiments and the Democrats' embrace of labor unions led to repeated charges that Franklin Roosevelt was being manipulated by those on the far left. One brochure opposing his reelection in 1936 stated that "Most of Mr. Roosevelt's advisors, since he has become President, are instructors or graduates of Harvard who believe in socialism to an extreme degree, and communism also." Meanwhile, his wife Eleanor Roosevelt, who showed sympathy toward blacks, was condemned as a "nigger lover." When her husband sought a third term and openly supported the Allies after the war started in Europe, he was called a dictator and a warmonger. Some anti-Semitic literature claimed Roosevelt was of Jewish ancestry and that the effort to get the United States into the war was a Jewish conspiracy. On the other hand, Wendell Willkie, Roosevelt's opponent in 1940, having come from a German background, stood accused of being a Nazi sympathizer. "The Nazis Endorse Willkie," read the title page of one leaflet.[12]

While pamphlets and leaflets continued to be published in considerable quantities, they no longer seemed as vital as they did at the turn of the century. The parties increasingly worked through newspapers, making available prepared plate matter and also issuing news releases from state and national headquarters. During the 1928 presidential campaign, the Democratic party's publicity bureau dispatched between 1,000 and 1,500 news stories; the Republican bureau emitted a similar amount. In the mid–1930s Democratic publicity director Charles Michelson started sending out a weekly column called "Dispelling the Fog," which presented the party's view on many subjects. The column usually ran 700 to 1,000 words and was mailed to about 7,000 daily and weekly papers. During major campaigns the Democrats also distributed the weekly "Clip Sheet," a compilation of news items reporting the achievements of the Roosevelt administration.[13]

Unlike the past when a partisan press was the norm, newspapers in this period grew increasingly independent, with fewer remaining strictly party organs. Almost all papers, whatever their affiliation, published statements from both camps. A few partisan sheets even carried advertising for the opposing side. By 1940 nearly half (48 percent) of all newspapers identified themselves as independent, and 24 percent were independent Democrat or Republican, with only 28 percent fully tied to a major party. To be sure, most newspapers claiming to be independent still endorsed a party and candidate at election time and often provided them with strong editorial support. Just as in previous decades, the majority of daily papers continued to lean toward the Republican ticket—60 percent or more favored Hoover in 1932, Landon in 1936, and Willkie in 1940. Yet the influence of newspapers on the outcome of presidential races—as can be seen by what happened in these contests—was questionable. Contemporary studies, in fact, indicate the newspaper editorial policy had little impact on voter attitudes, though one can argue that a sympathetic press might have made Roosevelt's victories even larger. In any case, down to World War II, newspapers were the chief carrier of political news, but this eventually would change. Indeed, by the late 1940s, the number of newspapers being published had declined sharply, with many people getting their news from other sources, especially radio.[14]

NEW TECHNOLOGY: RADIO AND MOTION PICTURES

Clearly the most important breakthrough in electioneering in this period was the advent of radio. Radio enabled candidates to reach much larger audiences and reach them more frequently than earlier politicians would have dreamed possible. The new medium was first employed by the major parties, albeit in a minor way, in the campaign of 1924. In the biggest broadcast, made on election eve, President Coolidge spoke over a hookup of some twenty-six stations. There is no evidence that radio exerted any impact on the race that year, but it would have a considerable effect on many subsequent ones. By 1928, thanks to improvements in transmitting facilities and reception, the new system had greatly expanded. The two leading networks, NBC and CBS, controlled 168 stations having a potential audience of 15 to 20 million. The national parties together spent over $900,000—more than 20 percent of their budgets—for radio, mostly for speeches by the main adversaries Herbert Hoover and Al Smith. (Each minute on the air was so expensive that Smith once told a Boston crowd to hold their applause.) Regardless of the high cost, the amount of airtime and the money appropriated for it continually increased. The two sides by the 1940s were purchasing over 100 hours on the national networks (now with an estimated 50 million listeners) and devoting over one-third of their funds—perhaps $2 million—to radio. At the same time state and local candidates also began to make extensive use of radio.[15]

With the development of the new medium, a candidate's "radio voice" often would determine how well he fared in the election. Following the defeat of Al Smith, whose scratchy voice made him a less-than-adequate radio performer, it became difficult for the parties to promote anyone who did not come across satisfactorily on the air. Many would claim that Franklin Roosevelt's phenomenal success as a campaigner had much to do with his voice quality and voice control behind a microphone. Besides the overall sound, experts noted his excellent diction, friendly manner, and fine sense of humor. His "fireside chats" gave the impression that he was speaking personally to each radio listener. Party hopefuls who did not possess such a pleasing radio voice tried to avoid on-the-air speechmaking. They instead depended on trained announcers, who provided brief testimonials or statements on the issues. But over the years it became more and more difficult to shun live radio appearances.[16]

In general, radio would have a profound influence on the style of political discourse. Given the high expense for airtime, addresses had to be shorter and to the point. They often focused on a single subject. Listeners, who could change the station by turning a knob, would refuse to put up with a long meandering discourse. On the national networks candidates were less apt to make class or sectional appeals and had to be concerned about offending particular groups. They also had to be careful not to make a serious error before so large an audience, for they no longer could claim they were being misquoted. In the late 1920s some commentators believed that the new invention would soon rationalize campaigning and put an end to the heavily gesticulating demagogic type of orator. However, certain individuals, such as Senator Huey Long of Louisiana and "radio priest" Father Coughlin, proved adept at manipulating listening audiences with their down-to-earth, emotional style of speaking.

Formal speechmaking dominated the airwaves in the 1930s and 1940s, but other methods of reaching listeners were introduced as well. In 1936 the Republicans started presenting dramatized messages—in one, a marriage license clerk warns a prospective bride and groom about the growing national debt under the Democrats. Even though the networks balked at such dramatizations, many independent stations willingly sold time for them. Another controversy that year grew out of the attempt by Senator Arthur Vandenberg of Michigan to "debate" with President Roosevelt, that is, deliver rebuttals to recorded excerpts of previous presidential speeches. CBS originally refused to accept this format, but after much negotiation finally agreed to put it on. By the 1940s the parties were arranging elaborate preelection-night programs, where stars of stage and screen performed and then delivered testimonials for the candidate. Perhaps more effective than dramatizations or spectaculars, at least for state and local aspirants, was the use of spot announcements. These thirty-second or one-minute statements appeared on the air throughout the day and brought the candidate much-needed exposure.[17]

Although it had limited impact in comparison to radio, motion pictures provided an even more effective way to reach the voters. As early as 1924, each of the three major presidential candidates—Coolidge, Davis, and La Follette—appeared in brief "talking pictures" that subsequently ran in many theaters. In 1928 Al Smith and New York gubernatorial candidate Franklin Roosevelt began employing specially equipped trucks that showed sound pictures on a screen or against a convenient wall. "It isn't like the old days," said one spectator in New York's Times Square. "Then a candidate had to be able to shout above the noise to get a hearing." During the 1930s the major parties started preparing short documentaries to appeal to such groups as farmers, laborers, and blacks. The film, "The Plow That Broke the Plains," which treated New Deal agricultural policy in a favorable light, was particularly effective. Twenty- to thirty-minute movies on the life of the candidate—the first one featuring Alf Landon in 1936—also were introduced. Furthermore, the motion picture industry produced the forerunners of televised political spots when in the 1934 California gubernatorial campaign it staged "interviews" with a variety of individuals, who criticized the radical proposals of candidate Upton Sinclair, and then had these incorporated into regular newsreels.[18]

THE OLD AND THE NEW

Despite the changes brought about by the new technologies and public relations methods, certain aspects of campaigning did not differ too much from in the past. In the southern and western states, barbecues and picnics continued to be held where food and drink were served and where one still could hear some old-fashioned oratory. But much of the region's vote-getting activities combined the old and the new. Lyndon Johnson's first race for Congress from the huge Tenth District in Texas in 1938 provides a good example. The twenty-eight-year-old Johnson was unknown to most of the area's constituents and, compared to his rivals, lacking in organization. To overcome this Johnson and his small band of followers worked hard to get his name and face known and sought out influential persons to gain backing and obtain funds. Johnson used the money he raised to buy space in weekly newspapers, send out calling cards, hold barbecues, and offer payment to a few sheriffs and county commissioners for their support. But mainly the candidate spent a great deal of time traveling the backroads, going to small towns to seek votes "one by one." Unlike his competitors, he visited even the tiniest villages, making short speeches and shaking people's hands. During the last two weeks of the campaign, he bought some radio time in Austin to present spot announcements. Moving away from traditional campaigning and exerting more energy than any of his adversaries, he was able to win by a narrow margin.[19]

In the machine-run cities of the North, the vote-getting operation had been altered only slightly since the late nineteenth century. A Democratic committeeman in Pittsburgh, describing his duties in the 1930s, stressed many of the same functions that were performed in previous generations: "I knocked on doors to get out the vote; I collected money from people for the campaigns; I served as a judge of elections."[20] Of course, with the parties not as strong as they once were, urban politicians had to do more than before to maintain voter loyalties. In those cities still heavily populated by the foreign-born and their descendants, everyone from the boss to the precinct worker knew that the best way to accomplish this goal was through personal connections. The most successful learned how to "fall into the lingo of the tavern, the dance hall, the gambling den, the church festival or the political backroom at will." To solidify support they also promised patronage appointments and additional neighborhood services. Black voters were courted in a similar manner, for it was well known that "The Negro votes for the man who is his friend." Black and white precinct workers became adept at dealing with all types of individuals. A smooth operator in the Chicago ghetto boasted that he "could pray with an old woman, talk craps with a gambler, and talk with men about their women or anything they wanted to talk about."[21]

House-to-house canvassing was the principal method by which precinct captains remained in touch with the voters. (Some also sent out personal letters.) Efficient captains saw that a thorough canvass was made before each general or intermediate registration, so they could be sure that the names of all their potential supporters were on the books. Considering the high mobility of the population, this was no simple task. Canvassing techniques varied from one neighborhood to the next. In some places there was easy access to people, but in high-rent districts it was impossible to get by the doorman or butler without an introduction. Women often engaged in daytime canvassing and would try to reach other women. If a woman answered and claimed she was busy with housework, the canvasser offered to help with the chores while conveying her message about registering and voting. Shortly before election day, each of the parties employed "sound trucks" equipped with a public address system to traverse residential areas urging people to vote and, of course, to vote for the right ticket.[22]

Not only precinct workers but officeholders themselves, particularly a congressman seeking reelection in a competitive district, had to be extremely active. When not in Washington he was forced to spend a great deal of time "mending fences," that is, paying attention to the needs of his constituents. As one writer in the mid–1930s described the situation:

He will be beseiged by an army of political fortune hunters whose theme song seems to be, 'What have you got for me?' The unemployed look to him for employment, the employed want better jobs and higher wages, the farmers and business men want to know what he has done for agriculture and business, and the Chamber of Commerce and the civic league want bigger and better public works. He meets them all, relates his accomplishments and promises to do more next time. He calls upon local leaders in every walk of life to inquire what he can do for them, and they as a rule are not backward in telling him. Hotel managers, poolroom, barber shop, restaurant and drug store proprietors, and all such whose business brings them into contact with the public are key men. Ministers of the gospel, and spokesmen for ethnic, economic, veterans', educational and women's organizations are on his list of those 'to be seen.'

. . .

In the open country, he passes up no crossroads stores and as few service stations as possible, and his calling list in each county has on it scores of farmers who enjoy an influence in their townships at least equivalent to that of the chamber of commerce nabobs in the cities. . . . He calls on men and women he went to school with; on fellows he may have soldiered with; on widows he has got pensions for; on young men for whom he has done favors. . . . It is not unusual for him to speak several times a day at places many miles apart. . . . One Congressman during two days of his 1934 campaign traveled 397 miles, took part in no less than a dozen meetings, dinners and picnics, and shook hands with close to 4,000 people.[23]

To enable the candidate to attend all these gatherings and reach so many of his constituents, the automobile, which had been used to a limited degree earlier in the century, now became invaluable. In urban areas the automobile permitted the office seeker to travel easily through the different neighborhoods. During the 1920s the parties began arranging "motor caravans," later called motorcades, where dozens of local dignitaries in open cars accompanied the candidate down the main thoroughfares of a city as crowds of people looked on. In rural districts, the car made it possible for a candidate to greet the farmer on his own farm and the mountain dweller at his cabin or local store. Candidates for statewide offices, such as governor or U.S. senator, depended on the automobile to reach every part of their state. Some carried microphones along to give impromptu speeches. In the South and West senatorial aspirants such as Huey Long of Louisiana and W. Lee (Pappy) O'Daniel of Texas used cavalcades of automobiles to carry hillbilly bands who played music at each stop to help attract an audience for subsequent speechmaking.[24]

PRESIDENTIAL CAMPAIGNING

Although they traveled more by train than by car, campaigning by presidential candidates generally expanded during this period. The front-porch approach was no longer deemed so desirable in the new publicity-conscious age. As one political expert pointed out: "The voters want to see the candidate for office, and make their own estimate of his qualifications, before marking the ballots."[25] The lesser-known nominees—John W. Davis in 1924, Alf Landon in 1936, and Wendell Willkie in 1940—knew they had to go out and make themselves familiar to the voters. Even Herbert Hoover in 1928 and Franklin Roosevelt in 1932, who were fairly well known and had comfortable leads, thought it desirable to go on the hustings. As was true earlier, highly favored incumbents such as Calvin Coolidge in 1924 did not often leave the White House. But the trailing presidents could not afford to remain idle if they still had hopes of being reelected. In 1932 Hoover traveled 10,000 miles, delivering ten lengthy addresses and many shorter ones. Of course, the epitomy of presidential barnstorming occurred in 1948 when Harry Truman undertook his famous whistle-stop campaign, in which he covered almost 32,000 miles and gave 350 speeches.

Vice presidential nominees increased their campaigning as well, often taking on the largest burden of speechmaking and traveling. Also, running for a less dignified office than the presidency, they frequently were designated to make the more slashing remarks against the opposition. Not all number-two men played such an extensive and hard-hitting role. The biggest exception was John Nance Garner, chosen by the Democrats to run with Franklin Roosevelt in 1932. Garner, a conservative who showed minimal interest in the New Deal, proved to be a most reluctant campaigner, preferring to stay home in Texas rather than go out on the road. Late in the race, he finally agreed to give a few speeches, though they lacked real enthusiasm. In 1936 Garner made even less of an effort, delivering but one formal speech. He would, however, be the last candidate for vice president to remain so inactive. By the 1940s full-time campaigning on the part of the second man on the ticket—Harry Truman and John Bricker in 1944, Alben Barkley and Earl Warren in 1948—had become the norm.[26]

NATIONAL CAMPAIGNS

The upsurge in presidential and vice presidential activity was just one part of an overall effort to bring about greater efficiency in national campaigns. Another aspect involved the attempts by party managers to devise a successful strategy, something not given too much consideration before this time. Those in charge generally followed the precepts laid down in an anonymous work written in 1924 entitled *Behind the Scenes in Politics*. According to the book's author it was important for the candidate to seize the lead from the start and then maintain it. This was to be done by establishing the grounds for the campaign and refusing to meet one's opponent on his grounds. For example, in 1924, President Coolidge's strategists ignored his Democratic challenger and did not allow Republican speakers to be drawn into discussions of the Teapot Dome scandal. All of them dwelled instead on Coolidge's character and achievements. "The keynote of the policy," said the *New York Times*, "was a constant reiteration of Coolidge, in order to make the President's name stand as a symbol of everything the voter desired in the way of stability, order, and prosperity."[27]

Strategy was, in large part, still tied to various regional factors. Both parties normally counted on certain sections of the country for basic strength and saw others as virtually hopeless. The Democratic party sought to build on the eleven-state Solid South, plus the surrounding border areas that contained fully a third of the electoral vote (177 of 531). Greatest emphasis was placed on the West and Midwest, with little attention at first given to the East except for the large state of New York. The Republicans, having virtually no chance in the South, pinned their hopes on maintaining total control of the Northeast while, like the Democrats, looking for additional support in the Midwest and West. By the 1930s and 1940s voter allegiance outside the South was not as firm as before, making many states far more competitive. Except for rapidly growing Michigan and California, the most crucial half dozen continued to be the old doubtful states of New York, New Jersey, Pennsylvania, Ohio, Indiana, and Illinois. Together these eight accounted for more than 200 electoral votes—about 40 percent of the total.[28]

Besides looking at specific sections or states, party strategists increasingly thought about winning over major interest groups. Both parties naturally made a powerful pitch to farmers, trying to show their side's policies to be the most favorable to agriculture. The same was true in the realm of business and labor. Special literature was prepared and speakers dispatched to meetings of the leading associations in each field in order to gain endorsements. It still was common to seek support within different ethnic communities. Advertisements were placed in foreign-language newspapers, and speakers of a particular nationality were sent to areas where that group predominated. In addition, both parties began to court blacks, many of whom had moved to the North and become eligible to vote. Down to 1932, the vast majority of black voters remained tied to the Republicans—"the party of Lincoln." But with the coming of the New Deal, they started shifting sides as a result of Roosevelt's relief and jobs policies along with the publicity that the Democrats gave to these efforts.[29]

Now that women could vote, both parties enlarged their appeals for female support by stressing social issues, making a few high-level appointments, and seeking the endorsement of major women's groups. The women's division of each of the national committees gradually expanded its operations, increasing the amounts of literature directed at women. Mary Dewson, head of the Democratic Women's Division in the 1930s, helped to establish countywide organizations in several states, believing this would raise overall turnout by ten percent. Not only did the parties seek their votes, they also employed many women as workers. While the majority of them did canvassing and secretarial tasks, some were hired as speakers to address women's groups and occasionally mixed audiences. Wives began to accompany their candidate-husbands on tour, and a few even spoke out on their behalf. Belle La Follette in 1924 became the first presidential nominee's wife to deliver partisan speeches, and was followed by Eleanor Roosevelt in the 1930s. One woman, Belle Moskowitz, was a close adviser to Al Smith and served as his presidential campaign publicity director.[30]

As another means of stepping up efficiency, the parties eventually applied advanced statistical methods to campaign analysis. In the past party leaders could make only vague projections from their lists of "safe" and "doubtful" voters. Starting in 1932, however, the Democratic National Committee went beyond this and hired a Wall Street statistical analyst, Emil Hurja, to interpret voting trends and recommend where to channel resources. His contribution was soon recognized as invaluable.[31] A short time later scientific sample polling commenced under the auspices of the George Gallup organization and others. Their estimates would be taken into consideration by some candidates and party leaders, though not too seriously at first because of glaring inaccuracies. The Gallup and Crossley polls underestimated Roosevelt's totals in 1936 by seven percent and wound up five to twelve points away in the famous Dewey–Truman race in 1948. Dewey and a few congressional hopefuls such as Republican Jacob Javits of New York employed sample polling in the 1940s, but the large-scale use of this phenomenon would lay in the future.[32]

Not only in its concern with statistical analysis but in many other ways, the national committee operation broadened its scope of activities. Before the late 1920s the national organization barely functioned in the years between elections. According to Franklin Roosevelt, Democratic party headquarters "consisted of two ladies occupying one room in a Washington office building." The Republican counterpart was not much different. But after the defeat of Al Smith in 1928 and of Alf Landon in 1936, the Democrats and the Republicans set up full-time, well-staffed offices in the capital, with the number of workers in each office increasing perhaps fivefold (from about 100 to 500) during an election year. Older bureaus were expanded and new ones established. Both parties created large research divisions. At the start of each campaign, staff members produced detailed reports on national issues, particularly for nonincumbents. The committees also published material for party newcomers on how to organize a campaign and conduct precinct work. In addition, the Young Democratic Clubs of America (1932) and the Young Republican National Federation (1935) were set up to develop youth programs and encourage young people to become politically active.[33]

National party chairmen in this period generally went further than their predecessors in keeping track of operations around the country. Under the innovative James A. Farley of New York, who managed Roosevelt's first two presidential campaigns, much greater communication took place between the national chairman and state leaders. Farley became acquainted with the most important party figures from Maine to California and insisted on frequent reports—verbal and written—from them. But he did not feel that personal contacts alone were sufficient, especially if conditions seemed to be changing rapidly. Therefore, Farley created a huge newspaper-clipping bureau that received as many as 15,000 items daily. These, according to Louis Howe, Roosevelt's chief political adviser, "were passed through the hands of expert readers, and those which had a bearing on the situation were set aside, taken out and handed to expert condensers. . . . These men condensed into a few lines the importance of the clipping or editorial, and every national committeeman and every advisor at headquarters, as well as the campaign chairman . . . received copies every day."[34]

Farley also was concerned about the distribution of campaign literature, which he said had been handled rather inefficiently in former cases. "Huge bales of posters, pamphlets, and flyers were sent to state chairmen or county chairmen who, being too busy conducting meetings and doing other electioneering work, often left the literature to gather dust on the office shelves." He estimated that sometimes less than ten percent "actually found its way into the hands of voters who might be influenced by such propaganda." Farley and his aides sought to correct this situation by shipping material not to the chairmen but to the precinct worker directly, since he or she would be more likely to use it. Also, the literature was parceled out at first only in minimum quantities. "We learned that it was good policy to send a sample bundle or a small amount and have them ask for more, rather than to send too much without a request from them. The worker in the field who gets ten lithographs of the president soon has them distributed. . . . If he gets a huge bundle for the first time without asking, for some reason it seems to cause him to lose interest."[35]

To further encourage local workers, Farley made it a policy to communicate instructions to them straight from national headquarters rather than through an intermediary such as a county chairman.

The county or precinct worker . . . seems to feel that he has a new standing in his home community if he gets his orders directly from the 'generals' who are directing the campaign against the political enemy. It gives him a sense of satisfaction to be let in as part of the show, and the degree of loyalty awakened by this simple gesture is truly gratifying. The fellow out in Kokomo, Indiana, who is pulling doorbells night after night and respectfully asking his neighbors to vote the straight Democratic ticket, gets a real thrill if he receives a letter on campaigning postmarked Washington or New York; and we made sure that this pleasure was not denied him.[36]

The efficiency of chairman Farley in dealing with state leaders, precinct workers, and campaign literature also extended to the distribution of funds. In contrast to previous elections, when money was spent in a rather careless, unscientific manner, dollars were disbursed now only after much consideration and partly in accordance with statistician Emil Hurja's estimate of the party's chances in each state. As described in a *Fortune* magazine article in 1935:

Acting on the principle that success can do its own succeeding without any help from anyone, the Democratic National committee merely adapted its campaign expenditures to Mr. Hurja's figures. Down to 1932 political parties had largely used the scatter-gun method. A campaign chairman, with the evenhanded justice of a blind divinity, would spill his funds equitably and inefficiently over an entire map. Armed with the Hurja prognostication Mr. Farley . . . tempered the wind to the shorn lamb, turned the hose on the dry ground, and made his nickels last.[37]

CAMPAIGN FINANCE

The cost of financing campaigns, especially presidential campaigns, continued to rise above earlier levels in the three decades after 1920. Every one of the quadrennial quests for the presidency cost at least five million dollars, and some would go beyond ten million. Total expenditures by the major parties in the 1936 contest reached over fourteen million dollars—$8.9 million for the Republicans, $5.2 million for the Democrats. Gubernatorial and Senate race expenses rose as well, sometimes approaching $100,000 and in a few instances even more. In 1930 "Puddler Jim" Davis wound up spending over $600,000 just to gain the Republican Senatorial nomination in Pennsylvania. Not all contests were so costly, to be sure. "Alfalfa Bill" Murray won election as governor of Oklahoma in 1931 on the meager budget of $500. Numerous local campaigns were conducted on even less. Republican candidates for county offices in Maine in 1924 averaged only $103, and Democratic candidates just $30. Yet on the whole, the greater costs of running a campaign combined with the expanding population in most constituencies meant larger outlays of money were always necessary, even during hard times.[38]

Campaign expenditures generally fell into five categories: (1) publicity and propaganda; (2) headquarters expenses—rent, postage, staff salaries; (3) field activities—payments to organizers and speakers, hiring halls and entertainment; (4) grants to subsidiary groups; and (5) election-day expenses—sometimes referred to as "street money," which was used to get voters to the polls. The greatest amount, roughly half the total, went toward publicity. At first this mainly consisted of printed matter—pamphlets and other literature, as well as newspaper advertising. Later, radio commanded an increasing proportion—at least 20 percent of all spending in national campaigns. About 20 to 40 percent was allocated for staff and headquarters expenses, with the remaining 10 to 30 percent designated for field workers and subsidiary organizations. The distribution varied, of course, from state to state and from candidate to candidate. When old progressive Gifford Pinchot ran for the Senate from Pennsylvania in 1926, he spent 60 percent of his budget on advertising, while in 1930 New Jersey senatorial nominee Dwight Morrow allotted only 20 percent for that purpose, devoting 50 percent to headquarters expenses.[39]

Methods of financing went on in the old vein at first but gradually underwent change. On the state and local levels, considerable amounts of money continued to be raised through assessments on public employees. Even where the merit system operated, donations still were expected on the same graduated scale as existed earlier. Another source of state and local funding remained the candidates themselves. Certain wealthy individuals personally financed the major costs of their own campaigns or at least granted a percentage of their anticipated salary.[40] On the national scene, big contributions predominated as before. In 1928 both parties received roughly half their income in sums above $5,000. The system was altered only slightly in 1932, when about 40 percent of each party's funds were in gifts of that size. In 1936 the seemingly antibusiness philosophy of the New Deal encouraged a small number of Republican financiers to make greater allocations than ever, eight of whom would give over $100,000. Yet in subsequent years the overall proportion of funds from large donations gradually would fall because of the introduction of new kinds of financing.[41]

The Republicans for their part inaugurated a program of systematic fund-raising in the late 1930s to obtain money from the small as well as the large donor. Primarily through the efforts of Carlton G. Ketchum, a Pittsburgh businessman who became attached to the Republican National Committee after 1936, the party adopted methods formerly used in raising money for private causes. There was to be a single unified fund drive each year in each jurisdiction, with a certain proportion of the amount received going to the national organization and the remainder to be spent locally. The new committee came to be separately organized and staffed with skilled fund-raisers not politicians. While the attempt at mass funding did not always work out in practice, and wealthy individuals often would have to carry on as before and provide a considerable part of the total, the basic financing structure was established for the next several decades. In the 1940s an increasing percentage of funds would come through small and medium-size contributions.[42]

Unlike the Republicans, the Democrats never developed such an orderly fund-raising system. Theirs would be less formal and more dependent on a few major groups, particularly labor unions, to carry the load. Labor unions started contributing heavily to national campaigns in 1936. Unions previously had donated some money to political candidates, but in a rather haphazard and ineffective fashion. Now the prolabor stance of the New Deal helped create a strong financial bond between big unions (under the new organization known as the CIO) and the Democratic party. It is estimated that the United Mine Workers, headed by John L. Lewis, contributed up to $250,000 to Roosevelt's reelection bid. Another new source of funds for the Democrats that year came from the sale of a volume known as the *Book of the Democratic Convention*, which contained many advertisements from companies doing business with the federal government. A deluxe edition bound in leather and autographed by the president sold for $100. Proceeds reached several hundred thousand dollars, bringing a net profit of at least $250,000. A similar book in 1940 yielded $338,000.[43]

An even more important method of financing introduced at this point was the large fund-raising dinner. Partisan commemorative dinners had been held since the Jackson era (originally to celebrate the Battle of New Orleans and foster Democratic harmony), but during the mid–1930s they developed into a regular and essential part of the political financing process. The idea seems to have come from businessman Matthew McCloskey of Philadelphia, later treasurer of the Democratic National Committee, and was perfected by James Farley, who sought to raise money to pay off party campaign debts in 1936. As one contemporary noted: "Farley is the only political manager who has ever been able to sell $5 worth of groceries for $100." An elaborate $100 per plate dinner was given in Washington with the head of the party present, while smaller-scale dinners (at somewhat lower prices) took place simultaneously in other cities. In subsequent decades fund-raising banquets became common on all political levels, with moderately priced events set for rank and file supporters and higher-priced ones arranged for more select groups.[44]

Beginning in 1940 attempts were made to place a lid on the size of contributions to candidates for federal office. The Hatch Act, passed by Congress that year, limited to $5,000 the amount an individual could contribute to a party committee supporting a particular person. This provision did not, however, take into account the fact that a large gift could be divided so that it would seem like it had been given by various members of a family. Nor did the law affect donations to state and local committees; somebody legally

could give $5,000 to any number of them. Another new congressional re-
striction was the federal gift tax imposed on individual contributions of more
than $3,000. Yet this too could be circumvented by a person who sent checks
to several different committees. During 1943 Congress sought to restrict
donations by labor unions in the same manner as corporations had been
forbidden earlier. But unions easily got around this legislation by forming a
subsidiary group, which became the nation's first PAC, the CIO Political
Action Committee. So successful was this venture that support groups connected to each of the parties began setting up several such committees, with
names like the One Thousand Club or the President's Club, which could
not be tied to the federal funding limitations.[45]

Not only through finance but in other ways, organized labor emerged as
the most important interest group taking part in elections as the period wore
on. By the mid–1930s, as the labor movement established close ties to Franklin Roosevelt, union personnel would be extremely active on behalf of the
Democratic ticket, holding registration drives and encouraging fellow workers to vote. In certain industrial states they even sought to mobilize support
beyond their own union membership. While a personal conflict between
Roosevelt and union leader John L. Lewis reduced labor activities to some
degree in 1940, the CIO through its Political Action Committee came to be
a major force in the 1944 encounter. The CIO-PAC distributed great quantities of pro-Democratic literature and sponsored a heavy get-out-the-vote
campaign. Union heads were consulted on numerous high-level matters,
including the choice of the vice presidential candidate. "Clear everything
with Sidney," a reference by FDR to powerful union official Sidney Hillman,
became a catchword during the contest. While Republicans may have exaggerated the amount of union influence being exerted, organized labor would
continue to play a large role in most Democratic campaigns.[46]

THE PARTIES

The Republicans entered this era as the majority party and would remain
in that position throughout the 1920s. Outside the South, the GOP had
numerous strongholds, especially in small-town America. The party had not
altered its outlook much since the time of Lincoln. It still had its roots in
the Yankee tradition, which had spread across most of the northern half of
the country. It stressed long-held Protestant values such as hard work and
thrift; it also supported Prohibition and was critical of the cultural changes
associated with the city and the immigrant. The Republican party firmly
believed in free enterprise and in governmental promotion of business
through protective tariffs. But its adherents sharply opposed other forms of
intervention in the economy, seeing them as socialistic. Fervently nationalist

in foreign policy matters, party leaders would refuse all offers to join the League of Nations, taking an increasingly isolationist stance in world affairs.[47]

The Democrats, after having tasted power during the Wilson years, were again the minority party. The progressive element became dormant or sought other outlets; some conservatives went over to the opposing side. The party's only real source of electoral strength lay in the South, although there would be a few pockets of populism in the western states and growing support in northern cities. Indeed the Democratic organization would become almost irreconcilably split between the southern rural, traditionalist, nativist, prohibitionist faction and the northern urban, reformist, immigrant, antiprohibitionist side. The two found common ground only in their opposition to federal interference in their everyday lives. Power shifted toward the urban wing in the late 1920s, but sharp division remained until the Great Depression and the New Deal brought about a new coalition that embraced farmers and laborers from every part of the nation. Ideologically, it would move beyond Wilson's progressivism in domestic matters to a new kind of liberalism, yet it would follow his internationalist views in dealing with foreign problems.[48]

As in earlier periods, several third-party movements emerged in these years. They mostly followed the model of Theodore Roosevelt's Bull Moose effort in essentially being challenges by individual candidates rather than by established parties. Improvements in transportation and communication made it possible for well-known figures like Robert La Follette to reach large numbers of voters without depending much on local organizations. In fact, unlike some nineteenth-century third parties that lasted for two or more presidential contests, these were primarily one-shot experiments. In addition to La Follette's reform-minded Progressives in 1924, there would be William Lemke and the Union party in 1936, Henry Wallace and a new Progressive party in 1948, plus Strom Thurmond and the Dixiecrats that same year. To be sure, the Socialist party would operate throughout the period, but it never would obtain more than a tiny fraction of the total vote. (Two percent in 1932 was the highest figure.) The American Communist party, founded in 1920, also presented a presidential ticket each time, but it acquired an even tinier fraction, the largest being three-tenths of one percent in 1932.[49]

During the 1920s cultural issues sharply differentiated the major parties and strongly influenced voters' preferences. Questions regarding religion and social values such as Prohibition and Catholicism would be at the heart of each national contest. Then, with the onset of the Great Depression and throughout the subsequent decade, economic matters would dominate, causing a tremendous shift of allegiance. The Republicans, long connected with the idea of prosperity, became identified in many people's minds as the "party of depression," under whose reign there would be economic scarcity. Meanwhile, the Democrats, thanks to Franklin Roosevelt and the New Deal, came to be seen as the "party of the workingman" and as the party that provided government aid to the needy; they swiftly became the majority party. International issues would play an increasingly important role in partisan politics beginning in 1940 and, along with matters of federal control and bureaucratic waste, would swing some support back to the Republicans. However, by carrying forward their New Deal policies, the Democrats would, except for a brief period following World War II, remain in command of all branches of the government until the early 1950s.[50]

ELECTION OF 1924

The election of 1924 took place not long after the death of President Harding and the revelation of several acts of corruption, particularly the Teapot Dome scandal. The contest might have developed into a close one had the opposition fully been able to exploit the situation. But the Republicans were successful in overcoming the charges of corruption by focusing on the integrity of Harding's successor, Calvin Coolidge, whom they then nominated to run for a full term. The platform reflected the conservative attitudes of the party faithful. The Democrats showed much less unity; indeed their convention highlighted the differences between the northern, urban, "wet" faction led by New York Governor Al Smith and the southern, rural, "dry" faction headed by former Wilson cabinet member William G. McAdoo. The two sides became hopelessly bogged down on the issue of whether or not to condemn the Ku Klux Klan, and then went through a record 103 ballots before finally settling on compromise candidate John W. Davis, a Wall Street lawyer, to top the ticket. The Democratic platform criticized the Harding scandals and the isolationist policies of the Republicans, but its position on economic matters was hardly less conservative than that of their opponents.[51]

This left the door open for dissident elements in both parties to put forth an alternative candidate, Senator Robert La Follette of Wisconsin, the longtime progressive reformer. Supported by disgruntled farmers, the American Federation of Labor (AFL), the Socialists, and numerous intellectuals, La Follette's new Progressive party called for sweeping change. It favored nationalization of railroads, public ownership of waterpower, restricting the authority of the Supreme Court, limiting the use of injunctions against labor, and greater curbs on monopolistic business practices. La Follette's campaign, however, was handicapped by an almost total lack of organization and a paucity of funds. In addition, the candidate's ill health prevented him from making too many public appearances. Davis, the Democratic nominee, proved to be a more hardy campaigner, but he had a difficult time projecting an image distinct from Coolidge's. His speeches, besides criticizing Teapot Dome, tended to be legalistic and uninspiring. Rarely did they offer anything new.

The Republicans ignored Davis and the Democrats, concentrating mainly on La Follette's "radicalism." Coolidge's running mate, banker Charles

Dawes, would ask audiences, "Where do you stand—with the President on the Constitution with the flag or on the sinking sands of socialism?" Coolidge himself campaigned little, though he issued a number of statements denouncing La Follette's "foreign economic ideas" and extolling Republican contributions to America's prosperity. Prosperity seems to have been the key factor in the race, as Coolidge was elected by a huge majority. He took thirty-five states to twelve for Davis (all in the South) and one for La Follette (his own Wisconsin). The electoral count stood at 382 for Coolidge, 136 for Davis, and 13 for La Follette. In the popular vote, Coolidge amassed 15.7 million— more than the combined totals of his two adversaries, Davis having 8.3 million and La Follette 4.8 million. The small vote for the progressive position represented quite a shift from twelve years earlier, when Wilson and Roosevelt had dominated the polls.

ELECTION OF 1928

Calvin Coolidge's full term in office went well, at least on the surface, and he easily could have been renominated by his party in mid–1928. But some time earlier he had issued a statement saying that he did not wish to run again for the presidency. When the Republicans met at their convention, they designated Secretary of Commerce Herbert Hoover as the presidential nominee. Hoover, born in rural Iowa, was a self-made man. He had been a successful mining engineer and, during World War I, an able administrator of relief. His diligent service in the Commerce Department under Harding and Coolidge won him further plaudits, especially from the business community. The Republican platform praised the accomplishments of the incumbent administration, particularly its contribution to the country's economic well-being. It also promised continued enforcement of Prohibition.[52]

The Democrats named as their candidate Governor Al Smith of New York, the first Catholic ever to run for the nation's highest office. Smith was no less a self-made man than Hoover. Although having had limited formal education, Smith had worked his way up through the Tammany machine in New York City to become an assemblyman and then a four-term governor of the Empire State. As chief executive he inaugurated many reforms and helped reorganize the machinery of state government. Smith, representative of the city, the immigrant, and the anti-Prohibition interests, was disliked by many in his own party, yet northern urban Democrats, tired of being passed over by the southern rural bloc, managed to get him nominated. The Democratic platform contained a few progressive planks, but on economic matters stood almost on the same ground as the Republican document. Even the usual low-tariff stance was deliberately missing so as not to alienate manufacturers. Indeed, Smith selected wealthy General Motors executive John J. Raskob as chairman of the National Committee.

Smith, the underdog, conducted an energetic campaign. He traveled across the country delivering numerous speeches in which he criticized Republican policies and defended the right of a Catholic to seek the presidency. His message was well received in the Northeast, but not as favorably elsewhere. Smith, who had never shown much interest in the problems facing the South and West, had trouble attracting widespread support in those sections. Hoover, starting in a stronger position, covered far less territory and spoke fewer times, never even mentioning his opponent by name. Important addresses by both candidates were for the first time carried over the radio. While not as colorful a personality as the New Yorker, Hoover sounded better over the air than did Smith, whose harsh accent annoyed many listeners. In his public statements Hoover mainly focused on the theme of progress and prosperity, which he connected to the Republicans' fostering of free enterprise. So successful was the present system, he said, that, "We in America today are nearer to the final triumph over poverty than ever before in the history of any land."[53]

Although Hoover did not emphasize the religious issue and said he personally opposed any bigotry, several Republican spokesmen urged Protestant ministers to use their influence against the Catholic Smith. Some clergymen, particularly in the South, needed little urging to denounce Smith as an agent of the Vatican. "A Vote for Smith Is a Vote for the Pope," was whispered far and wide. Smith, it should be mentioned, did not play down his Catholicism in any way; he openly practiced his religion and allowed Catholics like Raskob to run his campaign. But it was not just Smith's Catholicism that aroused people's suspicions. They questioned his Tammany Hall connections as well as his unabashed New York City style—wearing flashy clothes including a brown derby, smoking big cigars, and bluntly ignoring Prohibition. For many, Hoover, the product of middle America, seemed closer to the ideal of what a president should be like than the machine-backed urbanite Smith.

The balloting resulted in an overwhelming victory for Hoover. The Republican nominee came out ahead in forty states and amassed 444 electoral votes to Smith's eight states and 87 votes. The popular tally stood at 21.4 million (58 percent) to 15 million (41 percent). Hoover also did better than any previous Republican in making inroads in the "Solid South," capturing almost the whole upper tier. Smith only took six southern states, plus heavily Catholic Massachusetts and Rhode Island. Surely Smith's religion, manner, and Tammany ties contributed to the magnitude of his defeat, but it is equally clear that even had he been a Protestant from rural America, he would have lost. Most of the country was enjoying good times, making it highly unlikely that any Democrat could have beaten Hoover. The election of 1928, however, served as an indication of a future party shift, for even in losing, Smith reversed a long-standing trend by gaining a majority of votes in the nation's twelve largest cities.

Hoover's administration started off with great expectations, but the Wall Street stock market crash of October, 1929, set off a chain of events that pushed the country into a severe economic depression. Factory production declined, banks began to fail, and many farmers lost their farms. At the same time unemployment rose precipitously—to a point where perhaps one-fourth of the labor force was out of work. Although sympathetic toward the people's plight, the president was reluctant to use federal power to deal with the emergency. Hoover continued to believe that the nation's economic system basically was sound and that heavy governmental intervention only would be harmful. When in 1932 he finally created a new agency, the Reconstruction Finance Corporation, to provide federal loans to hard-hit businesses and to the states for relief, it turned out to be too little and too late.

ELECTION OF 1932

Despite the country's worsening problems and dissatisfaction with the president's handling of them, the Republicans renominated Herbert Hoover in 1932. As in similar cases in the past, the party felt that repudiating the incumbent would signify a clear admission of failure. But as might be expected, the convention that designated him had trouble conveying the usual degree of enthusiasm. Except for the Prohibition issue, which the party now straddled, platform statements strongly defended Hoover's record and offered no hint of change. The essence of the Republican prognosis for handling the depression was contained in the platform preamble, which read: "The people themselves, by their own courage, their own patient and resolute effort in the readjustments of their own affairs can and will work out the cure." The administration simply would provide assistance.[54]

The Democrats, optimistic about their chances for the first time in sixteen years, chose Franklin D. Roosevelt as their nominee. Roosevelt, the party's vice presidential candidate in 1920, had been stricken with polio the following year, but even though confined to a wheelchair, he had managed to make his way back into politics by the end of the decade. Twice successful in running for the governorship of New York, the popular Roosevelt attracted liberal support yet maintained connections with big-city machines and southern traditionalists. Breaking precedent, Roosevelt flew to the convention in Chicago, becoming the first candidate to deliver his acceptance speech directly to the delegates. Regarding this action he stated, "Let it . . . be symbolic that in doing so I broke traditions. Let it be from now on the task of our party to break foolish traditions. . . . Ours must be a party of liberal thought, of planned action, of enlightened outlook. . . . I pledge you, I pledge myself, to a new deal for the American people."[55] Soon the term "New Deal" would be used to identify the Roosevelt philosophy and program.

Other than the demand for the repeal of Prohibition, specific parts of Roosevelt's agenda were slow in developing. In order to facilitate matters

FDR put together a group of academic advisers—later known as the Brain Trust—led by Raymond Moley of Columbia University, to prepare statements on various issues and programs. While previous candidates had hired trained experts at times, this marked the first systematic use of specialists in the creation of campaign position papers. Over the next several months the Brain Trust would serve not only as a policy-generating group but as a general clearinghouse for proposals submitted by persons representing the entire political spectrum. As Moley later described it: "We were at once working up the material for specific speeches, pushing ahead with the broad economic education of ourselves and Roosevelt, adopting or rejecting thousands of ideas that poured in on us, and trying to observe the elementary political maxim that no one who voluntarily offered suggestions or plans, however silly . . . must be sent away unhappy."[56]

In general, FDR and his handpicked national chairman, James Farley, ran the most thoroughly organized presidential campaign up to that time, effectively using all the resources at their command. With the Democrats clearly in a dominant position, candidate Roosevelt could have avoided campaigning personally if he had so wished. In fact some of his advisers, fearing problems would arise, warned him against going on tour. FDR nevertheless chose to travel across much of the country by train, meeting directly with the people, and put himself on public display. He believed that by doing this he would further the attack on Hoover's policies and, perhaps equally important, combat rumors about his health and alleged lack of vigor. In addition, Roosevelt was a man who loved to campaign, feeling himself buoyed by the enthusiastic crowds who came to see and hear him. Roosevelt said little of substance at most whistle-stops, saving his fire for a few major addresses on principal themes. Yet he managed to make a strong impression on his audience wherever he spoke.[57]

The Republicans, although in a seemingly hopeless situation because of the depression, did not give up easily. They took advantage of their party's incumbency and had many federal employees working for Hoover's reelection. While fund-raising proved more difficult than usual, a few wealthy contributors donated enough money to enable the GOP to outspend its opponents on radio time and various kinds of literature. At first the president planned to spend most of the campaign season in the White House and give only a few speeches. But with the November outlook dim he was forced to go on tour and defend his administration. In spite of cool receptions Hoover, at every public appearance, stuck to his guns and appealed to voters not to change the American system. He referred to Roosevelt's call for more government action as socialism and warned of its dire consequences.[58] Hoover, however, proved incapable of making any of his charges stick. Many people by this time had completely lost faith in anything the president had to say. Roosevelt and the Democrats had succeeded in making Hoover appear responsible for everything that had gone wrong with the country.

On election day Roosevelt won an overwhelming victory, acquiring roughly 22,280,000 votes (57.4 percent) to Hoover's 15,760,000 (39.7 percent). FDR carried 42 states with 472 electoral votes, his opponent just six states and 59 votes. Roosevelt triumphed in more counties than any previous presidential candidate, including 282 that had never gone Democratic before. He showed particular strength in the southern and western states and in the central plains region, areas hit hard by the depression. Although rigorous voter opinion studies still lay in the future, it appeared that Roosevelt did better among the many in the lower socioeconomic brackets, while Hoover fared well among the few in the higher socioeconomic brackets. The ensuing presidential campaigns would accentuate the differences even further.[59]

ELECTION OF 1936

After taking office in March 1933 Roosevelt initiated a comprehensive program to lift the country out of the depths of the depression. Various measures were enacted to aid industry and agriculture. New agencies were established for the purpose of providing jobs and better use of natural resources. All of these helped bring about progress—the number of jobless began to diminish and public confidence came to be restored—which benefited Roosevelt and the Democrats politically. Yet as the 1936 presidential contest approached, many problems in the nation persisted. Unemployment remained high, the budget was unbalanced, and prosperity had proved to be elusive. Many Republicans disliked all the government restrictions and the power exhibited by the New Deal agencies. Former president Hoover warned that continued Democratic rule would lead to further class conflict, eventual economic collapse, and other outrages.

The Republican convention echoed these views, with the platform condemning the existing administration and declaring that "America was in peril." Only the GOP, it said, could "save the Constitution" and preserve the "American way" from the dangers of radicalism. Yet the delegates picked as their standard-bearer a middle-of-the-road Republican, Governor Alfred M. Landon of Kansas, a one-time Bull Mooser, who seemed to accept some of the New Deal program. The Democrats, of course, renominated Franklin Roosevelt who promised to continue and expand the New Deal. The party platform talked about helping all Americans obtain "social justice," "equal opportunity," and a "more abundant life." An alternative group known as the Union party, whose backers included such right-wing leaders as the Reverend Gerald L. K. Smith and Dr. Francis Townshend, selected the agrarian populist congressman William Lemke of North Dakota as its candidate, though a lack of clear direction ruined the latter's effort from the start.[60]

The Democrats entered the campaign with a close-knit, smoothly functioning organization. Not only did the national headquarters operate with great efficiency, but state and local parties provided full cooperation. National chairman James Farley had maintained close connections with Democratic officials across the country over the years and it paid off. The Republican organization, on the other hand, still lay in disarray as a result of the defeat four years earlier. When the new national chairman, John Hamilton, took over, he had to rebuild almost the entire structure, and unlike Farley, who possessed a complete index of local officials, Hamilton had to start from scratch. Yet by raising an enormous amount of money, the Republicans were able to put together a rather elaborate publicity machine. What the party lacked in teamwork, it hoped to make up in propaganda. Large numbers of newspaper and advertising men were hired. While denouncing Roosevelt's Brain Trust, the Republicans formed a similar group to prepare issue-related material.

In focusing on the "American way," the Republican campaign seemed to show a longing for the "good old days" in contrast to the Democrats' emphasis on change and modernization. Party leaders went on to stage various activities connected to this theme. Indeed the ceremony preceding Landon's acceptance speech included an elaborate pageant depicting "frontier days" with men and women dressed in old western attire and driving covered wagons. In his address and on later occasions, Landon sounded like a typical midwesterner and talked extensively about traditional values. His words came across as sincere, but being a less-than-exciting speaker without a clear-cut program, he had trouble bringing about any shift in voter attitudes. At first, Landon took a moderate position in discussing the New Deal, claiming that a Republican administration could achieve reforms more effectively and without waste. But as this failed to attract much attention, some GOP officials began making extreme accusations, playing on the fear of strict federal control. There also were vicious attacks on Roosevelt by the conservative business group known as the Liberty League and by the demagogic radio priest Father Coughlin, who referred to the president as a "great betrayer and liar."

Roosevelt initially sought to remain above the battle and let other Democrats make public statements for him. However, all the bitter charges ultimately caused him to enter the fray. In his personal appearances and on the radio, the president constantly stressed his administration's role in lifting the country out of the depression and asked people to contrast their current situation with that of four years earlier. He hoped to achieve backing from all segments of society, but when the business and banking community squarely positioned itself on the other side, Roosevelt lashed out at the "economic royalists" who opposed him. At the conclusion of his Madison Square Garden speech in late October, he declared: "Never before in all our history have these forces been so united against one candidate as they stand today. They are unanimous in their *hate* for *me*—and I *welcome their hatred*." He went on to say, "I should like to have it said of my first Administration that in it the forces of selfishness . . . have met their match," and then added, at a break in the applause, "I should like to have it said of my second Administration that in it these forces met their master."[61]

Although the GOP won the state contest in Maine in September and a *Literary Digest* poll predicted a Republican victory in November, Roosevelt overwhelmed Landon on election day. In the biggest sweep since 1820, he won a majority in all the states except Maine and Vermont. (Farley said the famous slogan, "As Maine goes, so goes the nation," should be changed to, "As Maine goes, so goes Vermont.") Roosevelt took almost 61 percent of the popular tally, acquiring more than 27,700,000 votes to Landon's 16,600,000. (Lemke's total was less than 900,000, while the Socialists and Communists together garnered only about 270,000.) The Republicans also suffered disastrous defeats in the House and Senate races, their strength falling to 89 and 16, respectively. Roosevelt and the Democrats had put together a stronger political coalition than any in the preceding century, attracting heavy support not only in the South and in northern cities, but among a majority of farmers and laborers, white and black, throughout the country.

ELECTION OF 1940

Franklin Roosevelt's second term in office turned out to be much more troubled than the first. Although a few progressive measures passed, such as that setting up a standard minimum wage, many others met with rejection, as did the president's attempt to "pack" the Supreme Court. His efforts to "purge" conservative Democrats during the 1938 congressional contest also failed. With the New Deal waning, most people expected FDR to announce his intention to retire before the 1940 presidential race. But as war had broken out in Europe, creating a severe world crisis, Roosevelt decided to break the two-term tradition and run for a third time. He firmly believed that the circumstances required his experienced hand at the helm. The absence of any major rival made his party renomination a foregone conclusion. Secretary of agriculture Henry A. Wallace of Iowa was designated for the vice presidency, replacing John Garner who opposed the third-term concept.[62]

In choosing their presidential nominee the Republicans ignored the regular party membership and opted for a real dark horse—Wendell L. Willkie of Indiana. Willkie, a high-powered lawyer and utility company executive, had never held public office and until a short time before had been a registered Democrat. The little-known Willkie had been brought to popular attention through a wide-ranging media effort; it was hoped that his winning personality and impressive business background would make up for his lack of political experience. The party platform condemned FDR's third-term quest as an attempt to establish a dictatorship. It also contained some well-worn attacks on the New Deal, though Willkie, a moderate, did not object as much to the reform programs themselves as to the inefficiency in their operation.[63]

In his acceptance speech and in later statements, Willkie hit hard on the theme of Roosevelt becoming a dictator and on the inability of the New Deal to restore full prosperity. Yet while he talked of the need for new leadership, he had trouble delineating a positive program. Willkie did, to be sure, display enormous energy as a campaigner. Over the course of several months he traveled as much as anyone since Bryan, delivering 540 speeches before an estimated 12 million people. Unfortunately, this burdensome schedule often caused his voice to give out, making him sound rasping and hoarse. Willkie also suffered from the disorganized state of his campaign. A novice in politics, he made many mistakes, especially devoting too much effort toward trying to win over Democrats. In addition, the candidate was unwilling to take advice from longtime Republicans, relying too heavily on the outsiders who had helped him gain the nomination. As the campaign progressed, so did the disorder within his own ranks, which proved difficult to contain. The Democratic machinery, on the other hand, ran much more smoothly. Under the leadership of Ed Flynn, "the boss of the Bronx," who had replaced James Farley as national chairman, the party again put together a strong vote-getting effort.

Roosevelt himself did not campaign much in the early stages of the race, preferring to remain in Washington and focus on his role as commander in chief. In September he announced his controversial "destroyers for bases" agreement with England, providing substantial military aid for the struggle against Germany. The overall plan was more or less acceptable to Willkie, who instead denounced the bypassing of Congress, calling it the most dictatorial and arbitrary act of any president. As Willkie fell behind in the late stages of the contest, he and his associates, in a cynical appeal for votes, sharply denounced Roosevelt as being a warmonger. "If his promise to avoid war is no better than his promise to balance the budget," exclaimed Willkie, our boys are "already almost on the transports." Such charges eventually led Roosevelt to forsake his silence and deliver a series of stirring speeches in which he specifically denied his opponents' accusations. "I have said this before, but I shall say it again and again and again: Your boys are not going to be sent into any foreign wars."[64] He also taunted isolationist Republicans in Congress who had long sought to block his preparedness proposals, singling out three men in particular—"Martin, Barton, and Fish." The rhythm of this phrase quickly caught the public's fancy.

On election day the majority of voters showed they still preferred Roosevelt, giving him approximately 27 million votes to 22 million for Willkie, and a total of 449 votes to 82 in the electoral college. Outside of Maine and Vermont, the Republicans' only real strength lay in some of the isolationist-leaning areas of the Midwest and the Great Plains region. Yet the president's margin of victory was somewhat smaller than in 1936, as he received 54.8 percent compared to 60.8 percent four years earlier. As expected, Roosevelt ran strongest in the large cities and in the traditionally Democratic South.

In the final analysis, the outcome hinged more on leadership capacity than on issues—the majority seemed unwilling to trust an unknown in high office at such a critical time. Moreover, many people remained grateful for what FDR had done to alleviate some of the worst aspects of the depression.

ELECTION OF 1944

Less than a year after Roosevelt's third inauguration, the United States was plunged into World War II. Millions of men and women became involved in fighting the Axis powers overseas or handling the wartime emergencies at home. Although a global war was being waged, the political system within the country continued to operate almost as usual. With the depression no longer an issue, the Republicans picked up several seats in the 1942 congressional elections and thought they might have a chance at capturing the presidency in 1944. For its nominee the GOP chose Thomas Dewey, the young (age 42) and energetic governor of New York, thwarting the comeback attempt of Wendell Willkie. Despite showing signs of strain and aging, Franklin Roosevelt was nominated for a fourth term by the Democrats without opposition. A struggle did develop over the vice presidential selection, however, when many party regulars opposed the retention of liberal Henry Wallace on the ticket. The designation ultimately went to Senator Harry S Truman of Missouri, a moderate, who had gained wide respect in carrying out a special investigation of military spending.[65]

The campaign, though heated in some respects, did not attract as much interest as the previous one because of the wartime conditions. Roosevelt for the most part avoided politicking, leaving the work to surrogates, and instead concentrated on running the war effort. Dewey, who was much more active than the president, tried to get attention by denouncing the tired and quarrelsome "old men" in Washington. While Dewey, like Willkie, accepted certain aspects of the welfare state, he claimed that the Democrats had not really solved the economic problems of the nation and that, after "twelve long years" of New Dealism, it was "time for a change." As the contest wore on, the Republicans stepped up their attacks on the administration's high taxes, large national debt, and alleged government waste. They also carried on a whispering campaign, questioning the health of FDR and criticizing the activities of his wife and sons. One statement even made reference to his dog, Fala.

All of these remarks finally pushed Roosevelt into action. He gave several speeches defending his policies and countering the GOP assaults. The highlight was an appearance before the Teamsters' union in Washington, where he ridiculed his opponents—especially in a passage about his dog.

The Republican leaders have not been content to make personal attacks upon me—or my wife—or my sons—they now include my little dog, Fala. Unlike the members of my family, Fala resents this. When he learned that the Republican fiction writers had concocted a story that I left him behind on an Aleutian Island and had sent a destroyer back to find him—at a cost to the taxpayer of two or three, or eight or twenty million dollars—his Scotch soul was furious. He has not been the same dog since. I am accustomed to hearing malicious falsehoods about myself but I think I have right to object to libelous statements about my dog.[66]

From then on Dewey had little chance, as Roosevelt in his inimitable style demonstrated he was still in command. Moreover, to spike rumors about his physical condition, the president spent an entire day riding around New York City in the rain in an open car and then delivered a climactic speech at Madison Square Garden that night.

On election day, Roosevelt, with the help of organized labor, the urban machines, and absentee ballots from those in the armed forces, again triumphed by a large margin. He obtained 25.6 million votes to Dewey's 22 million and amassed 432 electoral votes to the latter's 99. The war seemed to be proceeding toward a successful conclusion and not too many people wished to change horses in midstream. The majority perhaps also felt that the more experienced Roosevelt would be better at handling the complex negotiations regarding the postwar world than any newcomer. Furthermore, many Americans were registering their appreciation for what the president had accomplished in his previous twelve years in office. Yet this encounter was the closest of the four that FDR had been involved in and foreshadowed problems that the Democrats would have to face in the near future when he passed from the scene. In fact, Roosevelt would die shortly after starting his new term, and Harry Truman would take over the presidency in April 1945.

ELECTION OF 1948

In the postwar period the Republicans began to make significant political gains. Now that the war was over and memories of the depression were fading, many voters seemed unconcerned about further governmental reforms. In 1946 they would give the GOP their first majority in Congress in eighteen years. Also, the electorate became increasingly disenchanted with President Truman, who in many ways did not provide the kind of charismatic leadership exhibited by his notable predecessor. Labor strife, foreign problems, and charges of Communists in the federal government constantly plagued the Truman administration. As the summer of 1948 rolled around, the Republicans looked as if they were in an insurmountable position for the upcoming presidential race. The convention once again nominated the able governor of New York, Thomas Dewey, who had put up a strong fight against Roosevelt four years earlier. The platform, as usual, condemned the excesses of the New Deal and also noted the failures of Truman, stressing once more that it was time for a change.[67]

Democratic leaders had no great enthusiasm about renominating Truman. Many hoped they could dump him and draft World War II hero General Dwight D. Eisenhower as the party's standard-bearer. But when the latter refused the call, the Democrats had no recourse but to accept Truman. The Truman candidacy, lacking much support to begin with, became even more doubtful when many southern Democrats walked out of the national convention protesting the civil-rights plank in the platform. These dissidents would create the States' Rights or "Dixiecrat" party and make Governor Strom Thurmond of South Carolina its designee. Coupled with the bolt by some left-wing Democrats, who joined socialist, communist, and pacifist elements to form the Progressive party under former vice president Henry Wallace, Truman's chances appeared hopeless. Except for William Howard Taft in 1912, no president faced so desperate a situation as Truman.

Dewey seemingly had everything operating in his favor—plenty of money, an efficient staff, and every poll placing him far in front. Given this situation, Dewey did not feel the need to campaign very vigorously. He and his aides believed that to engage in direct combat with the president might create some sympathy for the latter. This had happened to a large extent in 1944. Also, discussing specific issues in detail might, he thought, point up divisions within his own party. Therefore, he decided that he should remain above the battle and not say anything controversial. His bland speeches, however, tended to backfire on him. As one observer wrote: "The candidate, with his crisp executive manner and his rich commanding baritone, exuded so much confidence that he put his followers to sleep."[68] But for a long time it did not seem to matter, for during the summer Truman did not appear to be gaining any ground. In fact, one of the major pollsters felt there was no need to continue measuring public opinion, so one-sided had the contest become.

Despite the predictions of his impending defeat and doubts even among members of his own staff, Truman refused to give up. Convinced that he could still win, the president launched a hard-hitting, long-distance, whistle-stop campaign. Traveling across the country by special train, Truman delivered hundreds of short speeches and several substantive ones in which he lashed out at the "do-nothing" Republican-dominated Eightieth Congress. He warned farmers, laborers, and consumers that another Republican victory might destroy all the gains made under the New Deal. Although Truman lacked Dewey's polish as a speaker, his natural homespun manner and sharp anti-Republican rhetoric struck a responsive chord with a great number of average Americans. "Give 'em hell, Harry," they shouted at many of his stops. Truman, of course, did not turn things around all by himself. The Democratic National Committee eventually was successful in getting party regulars to overcome their original doubts and work hard for the ticket. Very important, too, was the aid provided by labor union officials in talking up Truman's candidacy and getting out the vote.

Ultimately Truman would surpass Dewey and achieve the greatest upset in the history of presidential elections. He would acquire 24.1 million votes to Dewey's 21.9 million. (Thurmond and Wallace combined for only 2.3 million.) Even with the two additional candidates in the field, Truman was able to put together an impressive majority in the electoral college, taking 303 votes to Dewey's 189, winning heavily in the West and South. (Thurmond carried only four states in the Deep South for a total of 39.) Actually, it turned out that Wallace and Thurmond did less damage than was expected. Wallace's criticism from the left made Truman look like the candidate of the center, and Thurmond's white-supremacy stance gave the president stronger support among blacks. In general, Truman was able to maintain much of the New Deal coalition, as many voters had not forgotten the benefits brought them by the Democrats and feared that these might be taken away by the Republicans.

Although the Truman victory provided a great deal of drama, it marked the end of an era in terms of campaign practice. The primary methods used— whistle-stop speeches, radio advertising, heavy grass-roots party and union activity—soon would recede in importance. New political attitudes, new technology, and new conditions in society would, starting in the 1950s, bring about very different vote-getting techniques.

7

The Mass Media Age

1952–88

The period after 1950 witnessed some of the biggest changes in the history of American electioneering. Although some forms of electronic technology and public relations techniques had infused earlier campaigning, such innovations as television, computers, and advanced marketing methods would in many ways revolutionize the vote-getting process. Running for office was no longer a haphazard business based primarily on intuition. It became a science, relying on detailed statistical information and complex analytical tools. Old styles of campaigning—through rallies and other events—did not disappear, but were modified and incorporated into a new strategic framework. Such a framework involved a more precise, centralized "team" strategy than had been employed in the past. It included a formal blueprint or master plan, the wider use of specialized propaganda skills, growing emphasis on the media, and a large amount of opinion measurement and manipulation. Image makers, to a further extent than before, tried to put their stamp on political contests, as candidates were sold to the public in an increasingly systematic fashion.[1]

DECLINE OF PARTIES

Equally important in altering campaign practices, and somewhat related to the above-mentioned innovations, was the declining influence of political parties, especially at the grass-roots level. To be sure, parties had lost a certain measure of power before the television age. But the last quarter of a century would see a much greater erosion of strength. Whereas most voters in past eras primarily looked to the party for information and cues for action, they now began to pay more attention to other sources. Party identification fell from about 80 percent to 60 percent by the late 1970s, as the new generation—better educated and less tradition bound—refused to accept the strictures of party loyalty. An indication of this independent-mindedness was the strong shift away from straight-ticket voting. Between 1920 and 1950 only about 15 percent of all voters split their tickets, but this figure reached 40 percent by the late 1960s and over 50 percent in 1972 before leveling off. Parties came to be seen by some as corrupt organizations in need of far-reaching reform. Yet as political scientist Martin P. Wattenberg has argued, it is not so much a case of voters becoming alienated from the parties, but rather one of voters becoming more neutral in their evaluation of them. People, he says, now view parties as less relevant to the process of resolving the major issues of the day. The growing weakness of the parties contributed to the drop in turnout from around 60 percent in the 1950s and 1960s to an average of less than 55 percent in the five national elections between 1972 and 1988.[2]

There were obviously other causes of party deterioration, one being the movement of people to the suburbs. The new suburbanites proved less likely to join party organizations than their city-dwelling forebears. Parties also suffered from a rise in nonpartisan elections and a further reduction in patronage. Even the remaining urban machines had trouble satisfying demands for jobs. But perhaps the main reason for the parties' declining influence was their loss of control over the nomination process with the proliferation of primaries. As election analyst Austin Ranney has remarked: "The primary system freed forces driving toward the disintegration of party organization."[3] When primary contests were first instituted, party professionals usually had sufficient resources to control the outcome. Now it became possible for a person to win a party's nomination without the favor of high party officials. Candidates in some states, in fact, ran against the established leadership. In 1966 Milton Shapp of Pennsylvania successfully campaigned for the Democratic gubernatorial nomination on the theme, "the man against the machine."[4] Winning no longer required the regular organization's backing because the services the traditional party offered—headquarters, canvassing apparatus, and so on—were not so essential as before. The new technical skills and financial resources necessary for a modern campaign could readily be found elsewhere.

Regarding the presidency, the expanded primary system would make it possible for someone like Jimmy Carter, little known beyond his own state of Georgia and without much connection to the national organization, to become a party's standard-bearer. Presidential primaries, instituted in several states shortly after the turn of the century, had only limited influence on candidate selection before the 1950s. Then, when as a relative outsider, Senator Estes Kefauver of Tennessee won key victories against party-backed Democrats in 1952 and 1956, it seemed apparent that someone could succeed through this channel all the way to the top. John F. Kennedy in 1960 would be the first person to secure the nomination by his showing in the primaries. Winning primaries quickly became the only way to gain the top spot on the ticket. As the number of primaries increased (to roughly thirty states by the 1980s), the vast majority of convention delegates now were chosen by the people and unalterably bound to a particular individual. Less than one-third of the delegates still remained under party control. The party's smaller role in the nomination phase gradually led to a smaller role in the general election as well.[5]

As parties lost influence in the selection process, campaigning naturally became more candidate centered. In contrast to the past when electors were exhorted to remain loyal to the party, and party accomplishments were invoked to rouse the audience, now there was less frequent mention of the party name. Republicans, for a long time outnumbered among registered voters, particularly avoided party labels and overt partisan appeals in trying to win independent and cross-over votes. Rather than leaning on the party, candidates counted on their own personal ability to create an aura of competence that could capture the imagination of the electorate.[6] Given the availability of new campaign tools, they soon found the means of developing direct voter contact without regard to party organization. They gradually reduced their dependence on the old party professional and began working with a new kind of political operative.

RISE OF CONSULTANTS

In former times long-standing party professionals were relied on for their expertise in analyzing the electorate, determining proper strategy, and mobilizing voters on election day. But as their well-worn methods proved less effective and they failed to adopt new ones, many of the old campaigners faded into the background. "The party professional," as Robert Agranoff has written, "has given way to a different type of professional—the advertising and public relations man, the management specialist, the media specialist, the pollster—who performs services for candidates based on skills he has acquired in nonpolitical fields."[7] As was discussed in chapter six, Whitaker and Baxter in California had been involved in furnishing such services as far back as the mid–1930s. Yet not until more than two decades later did the engagement of political consultants start mounting. Only twenty-five members of Congress used professional management services in 1960, but five times that many did so in 1968, and the total would rise even further in the 1970s. By 1980 more than half of the sitting congressional incumbents and 75 percent of all senatorial candidates employed consultants. Even candidates for certain local offices would come to recognize the need for outside managerial assistance.[8]

Professional campaign firms varied in their range of services. At first only a few followed in Whitaker and Baxter's footsteps by managing the entire operation. Most public relations agencies that engaged in political consulting in the 1950s did so on a part-time basis and only gave limited assistance to their clients. But as successes were achieved, more specialized agencies entered the field and the types of services expanded. In some cases the management firms employed their own experts to handle each phase, in others they hired outside professionals to perform particular jobs—purchasing media time and space, producing television commercials, preparing radio ads, designing direct-mail projects, conducting public opinion polls, running canvasses, and raising money. Not every candidate needed or could afford such a wide array of services, but these and many additional ones now were available. Although they usually did not possess a strong ideological bent, most political consultants generally worked for candidates of only one political persuasion. In time the consultants' influence reached the point where a few of them acquired as much fame as the clients they handled.[9]

One person of particular importance among the new specialists was the pollster, whose research helped the candidate make crucial decisions. Earlier in the century party organizations had conducted polls, but these usually supplied just basic information about which side was leading. The Gallup, Roper, and Crossley polls of the 1930s and 1940s did not go much further. Public opinion in regard to issues and other factors only could be guessed at. In recent years, however, pollsters like Patrick Caddell and Richard Worthlin, supplied with "hard" data from private polls they commissioned, would be able to assess several facets of the race. Modern polls told not just who was ahead but the quality of that support—strong or weak. They also could show the candidate which issues to emphasize and which ones to avoid, plus which aspects of an opponent's as well as their own platform and personality were vulnerable. Constant updating allowed the campaign staff to respond quickly to changing attitudes. By analyzing census data pollsters gained the capacity to determine the demographic makeup of particular districts. This made it possible to tailor campaign appeals to fit the interests of the area's potential voters.[10]

The proliferation of consultants and professionally managed campaigns eventually led to charges of blatant manipulation of the electorate. Many critics, responding to such exposés as Joe McGinnis's *The Selling of the President*, a revealing look at the massive media effort employed in 1968 on behalf of Richard Nixon, have claimed that the so-called experts have distorted the process by deliberately presenting false images to the voters. Yet it can be argued that there always has been some distortion in the portrayal of candidates and inevitably some limits on what could be done. As one consultant has stated: "What we cannot do is create. We can't make the voters believe that a dummy is smart, a bent man straight, a follower a leader, a bad man good."[11] In addition, it should be mentioned that the consultants on one side usually were balanced by those on the other side, and that some individuals who had greater media exposure still were defeated.

Besides high-powered consultants, a new breed of lower-level participants began to appear on the campaign team. Such workers, often referred to as "amateurs" or "purists" would be more idealistic—apt to be heavily committed to a certain cause or to the whole liberal or conservative philosophy. Some were attracted by a particular candidate and the positions he or she represented. This trend, which had started to take hold by the early 1960s, was evident even in New York City, once the domain of the powerful Tammany Hall machine. One appraisal written at the time concluded: "There is a 'new look' among today's political activists. They are 'respectable,' solid middle-class citizens. The party 'hack' of fiction, films, and the traditional literature is hard to find among the young, well-educated affluent, and socially acceptable committeemen—and women—of the nineteen-sixties. Concomitantly, both the nature of political motivation and the character of political activity have changed. The contemporary politician considers his party organization an instrument for effectuating policy rather than a haven for personal security."[12]

As a result of the decline in old-time party workers, an increasing amount of grass-roots campaigning was taken up by political action committees and volunteer groups. Some were well-established organizations such as the AFL-CIO Committee for Political Education (COPE), which performed a multiplicity of functions—for example, conducting registration drives and "get-out-the-vote" efforts. Other permanent groups such as the National Farmers Union operated within a narrower framework, offering mainly financial aid to favored figures. Along with permanent interest groups, many ad hoc associations appeared. As in earlier times they formed according to ethnicity or occupation or simply as "Citizens for Kennedy" or "Volunteers for Nixon." Some cut across party lines—"Democrats for Eisenhower" or "Republicans for Johnson." Members of these groups usually walked precincts and handed out literature, or else worked at party headquarters doing clerical chores or serving on phone banks. While the number of people contacted may not have reached the levels of previous generations, the total began picking up in the late 1970s.[13]

Many of the campaign volunteers in this era would be women. Indeed, women would play a much greater role in the electioneering process than ever before. Especially from the mid–1960s onward, as the modern feminist movement began to develop, numerous women became politicized for the first time and started working for candidates sympathetic to their goals. Although most women initially served in low-level volunteer positions, some eventually moved up to higher posts, coordinating arrangements, acting as press secretary, and even managing entire campaigns. Susan Estrich of Harvard Law School would be in charge of the Dukakis presidential effort in 1988. Moreover, as women themselves chose to run for office in considerable numbers, the totals would rise even further. (Women candidates' staffs often were heavily female.) The increased participation of women in all facets of politics also caused office seekers of both genders to place a stronger emphasis on issues of high importance to women—such as health and welfare measures. This was particularly true after 1980 voting results indicated for the first time the existence of a "gender gap."[14]

The extent of new-style campaigning—the use of professional management, advanced technology, and "amateur" volunteers rather than old-time party apparatus and personnel—varied according to the level of office involved. Candidates running for statewide posts that required a large-scale campaign effort, such as governor or senator, were more likely to employ consultants and purchase the kinds of services they provided than candidates for city, county, and state legislative positions. The latter generally found the new techniques too expensive for their smaller needs. Indeed, a two-tiered system has developed whereby nominees for lesser offices continued to use several traditional methods of vote-getting—canvassing the district, making public appearances, distributing printed material, gaining endorsements from business, labor, and civic groups, and providing favors for constituents. Of course, there were no hard and fast lines, and many local office seekers engaged consultants for certain aspects of their campaign, for instance, undertaking polls, but generally they relied on older forms and the old party organizations.[15]

Although regular parties at the grass-roots level declined to a certain extent, they still retained some importance at election time. For local partisan races, especially those in which the candidates were not well known, the party label continued to carry some weight among the voters. During campaigns in most areas members of party organizations went on providing many of the usual services, signing up and contacting voters, albeit on a lesser scale. On the national scene too, the parties attempted to make a comeback. The Republicans especially (perhaps because of their minority position among registered voters) made a substantial effort to rebuild their party's internal structure. Regional directors were appointed to work with local leaders about upgrading the institutional apparatus. Better recruitment of candidates and training of staffs took place. Large amounts of money from national headquarters poured into state legislative races. Managerial assistance and other resources were offered to congressional candidates. Notwithstanding these moves to revitalize the parties, the focus often was on applying the new campaign tools to the party framework.[16]

IMPACT OF TELEVISION

By far the most significant campaign tool, indeed lately the most significant factor in campaigning, was television. Television, which came into mass use in the 1950s, drastically altered the nature of American political campaigns. Overshadowing all other sources of news, it provided the electorate with most of the information they received about a contest. It exposed more people to elections than had been exposed previously. However, while viewers gained awareness of both sides' arguments, substantive matters often were trivialized or ignored. One- or two-sentence answers to complex questions became the norm. Most attention was devoted to the candidates' personalities, not to the opinions they held. Regardless of their limitations, personable candidates who conveyed a likeable manner on the TV screen would have a greater chance of success than otherwise capable individuals who did not come across well. Whatever the shortcomings of the new medium, the public got a closer look at the candidates than ever before, and especially at their private lives. For better or for worse, politicians began to lose some of their mystique as the camera constantly followed them around.[17]

Over the years candidates and their staffs employed many different television formats to reach prospective voters. At first they purchased air time to present traditional speeches—broadcasted live, and usually fifteen minutes to a half hour in length. But a "talking head" giving an address not always was effective in attracting and holding an entertainment-conscious audience. Late in the 1952 presidential race, the Republicans introduced a new concept, the spot commercial: a brief thirty-second or one-minute appearance by the candidate on film. The initial versions, prepared by Madison Avenue advertising expert Rosser Reeves, were rather straight forward, not too sophisticated or elaborately designed. They featured General Eisenhower, the party nominee, responding to simple questions asked by average citizens. For example: Questioner—"Mr. Eisenhower, what about the high cost of living?" Eisenhower—"My wife Mamie worries about the same thing. I tell her it's our job to change that on November 4th." Other spot commercials over the next decade were fairly similar in style, with the candidate facing the camera and delivering a short statement.

Besides spot commercials, media consultants in national campaigns began putting together five- to ten-minute "trailers" (so-called because they usually were scheduled at the end of a slightly curtailed regular program). These productions sometimes tried to display the candidate in an informal atmosphere. The Democrats brought out one entitled, "The Man from Libertyville," which had Adlai Stevenson standing outside his small-town Illinois home helping his son and daughter-in-law with the groceries and then stopping to make a speech. Another new development was the staged conversation or panel show. On such a program the nominee would "converse" with typical Americans on prearranged topics as a means of helping him explain his position. One variation had the candidate engaged in a discussion with a prominent figure—for instance, Barry Goldwater talking with former president Eisenhower in 1964—in an attempt to reassure voters that Goldwater was not going to destroy the social security system or start a nuclear war.

The mid–1960s saw the triumph of the spot commercial and in them the beginnings of a more subtle and manipulative form of advertising. Sometimes startling pseudo-events were created to play on the viewer's emotions. The candidate would not be seen and often not even heard. The most controversial production was the anti-Goldwater commercial known as "Daisy," designed by media expert Tony Schwartz. In it a young girl picks petals from a daisy, counting them as she goes along. Then a harsh background voice begins a countdown ending with a nuclear explosion. Next, as a mushroom cloud is shown rising, the voice of Lyndon Johnson exclaims: "These are the stakes: to make a world in which all of God's children can live or go into the dark. We must love each other or we must die." Last, an announcer declares: "Vote for President Johnson on November 3rd. The stakes are too high for you to stay home." So much protest occurred after its initial airing that it was withdrawn by the networks, though it was replayed on several newscasts. Some commercials for Goldwater, Nixon, and Wallace (1964 and 1968) graphically focused on crime and other urban problems. A few displayed scenes of destruction and decay in the nation's cities, implying that such conditions were the fault of the Johnson administration and would only improve after the Democrats were ousted.

By the 1970s media experts had moved television advertising in a more artistic direction, frequently injecting colorful backgrounds, modern music, as well as the latest in graphics and other high-technology methods. While spot commercials continued to be the dominant mode, a few alternative forms appeared. Borrowing to some degree from the earlier "conversation" format, semidocumentaries were filmed which showed the candidate discussing a particular issue with different groups of people—blue-collar workers, small businesspeople, senior citizens. In 1976 President Ford's reelection committee composed an upbeat feature called "I'm Feelin' Good About America," which displayed a number of patriotic images—the Statue of Liberty, marching bands, American flags—subtly seeking to connect them with the man in the White House. In that and other campaigns media people staged "man in the street" interviews where several average-looking individuals appeared on camera, one after another, and briefly told why they were supporting a particular candidate.

In later years television would be utilized in some new ways. Incumbent congressional candidates would benefit from free advertising through "video feeds," whereby representatives in Washington would film their reactions to national events and have them made available to local stations back home. Cable channels would begin to be employed for campaign purposes, as they could target specific audiences. Mainstream television advertising would continue along more or less established lines, though greater emphasis was placed on an individual's character and values. Candidates often would be shown in casual settings at home (to indicate concern for family) or behind a desk at the office (to represent them as hard workers). Also, there would be an increase in negative campaign spots, focusing on the opponent's alleged shortcomings. But whether campaign commercials truly influenced the electors' evaluations of the nominees was debatable. In regard to high offices it has been argued that commercials simply reinforce already existing views and that people see in them what they wish to see. However, several studies have indicated that commercials do have a good deal of influence on campaigns for lower offices where the competitors are less well known. This is especially true where a well-crafted, heavily financed ad campaign is virtually unchallenged.

Perhaps the most compelling and dramatic contribution of television to the campaign process was the institution of the joint debate. Although a few direct exchanges between candidates had taken place on the radio—for example, Thomas Dewey had faced challenger Harold Stassen during the Oregon Republican primary in 1948—television made these into major theatrical events, indeed, the highlight of each race. Nationally, the meetings of the two parties' standard-bearers attracted tremendous public attention—over 100 million viewers in recent years—and in some cases were looked upon as a turning point. The Nixon–Kennedy debates in 1960, which inaugurated the TV encounters, were the best example. Face-to-face confrontations were avoided by front-runners Johnson and Nixon in 1964 and in 1972, but they became more or less fully established in the last several national elections beginning with Ford and Carter in 1976. Careful planning went into the debates, the candidates spending considerable time in preparation, even to the point of rehearsing with stand-ins. The television debates would be condemned by certain critics for their press conference format and for focusing on style rather than substance. Even so, the debates gave the public a chance to see the nominees for an extended period of time, under some stress, in a situation where they and their staffs were not in control. As time passed, televised debates spread to many state and local elections as well.[18]

As television became the most important advertising medium for office seekers beginning in the 1950s, radio was utilized less and less frequently. The 1952 presidential campaign would be the last in which radio expenditures roughly equalled those for TV. After that funds for radio programming continually diminished; in 1980 the outlay for radio was surpassed by an eight to one ratio. Yet some national as well as local candidates continued to make use of radio for spot announcements and speeches. Republican presidential nominees from Barry Goldwater to Ronald Reagan would find the medium particularly conducive to discussion of individual issues. Richard Nixon, who came across much better on radio than on television, delivered several topical addresses during the last weeks of both the 1968 and 1972 campaigns. Radio offered certain advantages over other medias. It was much cheaper—less than a third of the cost of television advertising—and could be targeted to more specific audiences.[19]

Newspapers also would have less impact on election campaigns than in the past. The number of daily papers published continued to decline. Many cities had just one remaining daily, which often would take an independent stance. Party papers were now a rarity. By the mid–1960s most people received the majority of their political information from television. Despite this trend the press retained a significant place in the electioneering process. Even though people most frequently learned about day-to-day events from television, a majority still read a daily newspaper and probably formed many of their opinions from the latter source. In general, newspapers supplied more in-depth coverage, as reporters wrote frequent and lengthy stories about major contests. Closer to home, where the average person was less aware of each candidate's qualifications, it was the local press that provided such data. Moreover, editorial endorsement by an influential newspaper often was pivotal in determining the outcome of state and local races.[20]

PRINTED MATTER AND MATERIAL OBJECTS

Still fairly common, especially on the state and local levels, was the distribution of various printed materials. In the 1960s about one-fourth of the expenditures by congressional candidates went for the printing and mailing of pamphlets and leaflets. By the 1970s members of Congress and state legislators depended more on periodic newsletters to keep their constituents informed of their activities, thus subtly aiding their reelection bids.[21] In addition, this era also would see the extensive use of the "direct mail" approach in the form of personalized letters. Whereas some candidates earlier in the century had sent letters to advertise themselves through the mail, the practice was considered expensive and of questionable value. Many such items, it was said, were thrown away unread. However, with the creation of the computer-generated letter, it became possible, through the identification of the voter's background, residence, occupation, and issue concerns, to put together paragraphs that appealed to several of their interests. The personalized stationery and signature helped, too. Also, many office seekers started to send out personally addressed "votergrams," which resembled telegrams, reminding the recipient to vote and offering assistance to those who had difficulty reaching the polling place.[22]

Campaign buttons continued to be popular electioneering devices at least down to the early 1970s. Their styles changed, however. Compared to former creations, more emphasis was placed on the candidate's name than face. Although numerous buttons contained slogans such as "I Like Ike," there were fewer satiric statements than in the past. To be sure, some clever phrases like "Goldwater in '64, hot water in '65," would appear in the 1960s, but this was a far cry from the output of previous decades. By the mid–1970s the major parties came to feel that buttons constituted too great an expense for the value they provided, and they began distributing fewer of them. In many instances thereafter, partisans had to pay cash to obtain them. While buttons declined, other display items once in limited use—bumper stickers, transit advertisements, billboards, and lawn signs—would be exhibited in increasing quantities. Generally they contained just the nominee's name and the office being sought. Inexpensive to produce, such materials proved valuable in helping candidates achieve name recognition.[23]

NATIONAL CAMPAIGNS

National campaigns in this era would become exceedingly drawn out as a consequence of the expanded primary system. Indeed, on the day after one presidential contest had ended, the next one was said to have begun. After lining up an initial core of support, those seeking the nation's highest office would have to spend more than a year or two on the road. They would use this time to raise money, build an organization, and meet prospective voters, particularly in the early caucus and primary states like Iowa, New Hampshire, Florida, and Wisconsin. Then came several months of nonstop campaigning in the primary encounters themselves, where each competitor hoped to capture the popular imagination. Presidential campaigns would be compared to marathon races where only those with tremendous stamina (plus a tight-knit organization, heavy financial backing, and an abundance of luck) could survive. The long primary competition resulted in many casualties and a divisiveness that often plagued the party in the general election. But there seemed to be no alternative for someone who wished to become the standard-bearer. No longer could a candidate successfully play a waiting game and hope to be selected by the party convention. After 1952 all those who received their party's nomination already had gained enough support beforehand to be chosen on the first ballot; the convention simply served to ratify the preconvention choice.[24]

With the candidate already chosen, the convention's main function was to instill spirit among the party faithful and, if there had been a grueling primary struggle, to heal all wounds in order to create a semblance of unity for the general election ahead. One important step was to have former adversaries embrace the nominee and his basic position. Sometimes this was achieved by offering one of them the vice presidency, for example, John Kennedy choosing Lyndon Johnson as his running mate in 1960. But in many cases the differences could not be resolved and bitterness lingered. Fights developed over numerous matters, especially the content of the party platform. The most extreme situation occurred at the Democratic convention in 1968, where followers of Robert Kennedy and Eugene McCarthy who opposed the Johnson administration's stance on the Vietnam War became so angered that they later withheld their support from the party ticket headed by Hubert Humphrey. To avoid such problems some candidates like Gerald Ford in 1976 and Jimmy Carter in 1980 would allow former rivals in the primaries to prevail on certain disputed provisions in the platform. In fact, the platform increasingly served as an integrative device "bringing about harmony among factions and cementing their allegiance to the party."[25]

The national conventions were held later in the summer than in previous eras (preferably at the end of August), on the theory that voters might lose interest if the gathering took place too early. In the television age campaign timing became extremely important. For this reason it was necessary to curb the use of one's financial resources and personnel at the outset so as not to exhaust them too quickly. In addition, managers sought to "pace" their candidates in the same manner as race horses, aiming to have them "peak" at just the right moment—shortly before the balloting. The number and kinds of appearances were regulated carefully with a marked increase taking place as election day neared. Certain themes were stressed in initial statements to the media and then abandoned for stronger ones. Generally, candidates began by emphasizing their own positions and followed with attacks on their opponent's positions, before finally concentrating on their vision for the future, which simply reiterated ideas first presented in their acceptance speech at the party convention.[26]

One major change, somewhat connected to the decline of parties, was the reduced role of the national committee and national chairman. Although Eisenhower and Stevenson depended primarily on the regular party apparatus as late as 1956, candidates beginning with John F. Kennedy in 1960 usually preferred to operate through their own handpicked organizations. Having relied on personal appointees in the primaries, they left in charge those whom they considered firmly loyal and devoted to the cause. The candidate's staff, which swelled in size (Nixon had 337 paid staffers in 1972), handled many of the same tasks as the national committee—appointing regional and state coordinators, contacting local officials to arrange events— and tried to work in conjunction with it. By and large the new system would be fairly effective, but in some cases a conflict of authority would occur. In addition, there would be problems of overlapping and adjustment between the newly selected campaign staffers and longtime party personnel.[27]

Together with the dependence on the personal staff came the growing use of the candidate's family. While wives and others formerly had gone along on tours, separate appearances had been rare and not viewed very favorably. However, as a result of the increase in primaries, the personalization of politics, and the gradual acceptance of women as campaigners, it seemed only natural that family members should serve as surrogates. The large Kennedy clan in 1960 was the first to act in this fashion, having sisters and brothers as well as mother Rose traveling around or hosting events on behalf of Jack. By the time of the Ford–Carter contest in 1976, numerous relatives of both standard-bearers were out on the hustings expressing their opinions. Of course not everyone was happy with this situation. A *Time* magazine article that year noted that elections were beginning "to sound like Book CXXXV of 'One Man's Family' " and obscuring the candidate's own message.[28] Yet as long as kinfolk could extend the nominee's message far beyond what he or she could achieve alone, the proliferation of family members on the campaign trail would continue.

Presidential campaigns came to be much more carefully coordinated than in the past. Although the Roosevelt era had seen the start of the public relations approach and a higher degree of efficiency, the campaigns run by James Farley in the 1930s were still somewhat opportunistic and without a definite plan. There was as yet no regularly functioning strategy board, no set agenda for organizational activity, no detailed daily schedule. When Roosevelt made a preelection trip, decisions about what should be said, who should ride on the train, and who should appear on the speaker's platform, sometimes were made only at the last minute. But beginning with Eisenhower's bid in 1952, one finds the adoption of a formal plan or "blueprint" approach to politics. For Ike's "kick-off" speech in Philadelphia's Independence Hall on September 4, a thirty-nine-page set of instructions was prepared. It covered everything down to the smallest detail—the distribution of noisemakers, flags, and programs—and even mentioned the way the candidate should place himself so that he could be photographed with his right hand on the Liberty Bell. Subsequent events that year and after would be arranged in a similarly exacting fashion.[29]

Not only daily activities, but overall campaign strategy would be worked out in a more precise manner. The nature of the appeals to be made, the types of advertising to be used, and the kinds of areas to be visited were never handled casually again. The candidates increasingly concentrated their energies on the most populous states—New York, Ohio, Illinois, Pennsylvania, Texas, and California—and since the South was no longer so solid for the Democrats, they paid considerable attention to that section. But the whole plan was determined to a large degree by up-to-date polling information as the campaign managers sought to pinpoint the places (or "markets") in which to devote the most resources. In 1976, Hamilton Jordan, in charge of Jimmy Carter's election team, prepared a memorandum that used a mathematical formula to work out each state's total allocation. Points were given according to size and Democratic potential, the latter based on existing party control of offices plus previous presidential turnout figures. A "percent of effort" of the whole campaign was allotted to each state; California, for example, received 6.9 percent. Then Jordan assigned a numerical value to the contribution of a day's campaigning by the candidate himself, by the vice presidential nominee, and by each member of their families. Finally, he calculated how much time each one should spend in a particular state.[30]

Of course it would be one thing to formulate a precisely detailed campaign strategy, another to carry it out. Sometimes campaign organizations were insufficient to make the plan fully operative. Organizational efficiency would not always be easy to achieve in a short time span. A further problem was a shortage of funds. The Democrats, in particular, lacked the money to undertake a strong "media blitz" at times. Frequently the issues that the strategists selected did not take hold with the public. Walter Mondale's call for a tax increase during the 1984 presidential contest alienated many potential supporters. Occasionally circumstances beyond the candidate's control (the taking of hostages in Iran in 1979–80) altered the focus of attention. In certain years too, gaffes and faux pas ruined the best of plans—George McGovern's statements surrounding the choice of Senator Thomas Eagleton as his running mate in 1972 being the clearest example.

The attempt to achieve precision-like campaigning brought importance to the role of the "advance men." (Actually, by the 1980s, some of them would be women.) These were members of the candidate's staff who traveled to future stops on the campaign schedule a few days or a week before the candidate's arrival to prepare for the impending event. Instead of depending entirely on local officials to take care of the details and certify that everything would happen according to plan, the advance man was given primary responsibility. It was his or her duty to check out the route to and from the planned event, look into any problems involving transportation, and examine the site of the event itself to determine whether facilities were adequate. If the candidate was to stay overnight, the advance man would investigate the proposed hotel accommodations and make meal plans. In many cases the advance man recommended alterations or arranged for backup equipment—a second car or public-address system. The advance man also worked with local leaders to deliver enthusiastic crowds and assured that the needs of the media contingent would be met.[31]

As was true before, there would be a difference between the campaign style of the incumbent or in-party and that of the challenger or out-party. The incumbent usually was better known and had more clearly understood issue positions. Therefore, it often benefited the candidate to play the role of the "statesman" and claim to be "too busy" to go out on the road very much. Because television normally gave presidential activities a good deal of publicity anyway, most incumbents, especially since 1972, spent a lot of time following what came to be called the "rose garden" strategy, employing the White House rose garden as a place to greet dignitaries, sign bills, and make announcements while the cameras recorded each event. The incumbent also increasingly used the prerogatives of the office, distributing patronage and offering financial aid to certain doubtful states. Challengers tried to counter the sitting president's advantages by criticizing the vulnerable parts of the incumbent's record and promising to do a better job if elected. Non-incumbents generally would travel and speak more frequently to get their names and positions known to the public.

The development of the jet-propelled airplane markedly changed the nature of presidential campaigning. The "campaign special" train of previous eras had allowed a candidate to "whistle-stop" slowly through a state and see thousands of well-wishers over the course of a week or so. But the new jet aircraft enabled the candidate to travel two to three thousand miles and see hundreds of thousands of supporters in a single day. Eisenhower in 1952 would be the last nominee to ride the rails extensively. To be sure, whistle-stopping briefly was used by some later candidates as a novelty, yet the chief mode of transportation after 1952 was the airplane. By the 1960s special planes equipped with press facilities regularly carried large entourages across the country. Campaign managers would schedule perhaps a breakfast meeting in New York, a midday press conference in Chicago, an afternoon speech in Kansas City, and an evening rally in San Francisco. Adding on local television and newspaper coverage, there was greater public exposure than had ever been possible before. Indeed the widespread media coverage proved more beneficial than the crowds present at each site, causing the candidates to accommodate media production schedules and sometimes provide media representatives with needed facilities.[32]

The airplane together with the growing importance of nightly TV network news in the 1970s eventually led campaign staffs to try to arrange "media events," that is, candidate appearances having a strong visual attraction. In planning such occasions staffers were not so concerned about displaying large numbers of people as in creating something eye-catching that in some way reflected the nominee's interests—a visit to a semi-automated factory or a stop at a wildlife preserve—and that was desirable fare for the evening news. (A few state and local candidates would walk across their entire district or make a dramatic entrance to a campaign site by balloon or parachute to draw media coverage.) This was, of course, free advertising and more effective than paid advertising because the message was somewhat subliminal. By the time of the 1976 presidential contest, media events dominated the candidates' daily schedules. As Jules Witcover has described it in his book *Marathon*: "Engineering 'free media' became the highest political art form. Getting the candidate on the network evening news was the *sine qua non* of each day's plan; everything else revolved around that objective. The bare arithmetics of campaigning in the television era—obtaining street crowds numbering tens of thousands at the very most, with perhaps a hundred or so actually shaking the candidate's hand, as opposed to the millions watching Cronkite or Chancellor or Walters—was overwhelmingly persuasive."[33]

If it had not been true before, certainly by the 1970s presidential campaigns had in essence become mass media campaigns. In fact, according to media analyst Thomas E. Patterson, for the "large majority of voters, the campaign has little reality apart from its media version." This represented a sharp contrast with the golden age of parties, when there was much deeper personal involvement. Moreover, in contrast to an earlier view which claimed that the media do not affect already well-established voter attitudes, studies by Patterson and others have shown that while the media may not directly change people's views, they can influence perceptions that may result in behavior modification. The media have "tremendous power in determining which news events, which candidates, and which issues are to be covered in any given day. Thus, a candidate's campaign must be focused, in large measure, around those sorts of issues, photographic opportunities, and events that will draw media attention." Perhaps equally important, certain subjects that did not fit into this framework were ignored. Increasingly, events that were visually appealing plus the "horse-race" aspects of the campaign—who was ahead in the polls and by how much—formed the bulk of preelection news programming.[34]

Although media events emphasizing the visual dominated what the public saw of the nominee, traditional speechmaking still went on in some form. In fact at most campaign stops, candidates gave a short speech—a "set" or "stock" speech, which varied only slightly according to the locality. A set speech was one that evolved over the course of the campaign, containing a few basic ideas—eliminate corruption, trim the bureaucracy, improve defense—plus certain applause lines aimed at sparking enthusiasm among the listeners. In the latter vein George McGovern in 1972, appealing to the average American, mentioned that businesspeople could take a tax write-off for a three-martini restaurant meal, but ordinary workers could not deduct the cost of the bologna sandwich in their lunchbox. Candidates also continued to deliver a few major addresses on key policy matters. These addresses would be prepared carefully with the aid of advisers and speechwriters, each position paper going through several drafts before completion. Presentations would occur at major party functions and sometimes be shown to party supporters nationwide on closed-circuit television.[35]

In attempting to sell their candidates through the media, campaign managers and consultants sought more than ever to develop a general theme that would capture the essence of the campaign. Some coined slogans that revolved around specific issues. Others made general calls to action, such as John F. Kennedy's "We've got to get the nation moving again" (1960). Campaigners still would evoke the images of past heroes, though only the Democrats, having the majority of registrants, would connect their candidates with their own party's tradition. Thus John F. Kennedy said that he stood "where Woodrow Wilson stood, and Franklin Roosevelt stood, and Harry Truman stood."[36] Republicans, being in the minority, often ignored party labels and rarely mentioned past Republicans. Interestingly, Ronald Reagan, though at the other end of the political spectrum from the New Deal, invoked the names of Franklin Roosevelt and his immediate successors, claiming that recent Democratic leaders "had abandoned the good and decent Democrats of the JFK, FDR, and Harry Truman condition."[37]

CAMPAIGN FINANCE

The cost of campaigns would rise precipitously in this period—more than twice as fast as the Consumer Price Index—after several decades of relatively slow growth. The total for all campaigns nationwide was $140 million in 1952, $300 million in 1968, and $1 billion in 1980. On the presidential level, where expenditures averaged between $5 million and $6 million during the

1930s and 1940s, the figures doubled in the 1950s ($11 million to $12 million) and then rapidly multiplied in the late 1960s and early 1970s. The Nixon–Humphrey–Wallace contest in 1968 surpassed $40 million, while the Nixon–McGovern encounter in 1972 went above $90 million. The lengthening of the election process through the expansion of primaries was one major reason for the rising costs. McGovern, for example, had to lay out $9 million simply to obtain his party's nomination. The heavy expense for polling and other consultants' fees represented another factor. But clearly the chief cause was the enormously high price of electronic campaigning—not only for airtime but for the huge production costs. Nixon's and Humphrey's backers in 1968 allocated almost $20 million for media advertising—roughly half their total budget. Amounts were even higher in subsequent election years.[38]

Presidential campaigns were not the only ones to become increasingly costly. In the mid–1970s the typical seeker of a House seat spent more than $100,000, while those vying for a place in the Senate had to raise nearly $1 million. By 1980 the average House winner spent $177,000, the average victorious U.S. Senator $1.2 million. During the 1980s the House figure would double and the Senate figure would more than triple. Gubernatorial contests in some of the larger states such as Texas, California, and New York went way beyond the million-dollar mark. Democrat Hugh Carey, in seeking the governorship of New York in 1974, spent close to $4 million. Meanwhile, Republican Lewis Lehrman, a wealthy drugstore magnate, spent three times that amount in trying (unsuccessfully) to defeat Mario Cuomo for that office in 1982. The California gubernatorial race in 1986 would cost the two participants in the neighborhood of $20 million.[39] Of course not all congressional and gubernatorial campaigns were that expensive. Some heavily favored incumbents such as Senator William Proxmire in Wisconsin used only a bare minimum for their reelection bids. (Proxmire claimed he spent only a small sum, for postage, in 1982.) Yet it became the practice in many places even for sure-winners to raise and spend a lot of money in order to gain big victories so as to discourage future competitors. Naturally, fund-raising had to be stepped up to immense levels to satisfy those needs.

For presidential contests the growing decentralization of the nation's financial power required a much wider-ranging effort than before. "Big-time money raisers came into their own in the 1952 election," wrote one expert, "men who knew better than others a particular source of funds and how to milk it dry. The days when one man could cover Wall Street, and not concern himself seriously with other sources or areas, were over."[40] Each party came to depend on a group of individuals who had contacts not only in New York, but all around the country—and particularly in the affluent states of Texas and California—among bankers, oilmen, real estate developers, union leaders, and others in high places who could be tapped for substantial contributions. During the next two decades, large donations remained the prime source of funds in presidential campaigns; businesspeople and professionals of various kinds primarily supported the Republicans, labor organizations and a few wealthy philanthropists backed Democrats. In 1968, 15,000 donors gave $500 or more, and 424 of those individuals gave at least $10,000, with the majority of the money going to the Republicans. Richard Nixon accepted an estimated $8 million from 285 "fat cats" in that year.

While fund-raising among "fat cats" continued, there were renewed attempts by the parties to obtain money through smaller contributions to reduce dependence on a few large donors. A "Dollars for Democrats" drive was undertaken in the late 1950s, though without very positive results; more successful was the GOP effort initiated in the early 1960s by William S. Warner, executive director of the Republican National Committee. At Warner's request the National Committee began soliciting ten-dollar memberships among persons whose names appeared on several commercial mailing lists. The appeal brought in $700,000 in 1962 and over $1 million in 1963. The Goldwater presidential campaign in 1964 was based to a considerable extent on small or moderate-sized contributions—approximately 650,000 people each gave $100 or less for a total of $5.8 million. George Wallace's third-party bid in 1968 attracted an even greater number of grass-roots supporters—750,000 individuals contributed small sums amounting to roughly $5 million or 76 percent of all the income he received.[41]

The direct-mail approach, aimed at bringing in small contributions, was raised to an even greater height in the 1972 presidential contest, especially in the George McGovern campaign. Senator McGovern had acquired numerous lists of names of people who had given money to liberal causes and, after consulting with direct-mail expert Morris Dees of Alabama, sent out a lengthy letter to those on the lists, discussing his ideas and calling for funds. A heavy response, far beyond expectations, enabled McGovern to accumulate $3 million in the preconvention period—helping him to secure the nomination—and $12 million in the general campaign, at a cost of about $4.5 million (for printing, postage, and related expenses). So successful was this venture that direct-mail solicitation among low-level contributors became the chief means of fund-raising by the 1976 primaries. Democrat Jimmy Carter, who sent out over a million letters, and Republicans Gerald Ford and Ronald Reagan, who proceeded more selectively, all followed this method. Around that time some congressional and senatorial candidates began using direct-mail procedures, too. Senator Jesse Helms of North Carolina and other conservatives, aided by mass-mail specialist Richard Viguerie, would raise enormous "war chests" for their campaigns.[42]

Besides direct-mail solicitation, party leaders continued to sponsor fund-raising dinners and other events to gain financial support. Ten-dollar to one-hundred-dollar-a-plate dinners were given to aid local and statewide office seekers, while one-hundred to one-thousand-dollar affairs were set up for national candidates. In just one evening shortly before the Democratic convention in 1976, Jimmy Carter raised $415 thousand dollars by attending a series of parties where people had paid up to a thousand dollars each to meet the prospective nominee. To entice contributors, celebrities from the sports and entertainment world often appeared with the candidate at these occasions. In addition, musical performers sometimes were persuaded to give special concerts to raise money for a particular candidate. By the late 1970s major campaigns would not be complete without folk, rock, pop, or country-western singers present at big political gatherings. Telethons, previously limited to health-related causes, became another device used by the parties to obtain funds. Beginning in 1972 national and regional telethons were held not only to help current campaigners but to pay off past debts.[43]

Owing to the large upsurge in fund-raising activities from the late 1960s onward and to growing public concern not just about the high amounts but about certain questionable practices being used, Congress began investigating the matter and put forth several reforms. In 1971 it passed the Federal Election Campaign Act (FECA), which tightened disclosure and reporting requirements for federal office seekers and initiated curbs on candidate contributions to their own campaigns. Three years later, after revelations of shady campaign activities surfaced in the Watergate hearings, much more stringent legislation was approved. The campaign law of 1974, subsequently amended in 1976 and 1979, stipulated that all contributions above $200 must be reported. Individuals were to be limited to donations of $1,000 to a single candidate, $20,000 to a national party committee, and $5,000 to other political committees; the total could not exceed $25,000 in any one year. However, state and local party committees had few limits on spending at the grassroots level, and in 1976 the Supreme Court ruled in *Buckley v. Valeo* that no restrictions could be placed on the amount of personal funds an office seeker could spend on his or her own campaign. Clearly the biggest reform introduced was the federal financing of presidential contests. The law permitted each side $20 million, plus an inflation allowance, which curbed spending to well below the 1972 level. Yet in looking at the 1980 contest, it can be seen that both major-party nominees spent far more than the $29.4 million granted by the federal government to each of them. Carter spent $53.9 million, Reagan $64.3 million, with much of the additional funding coming from state and local committees and from the newly emerging political action committees.[44]

Political action committees (PACs) were, in fact, becoming a major force in campaign finance, and in national politics in general, by this time. As legislation in the mid–1970s had begun restricting the amounts individuals could give directly to a candidate, more and more contributions would be funneled through political action committees. Such committees, established on a limited basis decades earlier, enabled corporations, labor unions, and other interest groups to set up special funds to finance the campaigns of preferred candidates. Now, with fewer alternatives available, this source would be more widely used. Under rulings by the Federal Elections Commission in 1975–76, PACs could collect up to $5,000 from each member and

contribute $5,000 per candidate at each election. They also would be free
to donate unlimited amounts to campaigns, though not directly to the candidate. Narrow ideological organizations such as the National Conservative
Political Action Committee (NCPAC), supported by heavy direct-mail funding, would develop enormous clout through this arrangement. They often
purchased large amounts of advertising aimed at defeating certain targeted
individuals without formally collaborating with those being assisted. The
overall number of PACs would increase tremendously—from 608 in 1974 to
1,653 in 1978, 3,371 in 1982, and 4,157 in 1986. They would raise untold
millions of dollars, most of it going to congressional candidates. In 1986
PACs poured an unprecedented $139.4 million into House and Senate cam-
paigns; about two-thirds of the money was designated for incumbents who,
according to statistics, were more likely to be elected and to exert influence
on legislation. Indeed, by the late 1980s, PAC money would help make it
possible for more than ninety percent of incumbent members of Congress
to be reelected each time.[45]

More than ever before, money was an essential ingredient for campaign
success, "the mother's milk of politics," according to a phrase originally
coined by the late California Democrat Jesse Unruh. The candidates who
acquired and spent the greatest amounts usually came out victorious. In
1978, for example, winners outspent their rivals in 26 of 30 Senate races,
and in recent presidential elections the heavier spenders have triumphed most
of the time. However, it is difficult to demonstrate that the bigger spenders
won because of the money factor alone—indeed, many long-term incumbents
attracted money because of their popularity. Moreover, it would be hard to
prove that these individuals would have lost if their opponents had superior
financial support. It is highly doubtful, for example, that Jimmy Carter would
have beaten Ronald Reagan in 1980 even with a few more million dollars.
(Actually, in comparing just the purchase of media time, Carter seems to
have outspent Reagan, yet he wound up losing in a landslide.) Several cases
can be shown in which simply spending lots of money did not automatically
produce an abundance of votes. In the most prominent instance, Texan John
Connally funneled millions into his 1980 Republican primary bid and did
not obtain a single delegate.[46]

Although a great deal of money would be spent on campaigns, especially
on television, and recent elections increasingly would involve the creation of
images, it should be realized that issues were not neglected. Indeed, it can
be argued that with the higher levels of education and public awareness,
there was more concern about issues than at most times in the past. To
maintain that Dwight Eisenhower, Richard Nixon, and Ronald Reagan each
won two elections simply because they outspent their rivals, produced slicker
television commercials, and were "better packaged" is misleading. Voters
responded not only to their perceptions of the candidates, but to the issues
and general programs these men espoused. And while the political parties

may have lost influence, they still stood in the public mind as the embodiment of certain philosophies of government. In addition, many people at election time continued to react as members of long-standing interest groups. They often voted because of a class, sexual, ethnic, or religious affiliation. The candidate's personal appeal and the way he was presented to the people were indeed factors but not necessarily overwhelming factors.

THE PARTIES

The two major parties began the 1950s possessing primarily the same outlooks and bases of support that had existed since the New Deal. On the Democratic side, the Truman–Stevenson following mirrored the Roosevelt coalition, with strong backing among organized labor, Catholics, Jews, northern blacks, and white southerners. The Democrats still opposed the power of Wall Street and the great corporations and appealed mainly to people of lower and middle income. In foreign policy, they continued to pursue Wilson's and Roosevelt's goal of fostering internationalism. The Democrats wished to strengthen the United Nations and sought cooperation among the big powers, though during both the Truman and Kennedy–Johnson regimes, they would become deeply engaged in armed conflict in Asia.

The Republicans, though they had come to accept some New Deal reforms, remained opposed to an expanded central government, especially the kind employed by the Democrats for social welfare and regulatory purposes. The Republicans supported big business and believed in a government sympathetic to free enterprise, not one that restrained it. Theirs was still the party of Middle America—white Anglo-Saxon Protestant America—and traditional values. In regard to foreign affairs, they were wary of internationalism and less apt to seek cooperation with major adversaries. Yet it was the leadership of this basically conservative party that later came to extend diplomatic relations to Communist China and achieve détente with the Soviet Union.

Over the years most of these attitudes and attachments would remain the same. Nevertheless, there would be a few significant shifts. By the mid–1960s, as the Democrats took a stronger stand on civil rights and enhanced their appeal among blacks, they gradually lost favor among southern whites. (Indeed, two-party competition would develop in the South for the first time since Reconstruction.) Then, as the party pursued policies beneficial to blacks, many Catholics and Jews, longtime cogs in the urban machine, began switching sides. At the same time, some affluent Americans who previously had been attached to the GOP would, because of its conservative foreign policy and social views, start moving toward the Democratic position. In the 1980s the Republicans had their largest following in the so-called Sunbelt of the South and West, while the Democratic strongholds were in the older states of the Northeast, a major reversal from the FDR era.[47]

In their appeals for votes the Democrats would be most successful when stressing domestic, particularly "bread-and-butter" issues. The perpetuation of the New Deal philosophy of government aid helped them to be seen as the "party of the workingman." The Republicans, despite the passage of time, remained somewhat tainted as the "party of the depression" or the "party of the rich." Yet by 1980, as the Carter administration encountered difficulty handling high inflation and interest rates, the Republicans were able to find increasing support for their conservative economic views. However, the GOP often would do better emphasizing foreign policy and defense matters. Although their side took a stronger anticommunist stand, called for heavier defense spending, and used harsher rhetoric against America's external foes, the Republicans were looked on as more likely to keep the peace than the Democrats. The latter had become stigmatized for having held the presidency during all the foreign wars that the United States fought during the twentieth century. The Republicans also would gain votes in the 1960s and thereafter by focusing on the "law-and-order" issue as well as on such causes as opposition to school busing for the purpose of achieving racial integration and support for school prayer.[48]

Minor parties played a smaller political role than in the past, perhaps owing somewhat to the general decline of parties. Yet a few individuals who ran as "third-party candidates" had considerable influence in presidential elections. The most important of these was Governor George Wallace of Alabama, who tried to capitalize on the "white backlash" against racial integration. Wallace did not campaign openly on the basis of race, but he used such terms as "law and order" to get his message across. Another independent with a specific cause was Senator Eugene McCarthy of Minnesota, who first ran as an antiwar candidate in the 1968 Democratic primary and then without any party backing in 1976, as he continued to criticize American foreign policy. Finally, there was Congressman John B. Anderson of Illinois, a liberal Republican, who sought to offer a more liberal alternative to Jimmy Carter and Ronald Reagan during the race for the presidency in 1980.[49] Presidential elections in this period particularly reflected the declining influence of the major parties. Not only could a few third-party candidates draw a considerable following, but the Republicans, despite their minority status, were able to win seven of the ten races for the White House between 1952 and 1988.

ELECTION OF 1952

The Democrats would be in trouble from the beginning of the 1950s. For several reasons President Truman's administration gradually lost popular support. The economy, after the postwar boom, began experiencing some ups and downs. Several instances of high-level corruption were revealed, leading to talk about a "mess in Washington." Worst of all, foreign problems caused a great amount of public frustration. The communist takeover in China (1949), followed by the North Korean attack on South Korea, soon led to the dispatch of American troops to the area. Although the enemy's advance was stopped, the war eventually reached an impasse. Communist expansionism abroad also sparked criticism of the government for being "soft on communism" at home. Senator Joseph McCarthy of Wisconsin, playing on fears of internal subversion, charged cabinet officials like Secretary of State Dean Acheson with being communist sympathizers. All these developments caused many Americans to believe that after twenty years of a Democrat in the White House, it was truly "time for a change."[50]

The Republicans in 1952 felt certain that this finally would be their year. Senator Robert Taft of Ohio seemed to be the favorite candidate of party regulars, but his highly conservative and isolationist views bothered the powerful eastern internationalist wing of the party. Ultimately the latter group was able to persuade General Dwight Eisenhower, military hero of World War II, who had never been in politics before, to compete for the nomination. The Republican convention, sensing the widespread popularity of "Ike," rejected Taft and chose the general to head the ticket. To pacify the conservatives, Senator Richard M. Nixon of California, who had developed a reputation as a hard-line anticommunist, was designated for the vice presidential slot. The Republican platform for the most part condemned the Democrats for all the nation's ills, though it was not very specific about what its side would do instead.[51]

In the Democratic corner, President Truman, seeing his popularity fading, eventually decided not to run again. After a good deal of backroom maneuvering, the party selected a somewhat reluctant Adlai E. Stevenson—the witty, urbane, and liberal governor of Illinois—as its nominee. Although not too well known outside his home state, Stevenson soon established himself as a bright and eloquent candidate. He promised to "talk sense to the American people," explaining that the problems of the age had no easy solutions and would require restraint, patience, and sacrifice. Faced with an uphill struggle because of his party's recent reverses, Stevenson sought to distance himself from the Truman administration. He even admitted that a mess existed in Washington and needed cleaning up. However, he did not differ too much from Truman on the issues, supporting the continuance of prolabor and social welfare legislation. Stevenson showed great courage at times, condemning excessive "red-baiting" before an American Legion convention and speaking about civil rights in Richmond, Virginia. But while he won praise from the liberal press, Stevenson was seen by many voters as too much of an intellectual, an "egghead," who could not relate well to the common people. He also was stuck with the negative Truman record which he could not shake off.

Eisenhower and the Republicans had a far easier time of it. After reconciling with the Taft forces, Ike and his supporters went on the offensive, attacking the evils of the Democratic administration (though promising not to disturb the social gains that had been made under the New and Fair Deals). In this contest, which ultimately hinged more on personalities than issues, Eisenhower had many advantages. His nonpolitical background appealed to the independent voter as well as to many Democrats. Although not the most forceful speaker, his grandfatherly and less-than-partisan pose gave people a feeling of security. Ike left the nastier side of campaigning to Richard Nixon, who relished accusing his opponents of having procommunist sympathies. Nixon denounced the intellectual Stevenson as "Adlai the Appeaser," with a "Ph.D. from Dean Acheson's College of Cowardly Communist Containment."

The Republican drive, which seemed unstoppable, suddenly came to a halt with the revelation that Nixon had received money from a secret fund set up for him by several businessmen. The whole credibility of the GOP campaign and its promise to clean up corruption appeared jeopardized. Ike even considered asking Nixon to resign from the ticket. But in an unprecedented move, the Californian went on national television and in an emotionally packed speech, successfully answered his critics. The fund, he said, had been used for legitimate political expenses and did not benefit him personally. He was not a rich man—his wife Pat wore a "Republican cloth coat." He had accepted but one family gift while in office, a small dog his daughter named Checkers. No matter what happened, he declared, he was not going to give up his child's dog. The public response to the so-called Checkers speech was highly positive. The next day, a smiling Eisenhower met with Nixon and told him, "You're my boy."

The Republican lead further solidified when in late October, Eisenhower, in discussing the Korean War, pledged to go to Korea to help bring an end to the hostilities. Stevenson had no chance to counter this. Although the pollsters, fearing another situation like 1948, remained noncommittal, it was clear to most observers that Eisenhower would win a massive victory. When the ballots were cast and counted, this view was substantiated. Ike garnered 55.1 percent of the popular vote to Stevenson's 44.4 percent. Minor parties had little effect this time—the old left, in particular, appeared dead. Ike took the entire North and West, plus a number of southern and border states, for a total of 442 electoral votes. Stevenson won only nine states, mostly in the Deep South, containing 89 votes. The president's coattails, while not too long, did manage to give the Republicans a majority in both houses of Congress for the first time in several years.

ELECTION OF 1956

As President, Eisenhower displayed a style in marked contrast to that of Roosevelt and Truman. Satisfied to reign rather than rule, Ike allowed his cabinet and personal advisers to make many important decisions. In terms of policy, his administration tended to follow a moderate course. While it cut spending slightly and did not initiate any long-range programs, it did not dismantle the New Deal and actually expanded some of its social welfare benefits. The president's manner and middle-of-the-road philosophy appealed to many Americans, who sought respite from the turmoil of previous decades. Even though he suffered a heart attack in 1955 and underwent an abdominal operation a few weeks before the Republican convention in 1956, Eisenhower was renominated unanimously by his party. Richard Nixon again was named for the vice presidency.

The Democratic nomination process saw Senator Estes Kefauver of Tennessee sharply challenge Adlai Stevenson for the top spot on the ticket. Yet in spite of losing a few primaries to Kefauver, Stevenson held on to the bulk of delegates at the convention and received the nod. In an open vote for the second spot, Kefauver obtained enough backing to defeat the bid of youthful Massachusetts Senator John F. Kennedy. Right from the start, the Democratic campaigners took the offensive, attacking Republican policy, especially in the realm of foreign affairs which, they said, hurt the country's prestige and weakened its defenses. They also criticized the farm program and lack of concern for low-income workers and the elderly. Regarding their opponents' individual capacities, Stevenson and Kefauver warned against Eisenhower's questionable health—they called him a "part-time President"—and Nixon's questionable character. "Nervous about Nixon" was the theme of many speeches and television commercials. But in the relatively good times of the mid–1950s, it was difficult to get many people to listen. While Stevenson made fewer "high-brow" speeches and catered more to ordinary folks, he had trouble overcoming Ike's broad popularity.[52]

The Republican campaign emphasized the themes of peace abroad and prosperity at home. Eisenhower was presented as the man who ended the Korean War and improved the economic situation. "America is happier than it was four years ago," declared Ike whenever he spoke. Actually, the president did not make many appearances; the major part of barnstorming was taken on by Nixon, who traveled 42,000 miles and gave hundreds of speeches. During the last two weeks of the contest, international tension developed over the revolt against communist rule in Hungary and the struggle by several powers for control of the Suez Canal. Stevenson tried to use these events to illustrate Republican ineffectiveness in foreign matters. But it came to little avail as Americans rallied to support Eisenhower.

On election day, Ike won by a wider margin than in 1952, engineering the biggest triumph since Roosevelt overwhelmed Landon twenty years earlier. Eisenhower rolled up 457 electoral votes to Stevenson's 73, and amassed 35.5 million popular votes (57.6 percent) compared to the latter's 26 million (42.1 percent). Again, the president captured not only most of the northern and western states but several in the South. Still, the Democrats kept their position as the majority party and won both houses of Congress, controlling the Senate, 49 to 47, and the House of Representatives, 234 to 201. This was the first time since 1848 that the winning president carried neither house along with him. The people liked Ike, but they preferred the other side for the other branches of government.

ELECTION OF 1960

Although Eisenhower continued to be popular personally, his second administration was not as successful as the first. Economic recession, political scandal, and troubles abroad increased the Democrats' majorities in both houses of Congress in the midterm elections of 1958. As the situation did not improve greatly during the next eighteen months, the Republicans approached the 1960 presidential contest with some apprehension. Vice President Richard Nixon was the obvious choice as Ike's successor and quickly was approved by the GOP convention. Over the years Nixon had endeared himself to party regulars by providing many favors and had gained in stature from his role as a government spokesman. Admired by supporters as a skillful leader, he was, nonetheless, seen by opponents as a slick opportunist; "Tricky Dick" had become a common sneer. The Republican platform stressed the danger of international communism and the need for responsible U.S. leadership. Such leadership had been provided by Eisenhower and would proceed, it was said, under Nixon.[53]

The Democrats, more optimistic than in the two previous presidential races, nominated Senator John F. Kennedy of Massachusetts. Kennedy had many strong assets: relative youth and good looks, wit and intelligence, a heroic war record, and an attractive wife. He also had several liabilities: a lack of administrative experience, a controversial millionaire father, and, most important, his Roman Catholic religion. No Catholic had ever been elected president, and though Al Smith's disaster had taken place a generation earlier, many still thought it impossible for a non-Protestant to reach the White House. However, Kennedy had shown himself to be such an effective vote-getter in the Wisconsin and West Virginia primaries that he was able to win a first-ballot victory at the party's convention. Lyndon B. Johnson of Texas, the powerful Senate majority leader who had sought the nomination himself, accepted the second spot on the ticket. The platform called for further civil rights legislation, an expansion of social welfare measures, and also for a stepped-up defense.

In his acceptance speech Kennedy presented not promises but challenges. The world was changing, he said, and the old ways would not always be effective. The nation was falling behind in certain respects. Thus it was necessary for Americans to move forward toward a "new frontier." Indeed his basic theme was to "get the country moving again," to confront the problems of the 1960s so as to build up America's status abroad and encourage economic progress at home. Nixon, on the other hand, asked voters to look back on the peace and prosperity achieved in the Eisenhower years and claimed that they would continue under him. He also tried to show that Kennedy's criticisms of America hurt the nation's prestige and that it would be unwise to trust a man of limited experience with the tremendous responsibilities of the presidency.

Nixon probably held a slight lead at the outset, making a good impression in most of the places he visited. But his pledge to campaign in all fifty states soon became a burden, particularly when a knee injury caused him to be hospitalized for almost two weeks. Kennedy operated more selectively. Concentrating on the large industrial areas, he convinced many people that he would bring into being an imaginative, forward-looking administration. Faced with questions about his religious views, Kennedy agreed to appear before a group of notable Protestant ministers. There he insisted he would not be influenced by the Vatican or by any church doctrine in determining what was best for the national interest. The ministers in attendance, skeptical at first, found his statement "complete, unequivocal, and reassuring."

The turning point in the campaign came with an unprecedented series of television debates between the two candidates. Nixon, although better known than Kennedy, agreed to the match on the premise that his debating skill and broad knowledge clearly would show him to advantage. Yet Nixon, who had used television effectively on earlier occasions, arrived for the first encounter less than fully prepared and looking pale from his recent illness. While he answered the questions in an adequate manner, he came across as haggard, nervous, and on the defensive. Kennedy, in contrast, impressed viewers as being fresh, alert, and coolly confident. His articulate responses helped overcome previous doubts people had about his qualifications for high office. During the next three debates Nixon looked better and improved his overall performance, but the damage from the initial meeting could not be undone. Kennedy moved ahead in the polls, and enthusiasm for his campaign grew as well.

Even with the impact of the debates, the race remained extremely tight. Nixon might have been able to regain the lead by having Eisenhower campaign heavily on his behalf. But wishing to show he was his own man, Nixon did not call on the president until the final week of the contest—too late to make a difference. Another development that aided Kennedy's chances and hurt Nixon's concerned their responses to the arrest of civil rights leader Martin Luther King in Atlanta, Georgia, in late October. Advised of the situation by his staff, Kennedy telephoned his sympathies to Mrs. King, and his influence may have helped King subsequently to gain release on bail. This action, in conjunction with Nixon's inaction, probably swung many black votes to Kennedy on election day.

Whatever the reasons, Kennedy won the presidency albeit by a tiny margin. Although the electoral college totals (303–219) showed him winning by a comfortable spread, the actual outcome across the nation was very close. Overall, Kennedy had a majority of less than 120,000 among almost 69 million ballots cast, just one-tenth of one percent. JFK won most of the eastern industrial belt and, thanks to Lyndon Johnson's efforts, did fairly well in the South. Nixon, meanwhile, carried a large part of the Midwest and Far West but not enough to change the verdict. The biggest issue of the campaign proved to be Kennedy's religion. While a handful of Protestants may have switched their votes to Nixon, many more Catholics than usual came out for Kennedy, giving him small victories in a number of key states.

ELECTION OF 1964

President Kennedy's New Frontier started off on a high note with talk of "Camelot" and truly idealistic goals. However, much of the progressive legislation the new president contemplated soon got bogged down in Congress. Kennedy also suffered foreign policy reverses such as the ill-fated Bay of Pigs invasion of Cuba (1961), though he succeeded in resolving the Cuban missile crisis (1962) and in achieving a nuclear test-ban treaty with the Russians (1963). Unfortunately, Kennedy never had a chance to accomplish anything further, as he was assassinated on a visit to Dallas, Texas, in November 1963. Lyndon B. Johnson took over the presidency and proceeded to push forward some of Kennedy's proposals, particularly in the area of civil rights. He then introduced his own program to help the poor and disadvantaged—later known as the War on Poverty. His call for medical care for the elderly, aid to education, and new job-training facilities were part of his vision of a Great Society. Johnson's hope to implement fully his plans rested on his being elected president in his own right in 1964.

The adoption of a more liberal stance by the Democrats led to a conservative reaction by the Republicans in nominating their standard-bearer in 1964. There long had been the belief by some in the party that a large bloc of American voters wished for a person with old-fashioned principles, and who offered a real alternative instead of being a "me-too" candidate. Thus the GOP bypassed moderate New York governor Nelson Rockefeller in favor of the leader of the right wing, Arizona Senator Barry Goldwater. While not fully victorious in the primaries, Goldwater sewed up the nomination by obtaining a majority of delegates at state party conventions and caucuses. Goldwater's book, *Conscience of a Conservative*, already had laid out many of his ideas—abolishing the graduated income tax, limiting social security and other forms of welfare, proceeding voluntarily in the area of civil rights, and intensifying the struggle against world communism. The Republican platform would reflect these views, focusing on the dangers to liberty from expanding federal programs and the need to adopt a more aggressive foreign policy.[54]

Yet despite the fervor of the Goldwater movement, his general election campaign, promising "a choice, not an echo," never went very far. The Republican party showed itself to be badly divided even at the convention, where Goldwater loyalists severely booed critical statements by Governor Rockefeller. This was followed by the senator's acceptance speech, in which instead of appealing for unity, he declared at one point: "Extremism in the defense of liberty is no vice... moderation in the pursuit of justice is no virtue."[55] While the words were later quoted out of context, Goldwater conjured up the image of someone who was uncompromising and who would lead the country into turmoil. No matter how hard he tried to shake the extremist tag in the following weeks, he always failed. Many of his earlier statements came back to haunt him. He was pictured as "trigger happy" because he had said that military commanders should be given the option of using nuclear weapons. His opinion that social security should be made voluntary was seen as a major threat to the system. Although his supporters shouted "In Your Heart You Know He's Right," many Americans, including longtime Republicans, found his candidacy frightening.

In contrast to Goldwater's extremist image, Johnson and his backers sought to present a man of moderation and restraint. They ran a consensus-type campaign in order to appeal not just to Democrats but to middle-of-the-road Republicans. Although LBJ had been tarnished by accusations of corruption, he was able to sidestep the issue by constantly stressing the benefits of his Great Society proposals. When the Vietnam War began to widen, Johnson put himself forward as the stronger peace candidate and stated his reluctance to send American boys to fight in a war several thousand miles from home. There was only one moment when Johnson faced a difficult situation. In mid-October, a close aide, Walter Jenkins, was arrested on a morals charge. This seemed to give credence to all the talk about corruption in the administration. But within a few days such international events as the fall of Premier Khrushchev in the Soviet Union and the detonation of the first nuclear bomb in China made people forget about Jenkins and see the need for Johnson rather than Goldwater in the White House.

At the polls Johnson put together the most sweeping victory since 1936. LBJ took forty-four states with a total of 486 electoral votes to Goldwater's six states and 52 votes. The latter only won in his home state of Arizona and in five states of the Deep South. In terms of the popular vote, Johnson's 61 percent exceeded Roosevelt's level as he garnered 43 million votes to just 27 million for his opponent. The House and Senate wound up heavily Democratic too, by margins of 295 to 140 in the House, and 67 to 33 in the Senate. In addition, Republicans came out on top in merely eight of the twenty-five governors' races. Many observers saw in the results a possible withering away of the Republican party, but circumstances over the next four years would prove that to be wishful thinking.

The big victory of Johnson and the Democrats led to further implementation of the Great Society agenda. The Office of Economic Opportunity introduced various antipoverty programs. Large amounts of money were spent to improve health, education, and welfare services. New civil rights legislation, which included protection of voting rights, was enacted. Yet for some members of the black community, change toward greater equality was not happening fast enough, leading to frustration and ultimately to widespread violence. An even greater immediate problem grew out of the expanding war in Vietnam. As the Johnson administration sent more and more troops there—eventually reaching half a million—without producing very positive results, people at home engaged in massive protests against continued involvement, leaving the nation deeply divided. Johnson's hopes for the Great Society and another four years in the White House were now severely jeopardized.

ELECTION OF 1968

When the 1968 presidential race began, antiwar Senator Eugene McCarthy of Minnesota, supported mainly by college-age youth, openly challenged President Johnson for the Democratic nomination. McCarthy's success in the New Hampshire primary and impending triumph in Wisconsin caused Johnson to announce that he would not seek another term. Meanwhile, Senator Robert Kennedy of New York, who long had been critical of the administration, entered the contest, and soon afterward Vice President Hubert Humphrey, a staunch defender of Johnson's policies, did likewise. Kennedy, a more popular figure than either McCarthy or Humphrey—especially among the poor and minorities—seemed headed for the nomination, but an assassin's bullet following his win in the California primary put an end to his quest. Humphrey, with the aid of party regulars, finally would be named to head the ticket at the Democratic convention in Chicago. Nevertheless, his selection was marred by factional hostility inside the auditorium and, more importantly, by an extremely brutal confrontation between local police and antiwar demonstrators outside. Indeed, like Goldwater in 1964, Humphrey found it exceedingly difficult to overcome divisions within his own party and a negative image stemming from the convention.[56]

By this time the Republicans already had held their convention. They had nominated Richard Nixon, who easily fought off competition by moderate Nelson Rockefeller and conservative Ronald Reagan. Nixon in some ways appeared an unlikely candidate, having lost the presidential contest in 1960 and the California governorship race in 1962. No national figure in the twentieth century ever had come back from such a position. Yet Nixon had campaigned widely for Goldwater and for congressional candidates in 1964 and 1966, which restored his popularity among party regulars. As his running mate, Nixon chose Governor Spiro T. Agnew of Maryland, who, it was hoped, would have strong appeal in the South. The southern vote had become highly competitive since the outspoken segregationist governor of Alabama,

George Wallace, had announced his candidacy through the American Independent party. Wallace, a champion of states' rights, lashed out at both
major parties and particularly the "pointy-headed bureaucrats" in Washington. He would run a revivalist-style campaign, emphasizing law and order
and a reduction of federal programs. While he had little chance of winning
overall, he hoped to prevent either of the top nominees from receiving a
majority in the electoral college.

In contrast to 1960, when he had campaigned frenetically and committed
numerous blunders, this time Nixon exercised caution and restraint. "Gone
was the old pugnacity, sock and slash style, and the tendency to buckle under
strain," wrote Theodore White.[57] Instead of traveling to all fifty states, he
restricted himself to the large industrial areas plus those on the southern
periphery. Instead of debating his opponents on national television head to
head, Nixon appeared at regional question-answer sessions, where the Re-
publican-picked panelists never asked anything hostile. Unlike the past,
Nixon established good relations with the press, and while he criticized the
Johnson regime, he sought to avoid bitter controversy. Without being specific
he promised to end the Vietnam War through new leadership. Though he
emphasized law and order, he did not attempt to compete with Wallace and
sound like a racist. All in all, his campaign ran very smoothly.

The Humphrey campaign, on the other hand, had trouble even getting
off the ground. No national organization had been fully established, no clear-
cut strategy had been devised, and no money was coming in. Humphrey
had alienated the liberal Democratic community, previously his chief backers,
forcing him to go begging for support. His early speechmaking efforts did
not go well either as they usually were marred by antiwar demonstrators.
By late September the polls showed him trailing Nixon by 15 points and
only 7 points ahead of Wallace. Yet the situation began to improve for the
vice president after he delivered a speech in Salt Lake City, implying a
willingness to deescalate the Vietnam War. Many liberal Democrats, even
Eugene McCarthy, eventually gave Humphrey their endorsement. Also,
members of the working class who had deserted to Wallace now returned to
the Democratic fold after union leaders demonstrated that the Alabama governor was no friend of organized labor. Humphrey, aided by his running
mate Senator Edmund Muskie of Maine, slowly narrowed Nixon's lead.
President Johnson's announcement, a few days before the election, of a halt
to the bombing of North Vietnam brought the contest to a virtual draw.

Humphrey started out well on election day, however, late returns from
the West gave Nixon the nod. In the popular vote Nixon ended up with an
edge of less than one percent, acquiring only 43.4 percent of the total to
Humphrey's 42.7 percent; Wallace finished a distant third at 13.5 percent.
The electoral tally provided Nixon with a bigger margin, as he ultimately
received 301 votes to Humphrey's 191 and Wallace's 46. Nixon's emphasis

on the incumbent administration's failings, especially regarding the Vietnam War and crime in the streets, proved enough to bring him success. The Democrats still maintained a majority in Congress, but it was clear that there would be some shift away from the heavy funding of government programs initiated under the Great Society.

ELECTION OF 1972

The Nixon presidency began in a relatively positive atmosphere in 1969 as the first astronauts landed on the moon and some of the earlier domestic divisiveness receded. Nixon succeeded to a degree in "Vietnamizing" the war in Southeast Asia, considerably reducing the number of American combat troops. His administration, however, was bothered by some hard-to-solve economic problems—rising inflation and unemployment. Moreover, vigorous antiwar protests resumed when in 1970 U.S. bombing attacks spread from Vietnam to Cambodia and Laos. But diplomatic breakthroughs in the direction of detente with Communist China and the Soviet Union helped ensure Nixon's renomination in 1972. Spiro Agnew, who had been effective playing the role Nixon used to play as vice president—criticizing liberals for example, as "nattering nabobs of negativism"—was kept in the second spot on the ticket.[58]

The Democrats in 1972 remained deeply divided. Many candidates engaged in a bitter struggle for the nomination. Middle-of-the-roader Edmund Muskie led at first but failed to win the early primaries. Hubert Humphrey, the former standard-bearer, entered the contest too late to succeed. Conservative George Wallace did well in several states, but in May was paralyzed by an assassin's bullet. Eventually, liberal Senator George McGovern of South Dakota, a longtime foe of American involvement in the war in Southeast Asia, who had created an enthusiastic and efficient organization, became the nominee. McGovern's designation by the Democratic convention was aided by new rules, which gave greater representation than ever before to youth, women, and minorities. Unfortunately for the candidate, many traditional Democrats—namely, organized labor—felt unhappy about his selection and did not provide him with adequate support in the months to come. Outside the party many people seemed skeptical about McGovern's call for huge cuts in defense spending; and his plan to give additional funds to the poor led to charges of socialism.

McGovern, who trailed badly in the polls at the time of the convention, would be set back even further as a result of a revelation regarding his running mate, Senator Thomas Eagleton of Missouri. It was disclosed that Eagleton had been hospitalized a few times under psychiatric care and also had received shock treatments. At first McGovern rallied around Eagleton and said he stood behind him "1,000 percent." Then when party pressure built up for Eagleton's resignation, McGovern appeared weak and indecisive in agreeing to drop him. According to campaign manager Gary Hart, "The events surrounding the selection of Senator Eagleton and his subsequent departure from the ticket cost McGovern any chance he had to win the presidency. In retrospect, all that took place thereafter was anticlimactic and politically inconsequential in terms of the final results. . . . We could not win with him or without him."[59]

To be sure, McGovern and his new running mate Sargent Shriver, a Kennedy in-law and former Peace Corps director, did campaign hard. They traveled back and forth across the nation many times, calling for an immediate end to American participation in the Vietnam War and for extension of government programs to help the disadvantaged. As news of deep Republican involvement in the Watergate episode became known, McGovern called the Nixon administration "the most corrupt in American history." But it fell on deaf ears, as most of the story was yet to be told, and the average person thought all the Democratic charges were just "politics." The McGovern forces, so adept in the primaries, lacked clear direction in the national contest and could not find any way of overcoming the president's lead. In fact, the gap kept getting larger. News from abroad hinting at an end to U.S. involvement in Vietnam further cemented McGovern's defeat and Nixon's victory.

As far as the presidential race was concerned, Nixon triumphed by an overwhelming margin. He won everywhere except in Massachusetts and the District of Columbia for a total of 520 electoral votes to 17 for McGovern, the largest electoral success since 1936. His proportion of the popular vote stood at 60.8 percent to McGovern's 37.5 percent, one of the highest amounts in recent times. Yet the results were deceptive, for in nineteen states, more votes were cast in senatorial and gubernatorial races. Indeed, the presidential turnout dropped six percent below that recorded in the previous contest in 1968. In addition, a heavy amount of ticket splitting occurred; the Democrats picked up two seats in the Senate and only lost a handful in the House. The majority of voters were still Democrats, but they preferred Nixon to McGovern as the lesser of two evils.

Nixon's second term would witness the final withdrawal of American troops from Vietnam but see many crises develop at home. Economic problems started to mount, particularly the rise of inflation, which largely had been brought about by soaring energy costs. At the same time political scandals involving the highest officers in the nation began eroding public confidence. Vice President Spiro Agnew was forced to resign after being charged with past illegal activities in Maryland. Revelations regarding the Watergate episode and its subsequent cover-up would compel Nixon's departure from office in August 1974. Watergate had involved a break-in at the Democratic party headquarters by persons associated with the president's reelection team. Nixon denied any complicity in the cover-up, but secret White House tape recordings revealed his involvement, which seriously damaged his credibility and led to his resignation. Longtime congressman Gerald

Ford of Michigan, who had taken over the vice presidency from Agnew, now moved into the Oval Office.

ELECTION OF 1976

Ford helped restore some integrity to the presidency at first by running an open and honest administration. Yet his pardon of Nixon led to rumors that a prior deal had been arranged and that Ford was just another politician. In addition, Ford had trouble straightening out the economic situation, and he acquired the reputation of a bumbler as news pictures showed him slipping or falling down in a variety of circumstances. Still, Ford sought election to the presidency in his own right in 1976 and, with the advantage of incumbency, was able to beat off a fierce challenge in the primaries by conservative Ronald Reagan to win the Republican nomination. Conservatives, however, would influence the content of the platform and also the selection of Senator Robert Dole of Kansas as Ford's running mate.[60]

The Democratic nomination was won by a little-known former governor of Georgia, Jimmy Carter. A Naval Academy graduate and successful peanut farmer, Carter had campaigned relentlessly in the primaries. He impressed voters as being honest and sincere, a "born-again Christian," who said he would "never lie to the American people." Unconnected with the Washington political scene, he appeared to be someone who could clean up the mess in the capital, and restore confidence in the government. Liberal Senator Walter Mondale of Minnesota was designated for the vice presidency, as the Democratic party displayed a good deal of unity at the national convention. In the weeks ahead, however, Carter made several mistakes and his early lead began to dwindle. His efforts to associate Ford too closely with the Nixon administration caused considerable resentment. His sometimes contradictory policy statements made him appear fuzzy on the issues. Most important, an interview in *Playboy* magazine, in which he said that in his heart he had lusted after women, brought into question his earlier moral and religious pronouncements.

Ford, not a particularly adept campaigner either, was able to improve his ratings simply by remaining in the White House and acting presidential. He and his supporters issued statements attempting to show Carter as slick but shallow, someone without high governmental experience who wanted power for its own sake. They also sought to demonstrate Republican achievements in the previous two years and how the economy gradually was improving. Ford, however, spoiled his comeback struggle when during one of his television debates with Carter he claimed that Eastern Europe was not dominated by the Soviet Union. Although there may have been some question about the statement's exact meaning, the response raised doubts among many viewers about Ford's competence in foreign affairs and his overall capability. A last-minute whirlwind tour and TV blitz brought Ford very close to victory, but not close enough.

Carter edged out Ford 50.1 percent to 48.0 percent in the popular vote, and 297 to 241 in the electoral college, the latter being the smallest gap since 1916. Carter, the first presidential candidate from the Deep South since Zachary Taylor in 1848, did extremely well among both black and white southerners. He also scored heavily among blue-collar workers in the northern industrial states. Ford carried almost the entire West and some of the farm belt, but was not as fortunate further east. In general, the less-than-buoyant economy and Ford's less-than-charismatic personality together with his pardon of Nixon and the feeling that Carter might raise the standards of morality in government gave the Georgian the victory. Carter would enter office with a heavy majority in Congress and high expectations for success.

ELECTION OF 1980

During his years as president, Jimmy Carter tried to tackle many pressing domestic problems. His inexperience in national politics and inability to mobilize the Democratic majority in Congress, however, made it difficult for him to accomplish his goals. His energy program eventually was stifled, and his attempts to stimulate the economy did not get very far. Double-digit inflation and high interest rates would prevail for much of his term in office. Carter, instead of taking responsibility, blamed it largely on a "national malaise." In foreign affairs he was somewhat more successful, achieving passage of the Panama Canal treaty, establishing full diplomatic relations with Peking, and furthering the Middle East peace process between Egypt and Israel. But the taking of American hostages by Iran in late 1979 would cause Carter increasing frustration as he sought reelection in 1980. He was able to use the issue at first to rally support for his renomination over Senator Edward Kennedy. But as the months passed, many Americans became increasingly upset at the president's failure to resolve the hostage crisis.[61]

Carter's Republican challenger would be former actor and governor of California Ronald Reagan, who easily had won the nomination by besting several rivals in the party primaries. Reagan, like Carter, came into the contest with a number of liabilities. At age sixty-nine he was the oldest major candidate to ever seek the presidency. In addition, his association with the Republican right wing gave rise to fears that he would threaten social programs and endanger world peace. However, at the convention and afterward, Reagan took pains to counter the extremist image by moving toward the center, choosing moderate George Bush as his running mate and promising not to dismantle existing programs. He also emphasized that he strongly believed in peaceful measures to resolve foreign conflicts and that he was not "trigger-happy." In general, the Republicans and Reagan would run a well-ordered campaign that particularly focused on the country's economic troubles and Carter's ineffective leadership. Reagan claimed that, if elected, he would cut taxes, increase defense spending, and at the same time reduce the federal budget deficit.

Although Reagan moved somewhat ahead in the polls in the early stages of the contest, a series of blunders and gaffes, including one about the amount of pollution caused by trees, led some people to question whether he was any more fit for the White House than Carter. The president, using his incumbency to advantage, seemed to be closing the gap in the final weeks of the race. However, Carter agreed to debate Reagan on television a short time before election day, and while on that occasion he showed more factual knowledge than his opponent, he came across as less presidential. Reagan, having better stage presence and a quick wit, gave people the feeling that he was a competent and reasonable man. He especially scored well in his concluding remarks when he asked voters if they were better off than they were four years earlier. Many apparently felt they were not. Carter's support also began slipping when rumors about an imminent release of the hostages proved ill-founded, reminding the public of the administration's failure to bring an end to the Iranian problem.

On election day, Reagan won a landslide victory, accumulating 489 electoral votes to 49 for Carter, who secured only six states and the District of Columbia. Reagan had 43 million votes (50.7 percent) to Carter's 34.7 million (41 percent), with 5.5 million (6.6 percent) going to independent candidate John B. Anderson. (Anderson's votes took a few states away from Carter, but not enough to make much of a difference.) Whether Reagan's election marked a triumph of conservatism is hard to ascertain. Surely Reagan had the support of fundamentalist Christians, or the so-called Moral Majority, which brought out many new voters. Yet Reagan did not seem to do appreciably better among white "born-again" Protestants than among those not "born again." In any case, some conservative shift occurred in the choice of senators, which led to a Republican majority in the upper chamber for the first time in twenty-six years, and there also was a reduction in the Democratic dominance of the lower chamber.

ELECTION OF 1984

Upon assuming the presidency Ronald Reagan sought to implement a hard-line foreign policy and a conservative domestic policy. Moving away from détente with the Soviet Union, he believed that the way to deal with the Russians was by further building up American military capability and by strongly backing anti-Soviet elements abroad. On the home front Reagan worked to promote economic growth through a combination of major tax cuts and reductions in spending on several federal programs. By means of his personality and speaking ability—he became known as the "great communicator"—Reagan was able to mobilize enough congressional support to achieve many of his goals. By late 1983 the economy had improved; inflation and interest rates as well as unemployment had fallen. Even though there was now a large federal deficit, one approaching $200 billion, the majority of people was happy with the Reagan administration and Reagan's leadership. When he decided to run for a second term in 1984, he was renominated unanimously by the Republican party.[62]

The Democrats, even more divided than usual, chose former vice president and Minnesota Senator Walter Mondale as their standard-bearer. Mondale, a liberal in the New Deal tradition and supported by organized labor, had gained the nomination only after a fierce struggle in the primaries. Among his rivals were Colorado Senator Gary Hart, who had called for "new ideas" to revitalize sagging Democratic fortunes and especially appealed to young urban professionals known as "Yuppies," as well as black activist Jesse Jackson, who had sought to put together a "rainbow coalition" of blacks and other minorities. As Mondale started his campaign against the Republicans, he seized the initiative in dramatic fashion by naming Congresswoman Geraldine Ferraro of New York as his running mate; it was the first time a woman had appeared on a major party's national ticket. However, the contribution of Ferraro, a feisty speaker out on the hustings, would be somewhat neutralized by disclosures of her husband's questionable business dealings and by critics of her pro-choice stand on abortion, who disrupted many of her personal appearances. The Democratic effort also would be hampered by organizational problems, particularly regarding the leadership of the national committee.

In contrast, the Republican organization ran smoothly and efficiently as it orchestrated a campaign based on positive rhetoric and patriotic images. President Reagan made relatively few appearances, but wherever he traveled there were plenty of American flags and other national symbols in the background. In his speeches Reagan emphasized four basic themes: economic growth, a strong defense, traditional values, and new frontiers. Mondale tried to make issues of the huge budget deficit facing the nation and of the administration's refusal to talk to the Soviet leaders about arms control. But his call for increased taxes to deal with the deficit alienated most voters, and the question about not negotiating with the Russians was eliminated after a hastily arranged meeting between Reagan and Soviet foreign minister Gromyko. The Democrats also sought to make an issue of the Republicans' close ties with the Moral Majority and its threat to the freedom of religion; but this too did not get very far. The personal popularity of the president coupled with general prosperity and good feelings in the country made it difficult for Mondale, a less-than-exciting campaigner, to create much of a contest.

The Democratic candidate's one moment of success came during the first televised debate between the contestants in early October, when in contrast to Mondale's sharpness, the president seemed tired and unsure of himself. Some people began to wonder whether the seventy-three-year-old Reagan could face another four years in the White House. Yet in the second debate, two weeks later, the president showed himself in better form and defused the age issue when he joked, "I am not going to exploit for political purposes my opponent's youth and inexperience."

With that statement, the outcome of the race was no longer in doubt. On election day Reagan went on to an overwhelming victory, capturing 59 percent of the popular vote (52.6 million votes to Mondale's 36.4 million) and 525 electoral votes to Mondale's 13, winning everywhere except in Mondale's home state of Minnesota and the District of Columbia. Yet the president's triumph was more a personal one than one for the Republican party, as the Democrats gained two seats in the Senate and kept their superiority in the House. Although some experts claimed that the old Democratic party was dying on the national level—having lost six of the past nine presidential contests by wide margins—the very fact that it continued to do well in congressional and statewide elections meant that the possibility of a comeback was very real.

ELECTION OF 1988

Democratic chances seemed to be improving during Reagan's second term, as the Republicans suffered several setbacks and lost their majority in the Senate in the 1986 midterm elections. While the economy remained sound in many ways, the budget deficit continued to grow as did the country's trade imbalance. Federal authorities had trouble handling the illegal drug problem and drug-related crime. There also were several scandals involving White House officials, especially the Iran–*Contra* affair. In this episode, the administration, going against its pledge not to deal with terrorists, secretly sold arms to the pro-terrorist government of Iran in return for a few American hostages. Apparently without the knowledge of the president and in violation of Congress, some of the president's men funneled proceeds from these arms sales to the rebel forces who were fighting the leftist Sandinista regime in Nicaragua. Critics asserted that this showed Reagan was losing control of national policy. Whether or not this was true, the impact of these revelations surely hurt the Republicans' hopes of a third straight national victory in 1988.

The Democrats, entering the race with brighter prospects than in the previous dozen years, went through a long primary fight before Governor Michael Dukakis of Massachusetts defeated black leader Jesse Jackson for the party nomination. A son of Greek immigrants, Dukakis had been elected to the governorship three times and had won high marks as a chief executive. Stressing administrative competence and claiming responsibility for the recent economic and social improvements in his state, Dukakis promised to do for America what he had done for Massachusetts. He talked about expanding the opportunities for every citizen, not just the well-to-do who had been the main beneficiaries of Reagan's policies. Dukakis chose as his running mate Senator Lloyd Bentsen of Texas and looked back to 1960 when another Massachusetts–Texas duo sought to take over the reins from an aging but still popular Republican whose second term was not faring so well.

Just as in the 1960 scenario, the GOP turned to its incumbent vice president, in this case party-loyalist George Bush. Like Nixon twenty-eight years earlier, Bush had more high-level experience than his rival, but there was concern whether he could fully emerge from the president's shadow. Many wondered not only about Bush's leadership ability but about his connections to the Iran–*Contra* scandal. Doubts also arose about his judgment when he selected the junior senator from Indiana, Dan Quayle, as the number-two person on the ticket. People had serious questions regarding Quayle's qualifications for the vice presidency and a row developed over whether his wealthy family had used its influence to get him into law school and into the National Guard during the Vietnam War. When the general election got under way in August, Bush found himself trailing Dukakis in the polls by as much as seventeen points.

Yet as the race unfolded, Bush, no longer in the background, proved to be his own man and an effective campaigner, quickly erasing his opponent's lead. Operating with a seasoned staff who had helped bring about Reagan's two victories, Bush managed to deflect much of the criticism heaped upon him and Senator Quayle by focusing on the shortcomings of Governor Dukakis's record in Massachusetts. Using a barrage of negative advertising, the Bush team was able to make Dukakis appear weak on defense and soft on crime. They also played on the public's fear of new taxes by pointing to the tax increases the governor had approved—they called his state "Taxachusetts"—and emphasized that Dukakis was a liberal on social issues, placing him outside the mainstream. They particularly targeted the fact that as governor he had vetoed a bill requiring teachers to lead their classes in the Pledge of Allegiance, thus making him seem less than patriotic. Although the Democrats complained that this was dirty politics, the margin of Bush's support kept on rising.

Meanwhile, Dukakis and his staff, without much experience in national campaigns, allowed the situation to drift. Instead of going forward aggressively, the Dukakis camp let Bush seize the initiative and wound up having to answer charges about their man day after day. Only at a relatively late stage did Dukakis begin to strike back, but by that time it was too late. The campaign simply became a nasty war of words, turning off many people who wished to hear about major issues rather than listen to attacks on personality. To be sure, with the nation in the throes of peace and enjoying (despite the deficit) relative prosperity, it was not easy to present issues that would attract public attention. When it came time to make a choice, most voters went along with the vice president, not wanting to risk bringing in a new regime led by a person without experience on the national level.

Bush was elected by a large margin; not as great as those in Reagan's two triumphs, but large nonetheless. He led by 54 percent to 46 percent in the popular vote and amassed 426 electoral votes to 112 for Dukakis. Bush was particularly strong in the South and West, receiving big majorities in many of the states in those regions. However, as in the Reagan years, the Republican coattails were not very long, as the Democrats strengthened their hold on the House and Senate, improved their position in the state legislatures, and gained a few governorships as well. The Democratic party had now lost seven of the last ten presidential contests by considerable amounts, yet it remained the majority party on most other levels. Whether the future would produce any change in this pattern was difficult to tell.

Notes

INTRODUCTION

1. Quoted in Lucille B. Griffith, *The Virginia House of Burgesses, 1750–1774*, rev. ed. (University, Ala., 1970), p. 63.

2. Basil Hall, *Travels in North America in the Years 1827–1828* (Philadelphia, 1829), p. 59.

3. Murray Edelman, *The Symbolic Uses of Politics* (Urbana, Ill., 1964).

4. Dan Nimmo, "Elections as Ritual Drama," *Society* 22 (May–June 1985): 31–38; Bruce E. Gronbeck, "The Functions of Presidential Campaigning," *Communications Monographs* 45 (November 1968): 268–80.

5. Richard Armstrong, *The Next Hurrah* (New York, 1988), pp. 25, 61.

6. Ernest R. May and Janet Fraser, *Campaign '72: The Managers Speak* (Cambridge, Mass., 1973), p. 214; Charles E. Merriam and Harold F. Gosnell, *The American Party System*, 3d ed. (New York, 1940), p. 355.

CHAPTER 1

1. This chapter is based on material in Robert J. Dinkin, *Voting in Provincial America* (Westport, Conn., 1977), and idem, *Voting in Revolutionary America* (Westport, Conn., 1982).

2. Lucille B. Griffith, *The Virginia House of Burgesses, 1750–1774*, rev. ed. (University, Ala., 1970), p. 62.

3. William Livingston et al., *The Independent Reflector*, ed. Milton M. Klein (Cambridge, Mass., 1963), p. 281.

4. *Pennsylvania Magazine of History and Biography* 21 (1897): 118.

5. Charles S. Sydnor, *Gentlemen Freeholders* (Chapel Hill, N.C., 1952), pp. 44–45.

6. Ibid., pp. 51–59.

7. Dinkin, *Provincial America*, pp. 109–12.

8. Douglass Adair, ed., "James Madison's Autobiography," *William and Mary Quarterly*, 3d ser., 2 (April 1945): 199–200.

9. *Pennsylvania Gazette*, September 29, 1737.

10. Dinkin, *Provincial America*, pp. 94–95.

11. RIHS Manuscripts, 2:101, Rhode Island Historical Society, Providence.

12. Robert Rogers, *A Concise Account of North America* (1765; reprint, New York, 1966), pp. 57–58.

13. Julian P. Boyd et al., ed., *The Papers of Thomas Jefferson* (Princeton, N.J., 1950–), 8:645.

14. John Eliot to Jeremy Belknap, May 9, 1777, in Belknap Papers, Massachusetts Historical Society, Boston.

15. Johann D. Schoepf, *Travels in the Confederation* (Philadelphia, 1911), p. 349.

16. Elizabeth Cometti, ed., *Seeing America and Its Great Men* (Charlottesville, Va., 1969), p. 36.

17. Jackson T. Main, *Political Parties before the Constitution* (Chapel Hill, N.C., 1973), esp. chap. 2.

18. Ibid.

19. William T. Hutchinson et al., eds., *The Papers of James Madison* (Chicago, 1962–), 9:364–65.

20. Quoted in E. Wilder Spaulding, *His Excellency, George Clinton* (New York, 1938), p. 189.

21. Worthington C. Ford, ed., *Correspondence and Journals of Samuel Blachley Webb* (1893; reprint New York, 1969), 3:98.

22. *Pennsylvania Evening Herald*, October 12, 1785, October 4, 1786.

23. Alice B. Keith and William H. Masterson, eds., *The John Gray Blount Papers* (Raleigh, N.C., 1952–65), 1:207.

24. Main, *Political Parties*, p. 205; Colonial Society of Massachusetts, *Publications* 11 (1907): 402.

25. Robert A. Rutland, *The Ordeal of the Constitution* (Norman, Okla., 1966), pp. 37–38, 117–18, 128, 138, 169, 199, 209.

26. Linda G. DePauw, *The Eleventh Pillar* (Ithaca, N.Y., 1966), pp. 125–26, 138; L. Marx Renzulli, *Maryland: The Federalist Years* (Rutherford, N.J., 1972), pp. 53, 75, 75n.

27. Van Beck Hall, *Politics without Parties* (Pittsburgh, 1972), pp. 274–75.

28. Irving Brant, *James Madison* (Indianapolis, 1941–61), 3:241–42.

29. J. Thomas Scharf, *History of Maryland* (Baltimore, 1879), 2:548.

30. Alfred M. Lee, *The Daily Newspaper in America* (New York, 1937), chaps. 1–3.

31. Ibid.

32. *Independent Gazetteer* (Philadelphia), October 7, 1786.

33. *New Hampshire Gazette*, February 4, 1785.

CHAPTER 2

1. David H. Fischer, *The Revolution of American Conservatism* (New York, 1965), p. 93; Noble E. Cunningham, Jr., *The Jeffersonian Republicans* (Chapel Hill, N.C., 1957), chap. 10.

2. John C. Miller, *The Federalist Era, 1789–1800* (New York, 1960), chap. 6. The quotation is in Harold C. Syrett, ed., *The Papers of Alexander Hamilton* (New York, 1961–79), 12:544.

3. Cunningham, *Jeffersonian Republicans*, p. 250.

4. Quoted in Daniel P. Jordan, *Political Leadership in Jefferson's Virginia* (Charlottesville, Va., 1983), p. 119.

5. Noble E. Cunningham, Jr., ed., *The Making of the American Party System, 1789–1809* (Englewood Cliffs, N.J., 1965), pp. 147–48.

6. Ibid., pp. 138–39.

7. Charles S. Sydnor, *Gentlemen Freeholders* (Chapel Hill, N.C., 1952), p. 55.

8. Quoted in Richard Beeman, *The Old Dominion and the New Nation* (Lexington, Ky., 1972), p. 38.

9. Quoted in Fischer, *Revolution*, p. 92n.

10. John A. Munroe, *Federalist Delaware, 1775–1815* (New Brunswick, N.J., 1954), p. 206.

11. Cunningham, *American Party System*, pp. 134–36.

12. Zephaniah Swift, *A System of Laws of the State of Connecticut* (Windham, Conn., 1795), 1:68.

13. Quoted in Carl E. Prince, *New Jersey's Jeffersonian Republicans* (Chapel Hill, N.C., 1964), p. 30.

14. Cunningham, *American Party System*, p. 133.

15. J. R. Pole, *Political Representation in England and the Origins of the American Republic* (London, 1966), p. 161.

16. Noble E. Cunningham, Jr., ed., *Circular Letters of Congressmen to Their Constituents* (Chapel Hill, N.C., 1978).

17. Alfred M. Lee, *The Daily Newspaper in America* (New York, 1937), p. 718; Frank L. Mott, *American Journalism*, 3d ed, (New York, 1962), p. 110.

18. Donald Stewart, *The Opposition Press in the Federalist Period* (Albany, N.Y., 1969), chap. 1.

19. Charles Warren, *Jacobin and Junto* (Cambridge, 1931), p. 226.

20. Mott, *American Journalism*, chap. 6; Mary E. Clark, *Peter Porcupine in America* (Philadelphia, 1937), pp. 150–51.

21. Cunningham, *Jeffersonian Republicans*, pp. 35–38.

22. Ibid., pp. 38–44. The quotations are on p. 43.

23. Marcus Cunliffe, "Elections of 1789 and 1792," in Arthur M. Schlesinger, Jr., ed., *History of American Presidential Elections* (New York, 1971), 1:3–32.

24. On foreign affairs, see Miller, *Federalist Era*, chaps. 8–10.

25. Cunningham, *Jeffersonian Republicans*, pp. 62–66.

26. Dumas Malone, *Jefferson and the Ordeal of Liberty* (Boston, 1962), chap. 18.

27. George Gibbs, ed., *Memoirs of the Administrations of Washington and John Adams* (New York, 1846), 1:384.

28. For the 1796 election, see Page Smith, "Election of 1796," in Schlesinger, ed., *Presidential Elections*, 1:59–80.

29. Cunningham, *Jeffersonian Republicans*, pp. 109–15.

30. Page Smith, *John Adams* (Garden City, N.Y., 1962), 2:898–900.

31. Noble E. Cunningham, Jr., "John Beckley: An Early American Party Manager," *William and Mary Quarterly*, 3d ser., 13 (January 1956): 40–52.

32. Stephen Kurtz, *The Presidency of John Adams* (Philadelphia, 1957), p. 114.

33. Ibid., chap. 6.

34. The electoral votes are found in ibid., pp. 412–14.

35. John C. Miller, *Crisis in Freedom* (Boston, 1951), pp. 178–79.

36. Beeman, *Old Dominion*, pp. 180, 204–10; James Callendar, *The Prospect before Us* (Richmond, Va., 1800), 1:26–27.

37. Noble Cunningham, Jr., "Election of 1800," in Schlesinger, ed., *Presidential Elections*, 1:101–34.

38. Cunningham, *Jeffersonian Republicans*, pp. 147–62.

39. Carl E. Prince, *The Federalist and the Origins of the U.S. Civil Service* (New York, 1977), pp. 254–55.

40. Cunningham, *Jeffersonian Republicans*, pp. 211–15.

41. Quoted in Cunningham, *American Party System*, p. 155.

42. *New York Commercial Advertiser*, April 25, 1800.

43. William Linn, *Serious Considerations* (New York, 1800), p. 19.

44. Quoted in Cunningham, *Jeffersonian Republicans*, p. 225.

45. Miller, *Federalist Era*, pp. 266–67, 262–63.

46. Kurtz, *Adams*, pp. 397–98.

47. Cunningham, *Jeffersonian Republicans*, pp. 176–85.

48. Delbert H. Gilpatrick, *Jeffersonian Democracy in North Carolina* (New York, 1931), pp. 118–19; Cunningham, *Jeffersonian Republicans*, pp. 191–92; Gibbs, *Administrations*, 2:404.

49. Marvin Zahniser, *Charles Cotesworth Pinckney* (Chapel Hill, N.C., 1967), pp. 222–33; Cunningham, *Jeffersonian Republicans*, pp. 231–39.

50. Miller, *Federalist Era*, pp. 268–73.

51. Fischer, *Revolution*, pp. 95–96; Keith I. Polakoff, *Political Parties in American History* (New York, 1981), p. 74.

52. Quoted in Fischer, *Revolution*, p. 59.

53. Ibid., pp. 60–72.

54. Cunningham, *American Party System*, pp. 118–22.

55. Howard B. Rock, *Artisans of the New Republic* (New York, 1979), pp. 51–53; Alfred Young, "The Mechanics and the Jeffersonians: New York Politics, 1789–1801," *Labor History* 5 (Fall 1964): 267.

56. Fischer, *Revolution*, pp. 110–28.

57. Benjamin W. Labaree, *Patriots and Partisans* (Cambridge, Mass., 1962), p. 130.

58. James M. Banner, Jr., *To the Hartford Convention* (New York, 1969), pp. 256, 257; Munroe, *Delaware*, pp. 206, 211; Samuel E. Morison, *Harrison Gray Otis* (Boston, 1969), p. 251.

59. Fischer, *Revolution*, p. 103.

60. Noble E. Cunningham, Jr., *The Jeffersonian Republicans in Power, 1801–1809* (Chapel Hill, N.C., 1963), p. 285.

61. Ibid., p. 282.

62. Ibid.

63. Herbert S. Parmet and Marie B. Hecht, *Aaron Burr: Portrait of an Ambitious Man* (New York, 1967), pp. 196–97.

64. Dixon R. Fox, *The Decline of Aristocracy in the Politics of New York* (New York, 1919), pp. 104–9; Cunningham, *Republicans in Power*, pp. 293, 295.

65. Elmer C. Griffith, *The Rise and Development of the Gerrymander* (Chicago, 1907), pp. 47–87.

66. Manning J. Dauer, "Election of 1804," in Schlesinger, ed., *Presidential Elections*, 1:159–69.

67. Irving Brant, "Election of 1808," in Schlesinger, ed., *Presidential Elections*, 1:185–221.

68. Norman K. Risjord, "Election of 1812," in Schlesinger, ed., *Presidential Elections*, 1:249–72.

69. Lynn Turner, "Elections of 1816 and 1820," in Schlesinger, ed., *Presidential Elections*, 1:299–321.

70. Richard P. McCormick, *The Second American Party System* (Chapel Hill, N.C., 1966), p. 23.

71. Ronald P. Formisano, "Federalists and Republicans: Parties Yes—System, No," in Paul Kleppner et al., *The Evolution of American Electoral Systems* (Westport, Conn., 1981), pp. 33–76.

CHAPTER 3

1. Quoted in J. Mills Thornton, *Politics and Power in a Slave Society* (Baton Rouge, La., 1978), p. 70; Charles G. Sellers, *James K. Polk: Jacksonian, 1795–1843* (Princeton, N.J., 1957), p. 473.

2. Richard P. McCormick, *The Second American Party System* (Chapel Hill, N.C., 1966); Douglas T. Miller, *The Birth of Modern America* (New York, 1970), pp. 155–56.

3. Quoted in Miller, *Birth of Modern America*, pp. 157–58.

4. Paul Kleppner, *Who Voted? The Dynamics of Electoral Turnout, 1870–1980* (New York, 1982), pp. 28–31.

5. James T. Chase, *Emergence of the Presidential Nominating Convention* (Urbana, Ill., 1973).

6. Quoted in Richard P. McCormick, *The Presidential Game* (New York, 1982), p. 162.

7. Quoted in Waldo W. Braden, ed., *Oratory in the Old South, 1828–1860* (Baton Rouge, La., 1970), p. 112.

8. Quoted in Irving H. Bartlett, *Daniel Webster* (New York, 1978), p. 152.

9. Edward Pessen, *Jacksonian America*, rev. ed. (Homewood, Ill., 1978), p. 160.

10. Quoted in David Crockett, *The Life of Martin Van Buren* (Philadelphia, 1837), p. 29.

11. Marquis James, *Andrew Jackson* (New York, 1937), p. 90.

12. Merrill D. Peterson, *The Jeffersonian Image in the American Mind* (New York, 1960), p. 109.

13. Quoted in John McFaul, *The Politics of Jacksonian Finance* (Ithaca, N.Y., 1972), p. 77.

14. See Ronald P. Formisano, *The Birth of Mass Political Parties: Michigan, 1827–1861* (Princeton, N.J., 1971).

15. Joel H. Silbey, *The Transformation of American Politics, 1840–1860* (Englewood Cliffs, N.J., 1967), p. 35.

16. John Quincy Adams, *Memoirs*, ed. Charles F. Adams (Philadelphia, 1874–77), 10:355–56.

17. Robert V. Remini, *The Election of Andrew Jackson* (Philadelphia, 1963), p. 102.

18. Quoted in Jean H. Baker, *The Politics of Continuity* (Baltimore, 1973), p. 3.

19. Quoted in Ronald P. Formisano, *The Transformation of Political Culture* (New York, 1983), p. 306.

20. Sellers, *Polk*, p. 354.

21. Alexis de Tocqueville, *Journey to America*, ed. J. P. Mayer (New Haven, Conn., 1960), p. 95.

22. Ada Sterling, ed., *A Belle of the Fifties* (New York, 1905), p. 21; J. F. H. Claiborne, *Mississippi* (Jackson, Miss., 1880), 1:425.

23. Bayard Tuckerman, ed., *The Diary of Philip Hone, 1828–1851* (New York, 1889), 1:116, 2:233.

24. Michel Chevalier, *Society, Manners, and Politics in the United States* (Boston, 1839), pp. 306–8.

25. Frank L. Mott, *American Journalism*, 3d ed. (New York, 1962), chaps. 13–15.

26. James M. Lee, *History of American Journalism*, rev. ed. (Boston, 1923), p. 150.

27. Allan Nevins and Frank Weitenkampf, *A Century of Political Cartoons* (New York, 1944), pp. 9–13, 32–69.

28. William B. Brown, *The People's Choice* (Baton Rouge, La., 1960), p. xiii.

29. M. J. Heale, *The Presidential Quest* (New York, 1982), chap. 8.

30. Remini, *Election*, pp. 84–86.

31. Tuckerman, *Diary of Philip Hone*, 1:324.

32. Quoted in Page Smith, *The Shaping of America* (New York, 1980), p. 720.

33. For the 1824 contest, see James F. Hopkins, "Election of 1824," in Arthur M. Schlesinger, Jr., ed., *History of American Presidential Elections* (New York, 1971), 1:349–81.

34. McCormick, *Presidential Game*, pp. 146–48.

35. James W. Tankard, Jr., "Public Opinion Polling by Newspapers in the Presidential Election Campaign of 1824," *Journalism Quarterly* 40 (Spring 1963): 361–65.

36. Samuel F. Bemis, *John Quincy Adams and the Union* (New York, 1956), pp. 24–25; James, *Andrew Jackson*, chaps. 3–4.

37. Remini, *Election*, chap. 1.

38. Ibid., chap. 3.

39. For the "Little Magician," see Robert V. Remini, *Martin Van Buren and the Making of the Democratic Party* (New York, 1959).

40. Robert V. Remini, ed., *The Age of Jackson* (Columbia, S.C., 1972), pp. 7–8.

41. Quoted in Remini, *Election*, p. 74.

42. Ibid., pp. 112–15.

43. Ibid., p. 124.

44. Ibid., pp. 121–135.

45. Ibid., p. 109.

46. Ibid., p. 108.

47. Ibid., pp. 76–80.

48. Ibid., pp. 102–3.

49. Ibid., pp. 154–56, 161–62.

50. Ibid., pp. 151–53.

51. Ibid., pp. 117–18.

52. Chase, *Nominating Convention*, chaps. 8–10.

53. Robert V. Remini, *Andrew Jackson and the Bank War* (New York, 1967), esp. chap. 3.

54. The 1832 campaign is treated in Remini, *Bank War*, chap. 4.

55. Lynn Marshall, "The Strange Stillbirth of the Whig Party," *American Historical Review* 72 (January 1967): 458–59.

56. For the Anti-Masons, see Lorman Ratner, *Anti-Masonry: The Crusade and the Party* (Englewood Cliffs, N.J., 1969).

57. For workingmen's parties, see Sean Wilentz, *Chants Democratic* (New York, 1984), chap. 5.

58. Daniel W. Howe, *The Political Culture of the American Whigs* (Chicago, 1979).

59. For the 1836 contest, see Joel H. Silbey, "Election of 1836," in Schlesinger, ed., *Presidential Elections*, 1:577–600.

60. The best study of the 1840 contest is Robert G. Gunderson, *The Log-Cabin Campaign* (Lexington, Ky., 1957). See also William N. Chambers, "Election of 1840," in Schlesinger, ed., *Presidential Elections*, 1:643–84.

61. Gunderson, *Log-Cabin Campaign*, p. 110.

62. Harriet A. Weed, ed., *Autobiography of Thurlow Weed* (Boston, 1883), pp. 490–91.

63. Gunderson, *Log-Cabin Campaign*, pp. 73, 135–39.

64. Ibid., pp. 148–50.

65. Ibid., p. 108; Glyndon G. Van Deusen, *Thurlow Weed* (Boston, 1947).

66. Gunderson, *Log-Cabin Campaign*, p. 158.

67. Glyndon G. Van Deusen, *The Jacksonian Era* (New York, 1959), pp. 146–47.

68. Gunderson, *Log-Cabin Campaign*, pp. 101–10.

69. Ibid., p. 221.

70. Ibid., pp. 165–72.

71. Quoted in Van Deusen, *Jacksonian Era*, pp. 148–49.

72. Roy F. Nichols, *The Invention of Political Parties* (New York, 1967), pp. 336–37. A list of all platforms is found in Donald B. Johnson and Kirk H. Porter, *National Party Platforms, 1840–1972*, 5th ed. (Urbana, Ill., 1973).

73. William J. Cooper, *Liberty and Slavery* (New York, 1983), pp. 187, 194–95.

74. For the 1844 contest, see James C. N. Paul, *Rift in the Democracy* (Philadelphia, 1951), and Charles G. Sellers, "Election of 1844," in Schlesinger, ed., *Presidential Elections*, 1:747–98.

75. Glyndon G. Van Deusen, *The Life of Henry Clay* (Boston, 1937), pp. 366–76.

76. For the origin of roorbacks, see William Safire, *Safire's Political Dictionary* (New York, 1978), p. 618.

77. Van Deusen, *Jacksonian Era*, pp. 188–89.

78. For the contest in 1848, see Holman Hamilton, "Election of 1848," in Schlesinger, ed., *Presidential Elections*, 2:865–96.

79. Frank B. Woodford, *Lewis Cass* (New Brunswick, N.J., 1950), pp. 265–66; Van Deusen, *Jacksonian Era*, pp. 252, 259–61.

80. Cornelius P. Cotter and Bernard C. Hennessy, *Politics without Power* (New York, 1964), pp. 13–16.

81. For the 1852 contest, see Roy F. Nichols and Jeanette Nichols, "Election of 1852," in Schlesinger, ed., *Presidential Elections*, 2:921–50.

82. *New York Herald*, August 17, 1852.

83. Charles W. Elliott, *Winfield Scott* (New York, 1937), pp. 634–41.

CHAPTER 4

1. Roy F. Nichols, *The Disruption of American Democracy* (New York, 1948), p. 21.

2. Allan Nevins, *Ordeal of the Union* (New York, 1947), 2:488.

3. For a general survey of the Republicans, see George H. Mayer, *The Republican Party, 1854–1966*, 2d ed. (New York, 1967).

4. Joel H. Silby, *A Respectable Minority* (New York, 1977).

5. John A. Garraty, *The New Commonwealth, 1877–1890* (New York, 1968), chap. 6. The quotation appears in Matthew Josephson, *The Politicos, 1865–1896* (New York, 1938), p. 224.

6. Silbey, *Respectable Minority*, pp. 177, 209, 230; Stanley P. Hirshson, *Farewell to the Bloody Shirt* (Bloomington, Ind., 1962).

7. Garraty, *New Commonwealth*, chap. 6.

8. Paul Kleppner, *The Third Electoral System, 1853–1892* (Chapel Hill, N.C., 1979): *Memoirs of Gustave Koerner* (Cedar Rapids, Iowa, 1909), 2:26–27.

9. The quotation is taken from Keith I. Polakoff, *Political Parties in American History* (New York, 1981), p. 249. See also Richard J. Jensen, *The Winning of the Midwest* (Chicago, 1971), pp. 123–25.

10. Paul Kleppner, "The Greenback and Prohibition Parties," in Arthur M. Schlesinger, Jr., ed., *History of U.S. Political Parties* (New York, 1973), 2:1549–81.

11. Jensen, *Winning*, chap. 1. The quotation is on p. 3n.

12. Quoted in ibid., p. 15.

13. Ibid., p. 11.

14. On clubs, see James Bryce, *The American Commonwealth*, 3d ed. (New York, 1894), 2:204–5.

15. Michael E. McGerr, *The Decline of Popular Politics* (New York, 1986), pp. 24–27.

16. Ibid., pp. 26–28.

17. Jean H. Baker, "The Ceremonies of Politics: Nineteenth-Century Rituals of National Affirmation," in William J. Cooper, Jr., et al., eds., *A Master's Due* (Baton Rouge, La., 1985), pp. 161–78. See also Jean H. Baker, *Affairs of Party* (Ithaca, N.Y., 1983).

18. *New York Times*, September 8, 1872.

19. *Colonel Alexander K. McClure's Recollections of Half a Century* (Salem, Mass., 1902), p. 184.

20. Francis B. Simkins and Robert H. Woody, *South Carolina during Reconstruction* (Chapel Hill, N.C., 1932), pp. 496–97.

21. Mildred Throne, *Cyrus Clay Carpenter and Iowa Politics, 1854–1898* (Iowa City, 1974), p. 95.

22. Francis P. Weisenburger, *Idol of the West: The Fabulous Career of Rollin Mallory Daggett* (Syracuse, 1965), p. 101.

23. *The Reminiscences of Carl Schurz* (New York, 1907), 2:195.

24. Allan Peskin, *Garfield* (Kent, Ohio, 1978), pp. 277, 385.

25. Giraud Chester, *Embattled Maiden: The Life of Anna Dickinson* (New York, 1951), p. 52; Earl D. Ross, *The Liberal Republican Movement* (1910: reprint Seattle, 1970), pp. 158–59.

26. Marvin R. Weisbord, *Campaigning for President* (Washington, D.C., 1964), p. 22; Ross, *Liberal Republican*, p. 154.

27. Mayer, *Republican Party*, pp. 13–14; Harry J. Sievers, *Benjamin Harrison* (New York, 1959), 2:405–6.

28. William B. Brown, *The People's Choice* (Baton Rouge, La., 1960).

29. Roger A. Fischer, *Tippecanoe and Trinkets Too* (Urbana, Ill., 1988), chaps. 3–4.

30. Frank L. Mott, *American Journalism*, 3d ed. (New York, 1962), pp. 388–91, 411–14; McGerr, *Decline of Politics*, chap. 5.

31. Allan Nevins and Frank Weitenkampf, *A Century of Political Cartoons* (New York, 1944), pp. 13–15, 72–171.

32. See the various campaign textbooks issued by both parties.

33. Nichols, *Disruption*, p. 27.

34. William E. Baringer, *Lincoln's Rise to Power* (Boston, 1937), p. 306.

35. Robert D. Marcus, *Grand Old Party: Political Structure in the Gilded Age* (New York, 1971), pp. 11–12.

36. Merrill D. Peterson, *The Jeffersonian Image in the American Mind* (New York, 1960), pp. 162–63, 195–97, 220–22; Claude G. Bowers, *The Tragic Era* (Boston, 1929), p. 487.

37. James A. Rawley, *Edwin D. Morgan* (New York, 1955), p. 61.

38. Jesse Macy, *Party Organization and Machinery* (New York, 1912), pp. 87–95.

39. See "Machine Politics in New York City," in *The Works of Theodore Roosevelt* (New York, 1926), 13:76–98.

40. For financing in this era, see George Thayer, *Who Shakes the Money Tree?* (New York, 1973), chap. 2. The quotation is from Thurlow Weed Barnes, *Memoir of Thurlow Weed* (Boston, 1884), p. 300.

41. Quoted in Josephson, *Politicos*, p. 222.

42. Quoted in Irving Katz, *August Belmont* (New York, 1968), p. 76.

43. Herbert E. Alexander, *Financing Politics* (Washington, D.C., 1976), p. 20.

44. Rawley, *Morgan*, pp. 244–45.

45. Josephson, *Politicos*, p. 222.

46. Quoted in ibid., p. 425.

47. Quoted in ibid., p. 345.

48. Quoted in Melvin Hammarberg, *The Indiana Voter* (Chicago, 1977), p. 34.

49. Quoted in Josephson, *Politicos*, pp. 431–32.

50. Jensen, *Winning*, p. 36.

51. Ibid., pp. 34–36; Garraty, *New Commonwealth*, p. 303.

52. Quoted in Josephson, *Politicos*, p. 430.

53. For the Know-Nothing movement, see Michael F. Holt's essay in Schlesinger, ed., *Political Parties*, 1:593–620.

54. William E. Gienapp, *The Origins of the Republican Party, 1852–1856* (New York, 1987).

55. Quoted in Mark Berger, *The Revolution in the New York Party Systems, 1840–1860* (Port Washington, N.Y., 1973), pp. 94, 95.

56. For the election of 1856, see Roy F. Nichols and Philip Klein, "Election of 1856," in Arthur M. Schlesinger, Jr., ed., *History of American Presidential Elections* (New York, 1971), 2:1007–33.

57. Pamela Herr, *Jessie Benton Fremont* (New York, 1987), chap. 18.

58. Quoted in Philip Klein, *President James Buchanan* (University Park, Pa., 1962), p. 257.

59. George W. Julian, *Political Recollections, 1840–1872* (Chicago, 1884), pp. 153–54.

60. Allan Nevins, *The Emergence of Lincoln* (New York, 1950), 1:374–404.

61. For the election of 1860, see Elting Morison, "Election of 1860," in Schlesinger, ed., *Presidential Elections*, 2:1097–1122.

62. Charles F. Adams, Jr., *An Autobiography* (Cambridge, Mass., 1916), p. 69.

63. Baringer, *Lincoln's Rise*, chap. 7.

64. Quoted in ibid., p. 310.

65. James G. Randall, *Lincoln the President* (New York, 1945), 1:182.

66. Quoted in William E. Baringer, "Campaign Techniques in Illinois," *Illinois State Historical Society Transactions* (1932): 252.

67. Quoted in Weisbord, *Campaigning*, pp. 37–38.

68. Robert W. Johannsen, *Stephen A. Douglas* (New York, 1973), pp. 786–91, 798–802. The quotation is from William L. Barney, *The Secessionist Impulse* (Princeton, N.J., 1974), p. 190.

69. Morison, "Election of 1860," 2:1117.

70. For state elections in 1862 and 1863, see Silbey, *Respectable Minority*.

71. For the election of 1864, see Harold Hyman, "Election of 1864," in Schlesinger, ed., *Presidential Elections*, 2:1155–78.

72. Quoted in ibid., p. 1170.

73. Silbey, *Respectable Minority*, chap. 5. The quotation is on p. 138.

74. *New York Tribune*, September 2, 1864.

75. *New York Times*, September 18, 1864.

76. Abram J. Dittenhoefer, *How We Elected Lincoln* (New York, 1916), pp. 87–88.

77. *New York World*, August 25, 1864.

78. Mary R. Dearing, *Veterans in Politics: The Story of the G. A. R.* (Baton Rouge, La., 1952), pp. 31, 36–37.

79. Silbey, *Respectable Minority*, pp. 213–15.

80. Dearing, *Veterans*, pp. 162–67; Josephson, *Politicos*, pp. 36–37.

81. Thomas B. Alexander, *Political Reconstruction in Tennessee* (Nashville, 1950), pp. 143–44, 155, 192.

82. For the 1868 campaign, see Charles H. Coleman, *The Election of 1868* (New York, 1933); John Hope Franklin, "Election of 1868," in Schlesinger, ed., *Presidential Elections*, 2:1247–66.

83. Quoted in Spencer B. King, Jr., *Georgia Voices: A Documentary History to 1872* (Athens, Ga., 1966), p. 328.

84. For the presidential contest of 1872, see Ross, *Liberal Republican*, and William Gillette, "Election of 1872," in Schlesinger, ed., *Presidential Elections*, 2:1303–30.

85. For the complicated developments of the election of 1876, see Keith I. Polakoff, *Politics of Inertia* (Baton Rouge, La., 1973).

86. Quoted in ibid., p. 130.

87. Quoted in ibid., p. 115.

88. Ibid., pp. 169–71.

89. Ibid., chaps. 6–7.

90. For 1880, see Herbert J. Clancy, *The Election of 1880* (Chicago, 1958), and Leonard Dinnerstein, "Election of 1880," in Schlesinger, ed., *Presidential Elections*, 2:1491–1516.

91. Quoted in Clancy, *Election of 1880*, p. 221.

92. For the race in 1884, see Mark D. Hirsch, "Election of 1884," in Schlesinger, ed., *Presidential Elections*, 2:1561–81.

93. See Allan Nevins, *Grover Cleveland* (New York, 1933), chap. 11.

94. For the national contest in 1888, see ibid., chap. 24, and Robert F. Wesser, "Election of 1888," in Schlesinger, ed., *Presidential Elections*, 2:1615–52.

95. Quoted in Wesser, "Election of 1888," 2:1638.

96. Quoted in Josephson, *Politicos*, p. 433.

97. Bryce, *American Commonwealth*, 2:209.

CHAPTER 5

1. Richard J. Jensen, *The Winning of the Midwest* (Chicago, 1971), esp. pp. 165–66; Michael E. McGerr, *The Decline of Popular Politics* (New York, 1986), chap. 6. The quotations are found on p. 147.

2. Jensen, *Winning*, pp. 167–75.

3. Ibid., pp. 174–75; Walter D. Burnham, *Critical Elections and the Mainsprings of American Politics* (New York, 1970), chap. 4.

4. Burnham, *Critical Elections*, chap. 4; J. Morgan Kousser, *The Shaping of Southern Politics* (New Haven, Conn., 1974); James W. Davis, *Presidential Primaries* (Westport, Conn., 1980), pp. 42–44.

5. *New York Herald*, October 26, 1892; George H. Knoles, *The Presidential Campaign of 1892* (Stanford, Calif., 1942), pp. 203, 222.

6. Quoted in Lewis L. Gould, *Reform and Regulation* (New York, 1978), p. 2.

7. *Outlook* 96 (October 1910): 523. See also Moise Ostrogorski, *Democracy and the Party System in the United States* (New York, 1910), p. 199.

8. *New York Times*, October 1, 7, 1892, October 9, 1900, October 20, 1908, October 29, 1920; James F. Byrnes, *All in One Lifetime* (New York, 1958), pp. 20–21.

9. Tom Johnson, *My Story*, ed. E. J. Hauser (New York, 1913), pp. 82–84.

10. Ostrogorski, *Democracy*, pp. 184–86.

11. Ibid., p. 187; Albert D. Kirwan, *Revolt of the Rednecks* (Lexington, Ky., 1951), pp. 113–14.

12. *Colonel Alexander K. McClure's Recollections of Half a Century* (Salem, Mass., 1902), pp. 184–85.

13. *Review of Reviews* 22 (November 1900): 550–55.

14. McGerr, *Decline of Politics*, chap. 5; Alfred M. Lee, *The Daily Newspaper in America* (New York, 1937), p. 182; Richard L. Rubin, *Press, Party, and Presidency* (New York, 1981), chap. 4.

15. McGerr, *Decline of Politics*, chap. 6.

16. *New York Times*, September 6, 8, 1908; Louis W. Koenig, *Bryan* (New York, 1971), pp. 336, 445–46; McGerr, *Decline of Politics*, pp. 160–66.

17. McGerr, *Decline of Politics*, pp. 161–62, 165–66.

18. Roger A. Fischer, *Tippecanoe and Trinkets Too* (Urbana, Ill., 1988), chap. 5.

19. *Outlook* 97 (February 25, 1911): 426–33.

20. Arthur F. Mullen, *Western Democrat* (New York, 1940), p. 126.

21. Claude G. Bowers, *My Life* (New York, 1962), p. 58.

22. Harold F. Gosnell, *Champion Campaigner* (New York, 1952), pp. 28, 31.

23. T. Harry Williams, *Huey Long* (New York, 1969), pp. 121–25.

24. Knoles, *Presidential Campaign*, p. 127; Ostrogorski, *Democracy*, p. 172; *New York Times*, October 27, 1904; October 1, 12, 1916, October 3, 4, 17, 26, 1920.

25. See Sidney Warren, *The Battle for the Presidency* (Philadelphia, 1968), chaps. 6–7.

26. For Stevenson and Reid, see Knoles, *Presidential Campaign*, pp. 167–70, 209–10; for Roosevelt, see Edmund Morris, *The Rise of Theodore Roosevelt* (New York, 1979), p. 730.

27. Freeman Hubbard, *Encyclopedia of North American Railroading* (New York, 1981), pp. 51–52; James M. Cox, *Journey through My Years* (New York, 1946), p. 267.

28. Marvin R. Weisbord, *Campaigning for President* (Washington, D.C., 1964), p. 25. Maine gave up its special election in 1949.

29. *Review of Reviews* 38 (October 1908): 432–38.

30. Ostrogorski, *Democracy*, pp. 162–63; *World's Work* 32 (October 1916): 663.

31. Ostrogorski, *Democracy*, pp. 164–70.

32. George Thayer, *Who Shakes the Money Tree?* (New York, 1973), chap. 3; Louise Overacker, *Money in Elections* (New York, 1932); Herbert E. Alexander, *Financing Politics* (Washington, D.C., 1976), pp. 64–67.

33. Herbert Croly, *Marcus Alonzo Hanna* (New York, 1912), p. 220.

34. Ibid., p. 326.

35. Alexander, *Financing Politics*, pp. 64–67.

36. Quoted in Jesse Macy, *Party Organization and Machinery* (New York, 1912), p. 246.

37. Robert F. Durden, *The Climax of Populism* (Lexington, Ky., 1965), pp. 62–63; *New York Times*, October 5, 1908.

38. Harold R. Bruce, *American Parties and Politics*, 3d ed. (New York, 1936), pp. 421–22.

39. Ibid., pp. 422–23, 426.

40. R. Hal Williams, *Years of Decision* (New York, 1978), chap. 1.

41. Lawrence Goodwyn, *Democratic Promise* (New York, 1976).

42. Ira Kipnis, *The American Socialist Movement* (New York, 1952).

43. Marc Carson, *American Labor Unions and Politics, 1900–1918* (Carbondale, Ill., 1958), esp. pp. 30–31, 44–46, 48, 49, 59–60, 67, 72.

44. Melvin G. Holli, *Reform in Detroit* (New York, 1969), pp. 17–18, 139, 141.

45. William L. Riordon, *Plunkitt of Tammany Hall* (New York, 1963), pp. 25–28.

46. Gould, *Reform and Regulation*, pp. 39–40.

47. John Hope Franklin, *From Slavery to Freedom*, 5th ed. (New York, 1980), pp. 258–67; Monroe Billington, *The American South* (New York, 1971), pp. 320–24.

48. For the 1892 contest, see Knoles, *Campaign of 1892*; H. Wayne Morgan, "Election of 1892," in Arthur M. Schlesinger, Jr., ed., *History of American Presidential Elections* (New York, 1971), 2:1703–32.

49. John D. Hicks, *The Populist Revolt* (Minneapolis, Minn., 1931), chap. 9.

50. Morgan, "Election of 1892," 2:1725.

51. Harold U. Faulkner, *Politics, Reform and Expansion, 1890–1900* (New York, 1959), chaps. 6–7.

52. The "battle of the standards" is chronicled in Stanley L. Jones, *The*

Presidential Election of 1896 (Madison, Wisc., 1964); and Paul W. Glad, *McKinley, Bryan, and the People* (Philadelphia, 1964).

53. Quoted in James A. Barnes, "Myths of the Bryan Campaign," *Mississippi Valley Historical Review* 34 (December 1947): 395–96.

54. Quoted in Weisbord, *Campaigning*, pp. 49–50.

55. Croly, *Hanna*, pp. 214–16.

56. For the campaign of 1900, see Walter LaFeber, "Election of 1900," in Schlesinger, ed., *Presidential Elections*, 3:1877–1917.

57. Richard Hofstadter, ed., *The Progressive Movement, 1900–1915* (Englewood Cliffs, N.J., 1963), pp. 1–15.

58. The campaign of 1904 is discussed in William H. Harbaugh, "Election of 1904," in Schlesinger, ed., *Presidential Elections*, 3:1965–94.

59. The campaign of 1908 is treated in Paolo Coletta, "Election of 1908," in Schlesinger, ed., *Presidential Elections*, 3:2049–90.

60. The campaign of 1912 is described in George Mowry, "Election of 1912," in Schlesinger, ed., *Presidential Elections*, 3:2135–66, and Warren, *Battle for the Presidency*, chap. 7.

61. For Woodrow Wilson's political rise, see Arthur S. Link, *Wilson: The Road to the White House* (Princeton, N.J., 1947).

62. *New York Times*, August 13, 1912.

63. Warren, *Battle for the Presidency*, chap. 7.

64. Ibid.

65. Quoted in William H. Harbaugh, *The Life and Times of Theodore Roosevelt* (New York, 1963), p. 421.

66. The 1916 contest is charted in Arthur S. Link, *Wilson: Campaigns for Progressivism and Peace, 1916–1917* (Princeton, N.J., 1965), and Arthur S. Link and William M. Leary, Jr., "Election of 1916," in Schlesinger, ed., *Presidential Elections*, 3:2245–70.

67. *New York Times*, November 4, 1916.

68. For the midterm election of 1918, see David Burner, *The Politics of Provincialism* (New York, 1968).

69. The presidential race of 1920 is recorded in Wesley M. Bagby, *The Road to Normalcy* (Baltimore, 1968), and Donald McCoy, "Election of 1920," in Schlesinger, ed., *Presidential Elections*, 3:2349–85.

70. On the League of Nations struggle, see Thomas A. Bailey, *Woodrow Wilson and the Great Betrayal* (New York, 1945).

71. Ibid., pp. 338–43.

CHAPTER 6

1. Al Smith, *Up to Now* (New York, 1929), pp. 52–54.

2. Arthur M. Schlesinger, Jr., "The Crisis of the American Party System," in Richard L. McCormick, ed., *Political Parties and the Modern State* (New Brunswick, N.J., 1984), pp. 71–85.

3. Ralph D. Casey, "Party Campaign Propaganda," *Annals of the American Academy of Political and Social Science* 179 (May 1936): 96–105; Robert B. Westbrook, "Politics as Consumption: Managing the Modern American Election," in Richard W. Fox and T. J. Jackson Lears, eds., *The Culture of Consumption* (New York, 1983), pp. 143–73.

4. Hugh Bone, *American Politics and the Party System* (New York, 1949), p. 603.

5. Casey, "Party Campaign Propaganda," pp. 99–100.

6. Ibid., pp. 96–97, and Casey, "Republican Propaganda in the 1936 Campaign," *Public Opinion Quarterly* 1 (April 1937): 27–44. See also Theodore M. Black, *Democratic Party Publicity in the 1940 Campaign* (New York, 1941).

7. Stanley Kelley, Jr., *Professional Public Relations and Political Power* (Baltimore, 1956), pp. 39–66.

8. Roger A. Fischer, *Tippecanoe and Trinkets Too* (Urbana, Ill., 1988), chap. 6.

9. Harold R. Bruce, *American Parties and Politics*, 3d ed. (New York, 1936), pp. 404–5.

10. Quoted in ibid., p. 393n.

11. Quoted in Casey, "Party Campaign Propaganda," p. 104.

12. Bone, *American Politics*, chap. 22.

13. Casey, "Party Campaign Propaganda," pp. 100–101; Black, *Democratic*, pp. 74–75.

14. Frank L. Mott, *American Journalism*, 3d ed. (New York, 1962), pp. 719–20, 771, 793.

15. Erik Barnouw, *A History of Broadcasting in the United States* (New York, 1966–70), 1:152–53, 2:144. Edward W. Chester, *Radio, Television, and American Politics* (New York, 1969), chap. 1.

16. For FDR, see Harold F. Gosnell, *Champion Campaigner* (New York, 1952), p. 221.

17. Barnouw, *History of Broadcasting*, 2:51–52, 206–7.

18. Erik Barnouw, *Documentary* (New York, 1974), pp. 114–18; *New York Times*, September 19, 1924, September 7, 1928, October 15, 21, 1928; Upton Sinclair, *I, Candidate for Governor, and How I Got Licked* (New York, 1935), pp. 150–56.

19. Robert A. Caro, *Path to Power* (New York, 1982), chap. 21.

20. Quoted in Bruce M. Stave, *The New Deal and the Last Hurrah* (Pittsburgh, 1970), p. 14.

21. Harold F. Gosnell, *Machine Politics*, 2d ed. (Chicago, 1968), esp. pp. 58–59; Gosnell, *Negro Politicians* (Chicago, 1935), pp. 139–40.

22. Gosnell, *Machine Politics*, pp. 61–63, 81–83.

23. Quoted in Peter H. Odegard and E. Allen Helms, *American Politics* (New York, 1938), pp. 549–51.

24. On motor caravans, see *New York Times*, September 16, October 18, 22, 1924, October 16, 1928.

25. James A. Farley, *Behind the Ballots* (New York, 1938), pp. 319–20.

26. Irving G. Williams, *The Rise of the Vice Presidency* (Washington, D.C., 1956), pp. 132, 145, 151, 163, 181, 218–19.

27. Howard R. Penniman, *Sait's American Parties and Elections* 4th ed. (New York, 1948), p. 515; Bruce, *American Parties*, p. 392.

28. Charles E. Merriam and Harold F. Gosnell, *The American Party System*, 3d ed. (New York, 1940), pp. 353–55.

29. On the shift of black voters, see Nancy J. Weiss, *Farewell to the Party of Lincoln* (Princeton, N.J., 1983).

30. Farley, *Behind the Ballots*, p. 160; *New York Times*, September 29, 1924, September 21, 23, 1928; Elisabeth I. Perry, *Belle Moskowitz* (New York, 1987).

31. Alva Johnston, " 'Prof.' Hurja, the New Deal's Political Doctor," *Saturday Evening Post*, June 13, 1936.

32. Bone, *American Politics*, p. 77.

33. Bone, *American Politics*, 3d ed. (New York, 1965), chap. 8.

34. *New York Times*, December 13, 1936.

35. Farley, *Behind the Ballots*, p. 159.

36. Ibid., pp. 159–60.

37. *Fortune* 11 (April 1935), p. 136.

38. On campaign finance, see George Thayer, *Who Shakes the Money Tree?* (New York, 1973), chap. 4, and Louise Overacker, *Money in Elections* (New York, 1932).

39. Overacker, *Money in Elections*, chap. 2.

40. Ibid., chaps. 5–6.

41. Penniman, *Sait's American Politics*, pp. 648–49.

42. Alexander Heard, *The Costs of Democracy* (Chapel Hill, N.C., 1960), chap. 8.

43. Thayer, *Money Tree*, pp. 70–71.

44. Ronald F. Stinett, *Democrats, Dinners, and Dollars* (Ames, Iowa, 1967), p. 15.

45. Thayer, *Money Tree*, pp. 71–74.

46. J. David Greenstone, *Labor in American Politics* (New York, 1969), chap. 1–2.

47. On the GOP, see Malcolm Moos, *The Republicans* (New York, 1956); George H. Mayer, *The Republican Party, 1854–1966* 2d ed. (New York, 1967), chap. 11.

48. For the Democrats, see David Burner, *The Politics of Provincialism* (New York, 1968).

49. Steven J. Rosenstone et al., *Third Parties in America* (Princeton, N.J., 1984), pp. 81, 93–102.

50. Nelson W. Polsby and Aaron H. Wildavsky, *Presidential Elections* 7th ed. (New York, 1988), chap. 4.

51. The contest of 1924 is discussed in David Burner, "Election of 1924,"

in Arthur M. Schlesinger, Jr., ed., *History of American Presidential Elections* (New York, 1971), 3:2459–90.

52. The election of 1928 is treated in Lawrence H. Fuchs, "Election of 1824," in Schlesinger, ed., *Presidential Elections*, 3:2585–2609, and Roy V. Peel and Thomas C. Donnelly, *The 1928 Campaign* (New York, 1931).

53. Aaron Singer, ed., *Campaign Speeches of American Presidential Candidates, 1928–1972* (New York, 1976), p. 7.

54. The election of 1932 is recorded in Roy V. Peel and Thomas C. Donnelly, *The 1932 Campaign* (New York, 1935); Sidney Warren, *The Battle for the Presidency* (Philadelphia, 1968), chap. 8; Frank Freidel, "Election of 1932," in Schlesinger, ed., *Presidential Elections*, 3:2707–39.

55. Singer, *Campaign Speeches*, pp. 68, 70, 77.

56. Quoted in Warren, *Battle for the Presidency*, p. 239.

57. Ibid., pp. 244–45.

58. Singer, *Campaign Speeches*, p. 112.

59. Kristi Andersen, *The Creation of a Democratic Majority, 1928–1936* (Chicago, 1979).

60. The 1936 campaign is discussed in William E. Leuchtenburg, "Election of 1936," in Schlesinger, ed., *Presidential Elections*, 3:2809–49.

61. Quoted in William E. Leuchtenburg, *Franklin D. Roosevelt and the New Deal, 1932–1940* (New York, 1963), p. 184.

62. The 1940 campaign is covered in Robert E. Burke, "Election of 1940," in Schlesinger, ed., *Presidential Elections*, 4:2917–46; Herbert S. Parmet, *Never Again* (New York, 1968).

63. On Willkie, see Steve Neal, *Dark Horse* (Garden City, N.Y., 1984).

64. Quoted in Burke, "Election of 1940," 4:2944.

65. The 1944 campaign is dealt with in Leon Freidman, "Election of 1944," in Schlesinger, ed., *Presidential Elections*, 4:3009–38.

66. The quotation is in ibid., 4:3081.

67. The 1948 campaign is treated in Richard S. Kirkendall, "Election of 1948," in Schlesinger, ed., *Presidential Elections*, 4:3099–3145; Irwin Ross, *The Loneliest Campaign* (New York, 1968); and Jules Abel, *Out of the Jaws of Victory* (New York, 1959).

68. Quoted in Paul Goodman and Frank O. Gatell, *USA: An American Record* (New York, 1972), p. 565.

CHAPTER 7

1. Brookings Institution, *The New Methodology: A Study of Political Strategy and Tactics* (Washington, D.C., 1967), p. vii; Ruth K. Scott and Ronald J. Hrebenar, *Parties in Crisis* (New York, 1984), p. 211.

2. Martin P. Wattenberg, *The Decline of American Parties, 1952–1980* (Cambridge, Mass., 1984), p. xi. See also Norman H. Nie et al., *The Changing American Voter* (Cambridge, Mass., 1979).

3. Austin Ranney, *Curing the Mischiefs of Faction* (Berkeley, Calif., 1975), p. 130.

4. Dan Nimmo, *The Political Persuaders* (Englewood Cliffs, N.J., 1970), pp. 127, 146.

5. James W. Davis, *Presidential Primaries* (Westport, Conn., 1980). A list of all primaries, 1968 to 1980, appears in Paul A. Smith, *Electing a President* (New York, 1982), app. C.

6. Robert Cantor, *Voting Behavior and Presidential Elections* (Itasca, Ill., 1975), p. 95.

7. Robert Agranoff, ed., *The New Style in Election Campaigns* 2d ed. (Boston, 1976), p. 5.

8. David L. Rosenbloom, *The Election Men* (New York, 1973), pp. 10–12, 50–54; Larry J. Sabato, *The Rise of Political Consultants* (New York, 1981).

9. Rosenbloom, *Election Men*; Sabato, *Political Consultants*; Sidney Blumenthal, *The Permanent Campaign* (Boston, 1980).

10. Sabato, *Political Consultants*, chap. 2.

11. Kathleen H. Jamieson, *Packaging the Presidency* (New York, 1984); Robert Spero, *The Duping of the American Voter* (New York, 1980). The quotation is found in Hugh L. LeBlanc, *American Political Parties* (New York, 1982), p. 294.

12. Alexandra Kayden, *Campaign Organization* (Lexington, Mass., 1978), chap. 3; Frank J. Sorauf, *Party Politics in America*, 4th ed. (Boston, 1980), chap. 4. The quotation is on p. 89.

13. Hugh Bone, *American Politics and the Party System*, 3d ed. (New York, 1965), pp. 366–72.

14. Ruth E. Mandel, *In the Running* (New Haven, Conn., 1981).

15. Stephen A. Salmore and Barbara G. Salmore, *Candidates, Parties, and Campaigns* (Washington, D.C., 1985), p. 72.

16. David E. Price, *Bring Back the Parties* (Washington, D.C., 1984). Paul S. Herrnson, *Party Campaigning in the 1980s* (Cambridge, Mass., 1988).

17. For the impact of television on campaigning, see Thomas E. Patterson, *The Mass Media Election* (New York, 1980); Edwin Diamond and Stephen Bates, *The Spot: The Rise of Political Advertising on Television* (Cambridge, Mass., 1984); Richard Joslyn, *Mass Media Elections* (New York, 1984); Doris A. Graber, *Mass Media and American Politics* (Washington, D.C., 1984); Nimmo, *Political Persuaders*, pp. 137–62.

18. Kathleen H. Jamieson and David S. Birdsell, *Presidential Debates* (New York, 1988); Judith S. Trent and Robert V. Friedenberg, *Political Campaign Communication* (New York, 1983), chap. 7.

19. Nimmo, *Political Persuaders*, pp. 133–35.

20. Edwin Emery and Michael Emery, *The Press in America*, 5th ed. (Englewood Cliffs, N.J., 1984).

21. Nimmo, *Political Persuaders*, pp. 125–29.

22. LeBlanc, *American Political Parties*, pp. 286–87. For the direct-mail phenomenon, see Richard Armstrong, *The Next Hurrah* (New York, 1988).

23. Roger A. Fischer, *Tippecanoe and Trinkets Too* (Urbana, Ill., 1988), chaps. 7–8.

24. William B. Keech and Donald R. Mathews, *The Party's Choice* (Washington, D.C., 1976); Gerald Pomper, *Nominating the President* (Evanston, Ill., 1963).

25. Scott and Hrebenar, *Parties in Crisis*, pp. 289–306.

26. Nimmo, *Political Persuaders*, p. 29; Diamond and Bates, *The Spot*, chap. 14.

27. John Kessel, *Presidential Campaign Politics* (Homewood, Ill., 1980), pp. 86–88.

28. Barbara Kellerman, "Campaigning since Kennedy: The Family as Surrogate," *Presidential Studies Quarterly* 10 (Spring 1980): 244–53. The quotation is found on p. 249.

29. Brookings Institution, *New Methodology*, pp. 6–7, 20–21.

30. Nelson W. Polsby and Aaron H. Wildavsky, *Presidential Elections* 7th ed. (New York, 1988), chap. 4; Jules Witcover, *Marathon* (New York, 1977), pp. 134–37, 518–19.

31. Jerry Bruno and Jeff Greenfield, *The Advance Man* (New York, 1971).

32. Bone, *American Politics*, 3d ed., p. 378.

33. Agranoff, *New Style*, pp. 27–28; Witcover, *Marathon*, p. 15.

34. Patterson, *Mass Media*, p. 3; Trent and Friedenberg, *Campaign Communication*, pp. 150–53.

35. Trent and Friedenberg, *Campaign Communication*, chaps. 5–6.

36. Quoted in Richard A. Watson, *The Presidential Contest*, 2d ed. (New York, 1984), pp. 67–68.

37. Ibid., pp. 60–61. The Reagan quotation is in Elizabeth Drew, *Campaign Journal* (New York, 1985), p. 668.

38. For financing in the 1950s and 1960s, see George Thayer, *Who Shakes the Money Tree?* (New York, 1973), pp. 76–205; Herbert E. Alexander, *Financing Politics* (Washington, D.C., 1976), and Alexander Heard, *The Costs of Democracy* (Chapel Hill, N.C., 1960).

39. Michael J. Malbin, ed., *Money and Politics in the United States* (Washington, D.C., 1984), chaps. 2, 6; Frank J. Sorauf, *Money in American Elections* (Glenview, Ill., 1988).

40. Quoted in Thayer, *Money Tree*, p. 78.

41. Kessel, *Campaign Politics*, pp. 112–17.

42. Alexander, *Financing Politics*, pp. 90–94.

43. Scott and Hrebenar, *Parties in Crisis*, pp. 244–47.

44. For legal reforms, see Malbin, *Money*, chap. 7.

45. On political action committees, see ibid., chap. 4.

46. Ibid., chap. 2.

47. For the parties in this period, see Arthur M. Schlesinger, Jr., ed., *History of U.S. Political Parties* (New York, 1973).

48. Polsby and Wildavsky, *Presidential Elections*, chap. 4.

49. Steven J. Rosenstone et al., *Third Parties in America* (Princeton, N.J., 1984).

50. The election of 1952 is covered in Barton J. Bernstein, "Election of 1952," in Arthur M. Schlesinger, Jr., ed. *History of American Presidential Elections* (New York, 1971), 4:3215–66.

51. For Nixon's "Checkers" speech, see Stephen E. Ambrose, *Nixon* (New York, 1987), pp. 288–91.

52. The election of 1956 is treated in Charles A. H. Thomson and Frances Shattuck, *The 1956 Presidential Campaign* (Washington, D.C., 1960).

53. For the 1960 election, see Theodore H. White, *The Making of the President, 1960* (New York, 1961).

54. For the 1964 election, see Theodore H. White, *The Making of the President, 1964* (New York, 1965).

55. Ibid., p. 217.

56. For the 1968 election, see Theodore H. White, *The Making of the President, 1968* (New York, 1969), and Lewis Chester et al., *An American Melodrama* (New York, 1969).

57. White, *1968*, p. 332.

58. For the 1972 election, see Theodore H. White, *The Making of the President, 1972* (New York, 1973).

59. Gary Hart, *Right from the Start* (New York, 1973), p. 264.

60. The 1976 contest is analyzed in Elizabeth Drew, *American Journal* (New York, 1977), and Witcover, *Marathon*.

61. For the 1980 election, see Jack W. Germond and Jules Witcover, *Blue Smoke and Mirrors* (New York, 1981), and Elizabeth Drew, *Portrait of an Election* (New York, 1981).

62. For the 1984 election, see Jack W. Germond and Jules Witcover, *Wake Us When It's Over* (New York, 1985), and Drew, *Campaign Journal*.

Bibliographical Essay

Readers who wish to pursue further the subject of campaigning might want to consult either certain general works on American elections or books and articles that deal with specific aspects. Arthur M. Schlesinger, Jr., ed., *History of American Presidential Elections*, 4 vols. (New York, 1971), contains narrative descriptions together with related documents from each quest for the presidency up to the year 1968. Eugene H. Roseboom and Alfred E. Eckes, *A History of Presidential Elections*, 4th ed. (New York, 1979), furnishes a more concise treatment, without documents. Sidney Warren, *The Battle for the Presidency* (Philadelphia, 1968), examines eleven of the most significant contests through 1964. All of the above books focus more on personalities and issues than on strategies and tactics. Richard J. Jensen, "Armies, Admen, and Crusaders: Types of Presidential Campaigns," *History Teacher* 2 (1969): 33–59, marks the first attempt to categorize different general approaches to campaigning. Marvin R. Weisbord, *Campaigning for President* (Washington, D.C., 1964), provides a brief summary of activities undertaken by presidential nominees through the 1960 election. Roger A. Fischer, *Tippecanoe and Trinkets Too* (Urbana, Ill., 1988), is an up-to-date, thoroughly researched survey of the uses of material culture in national campaigns, and William B. Brown, *The People's Choice* (Baton Rouge, La., 1960), is an excellent study of presidential campaign biographies. A popular account of the history of campaign finance is George Thayer, *Who Shakes the Money Tree?* (New York, 1973), though it should be supplemented for the modern period by Frank J. Sorauf, *Money in American Elections* (Glenview, Ill., 1988).

There are several important studies that treat electioneering in particular eras. For the century before 1789, see Robert J. Dinkin, *Voting in Provincial America* (Westport, Conn., 1977), and idem, *Voting in Revolutionary America* (Westport, Conn., 1982), as well as the classic work of Charles S. Sydnor, *Gentlemen Freeholders* (Chapel Hill, N.C., 1952). The early national period is well covered in Noble E. Cunningham, Jr., *The Jeffersonian Republicans* (Chapel Hill, N.C., 1957), and idem, *The Jeffersonian Republicans in Power* (Chapel Hill, N.C., 1963), especially when read along with David H. Fischer, *The Revolution of American Conservatism* (New York, 1965). Richard P.

McCormick, *The Second American Party System* (Chapel Hill, N.C., 1966), and idem, *The Presidential Game* (New York, 1982), provide fine introductions to the politics of the Jacksonian years. However, the campaigning innovations of that era probably are best observed in Robert V. Remini, *The Election of Andrew Jackson* (Philadelphia, 1963), which deals with party formation and the contest in 1828, and Robert G. Gunderson, *The Log-Cabin Campaign* (Lexington, Ky., 1957), which closely examines the lively, precedent-setting activities of 1840. Two recent works by Jean H. Baker, *Affairs of Party* (Ithaca, N.Y., 1983), and "The Ceremonies of Politics: Nineteenth-Century Rituals of National Affirmation," in William J. Cooper, et al., eds., *A Master's Due* (Baton Rouge, La., 1985), tell a great deal about electioneering in the so-called golden age of parties, as does Richard J. Jensen, *The Winning of the Midwest* (Chicago, 1971), though the most illuminating study of preelection practices in the last half of the nineteenth century and the early twentieth century is Michael E. McGerr, *The Decline of Popular Politics* (New York, 1986). Two still-valuable contemporary works are James Bryce, *The American Commonwealth*, 3d ed. (New York, 1894), and Moise Ostrogorski, *Democracy and the Party System in the United States* (New York, 1910).

Important contemporary studies of politics in the 1920s are Frank R. Kent, *The Great Game of Politics* (Garden City, N.Y., 1923) and the anonymously authored *Behind the Scenes in Politics* (New York, 1924). Pioneering articles by Ralph D. Casey, "Party Campaign Propaganda," *Annals of the American Academy of Political and Social Science* 179 (May 1936): 96–105, and "Republican Propaganda in the 1936 Campaign," *Public Opinion Quarterly* 1 (April 1937): 27–44, tell much about the changes in campaign styles in the 1930s. Also valuable for the FDR years are James A. Farley, *Behind the Ballots* (New York, 1938), and Theodore M. Black, *Democratic Party Publicity in the 1940 Campaign* (New York, 1941). Among the noteworthy investigations of the origins of campaign management are Stanley Kelley, Jr., *Professional Public Relations and Political Power* (Baltimore, 1956), and Robert B. Westbrook, "Politics as Consumption: Managing the Modern American Election," in Richard W. Fox and T. J. Jackson Lears, eds., *The Culture of Consumption* (New York, 1983), pp. 143–73. The first chapter of Edward W. Chester, *Radio, Television, and American Politics* (New York, 1969), provides a short survey of the use of radio in national politics. The subject also is treated in Erik Barnouw's *A History of Broadcasting in the United States* (New York, 1966–70). Harold F. Gosnell, *Machine Politics*, 2d ed. (Chicago, 1968), and idem, *Negro Politicians* (Chicago, 1935), are informative on the politicking of the inner city. Louise Overacker, *Money in Politics* (New York, 1932), gives an in-depth look at campaign finance in this era.

For the modern period, the series of volumes by Theodore H. White, *The Making of the President* (New York, 1961–73), give the reader a close-up view of the drama and complexity of campaigns in the mass media age, as does his more analytical overview *America in Search of Itself* (New York, 1982). Other important general works that deal more with campaign practices include Robert Agranoff, ed., *The New Style in Election Campaigns*, 2d ed. (Boston, 1976); Dan Nimmo, *The Political Persuaders* (Englewood Cliffs, N.J., 1970); and Stephen A. Salmore and Barbara G. Salmore, *Candidates, Parties, and Campaigns* (Washington, D.C., 1985). Nelson W. Polsby and Aaron H. Wildavsky, *Presidential Elections*, 7th ed. (New York, 1988), provides much information on national contests; Larry J. Sabato, *The Rise of Political Consultants* (New York, 1981), is the best study of the growing business of campaign management; Richard Armstrong, *The Next Hurrah* (New York, 1988), is a good introduction to the direct-mail phenomenon; Kathleen H. Jamieson, *Eloquence in an Electronic Age* (New York, 1988), is an excellent discussion of the decline of speechmaking. For the impact of television, see Thomas E. Patterson, *The Mass Media Election* (New York, 1980); Edwin Diamond and Stephen Bates, *The Spot: The Rise of Political Advertising on Television* (Cambridge, Mass., 1984); Doris A. Graber, *Mass Media and American Politics* (Washington, D.C., 1984); and Kathleen H. Jamieson, *Packaging the Presidency* (New York, 1984).

Index